Netaji: Collected Works
Volume 1

An Indian Pilgrim
An Unfinished Autobiography

**Netaji in Badgastein, Austria, in 1937 when
he wrote *An Indian Pilgrim***

Netaji: Collected Works
Volume 1

An Indian Pilgrim
An Unfinished Autobiography

Subhas Chandra Bose

edited by
Sisir Kumar Bose
and
Sugata Bose

Orient BlackSwan

AN INDIAN PILGRIM: AN UNFINISHED AUTOBIOGRAPHY

ORIENT BLACKSWAN PRIVATE LIMITED

Registered Office
3-6-752 Himayatnagar, Hyderabad 500 029, Telangana, India
e-mail: centraloffice@orientblackswan.com

Other Offices
Bengaluru, Chennai, Guwahati, Hyderabad, Kolkata,
Mumbai, New Delhi, Noida, Patna

© Netaji Research Bureau 2022
First published in hardback by Netaji Research Bureau in 1980
First published in paperback by Netaji Research Bureau in 1997
This new edition by Orient Blackswan Private Limited 2022
Reprinted 2023, 2024, 2025, 2026

ISBN 978-93-5442-308-6

041946

Typeset in
Charter BT 11/13pt
by Shine Graphics, Delhi 110 094

Printed in India at
Yash Printographics, Noida 201 301

Published by
Orient Blackswan Private Limited
3-6-752, Himayatnagar, Hyderabad 500 029, Telangana, India
e-mail: info@orientblackswan.com

CONTENTS

Part III
APPENDICES

PLATES

Frontispiece: Netaji in Badgastein, Austria, in 1937 when
he wrote *An Indian Pilgrim*

ACKNOWLEDGEMENTS

We would like to thank Professor Krishna Bose and Professor Leonard A. Gordon for editorial advice, Kartic Chakraborty for secretarial assistance, Naga Sundaram for archival support and Manohar Mandal and Munshi for unstinted, practical help in running the Bureau's publication division.

We take this opportunity once again to express our deep appreciation to Netaji's wife Emilie Schenkl and their daughter Anita Pfaff for having generously assigned the copyright in Netaji's works to the Netaji Research Bureau.

Sisir K. Bose
Sugata Bose

PREFACE

To the 2022 Edition of *An Indian Pilgrim*

Sugata Bose

My father Dr. Sisir Kumar Bose was busy seeing patients one day in 1980 when the son of a colonial-era police officer, who had recently died, arrived at our home with a large cigar box that had belonged to Sarat Chandra Bose. In it my father found eighteen letters written by Emilie Schenkl to Subhas Chandra Bose in the 1930s and the letters exchanged between Subhas and Sarat in 1920–1921 as Subhas deliberated on his decision to resign from the Indian Civil Service. Subhas had taken the 1920–1921 correspondence with him to Badgastein in late 1937 and quoted from the letters in chapter 9 of the manuscript *An Indian Pilgrim*. He wrote the ten chapters of the book by hand in pencil in three exercise books, which are preserved in the archives of the Netaji Research Bureau. It seems clear that an intelligence operative had pilfered the cigar box in which Subhas Chandra Bose had carefully kept the precious letters but that a descendant was good enough to return them through my father to Netaji Research Bureau.

It was Sisir Kumar Bose's idea to put together Netaji's unfinished autobiography ending in 1921 with letters composed by the young Subhas between 1912 to 1921. That editorial move provided the rare double first-person perspective that won the praise of readers and reviewers when the book appeared in 1965. By the time the book reappeared in 1980 as Volume 1 of Netaji's *Collected Works*, it was possible to include the full versions of the letters from Subhas to Sarat written in 1921. My father and I jointly wrote the editors' introduction to the 1997 centenary edition of *An Indian Pilgrim*, which is being reprinted in this new edition being on the occasion of Netaji's 125th birth anniversary year and the 75th anniversary of Indian independence. There is little to add to the comprehensive 1997 introduction except in one respect.

In January 2002 the renowned historian Ranajit Guha delivered the Netaji Oration at the Netaji Research Bureau, Netaji Bhawan, titled "Nationalism and the Trials of Becoming", offering the most sophisticated interpretation of Netaji's unfinished autobiography (*The Oracle*, 24, 2, August 2002, available in print and at www.netaji.org). "In paying our homage this evening to a historic instance of life's triumph," Guha said in January 2002, "let us invoke the spirit of the new by reading, once again, the story of that life as told by Netaji himself in his autobiography. In my own reading of that text I am deeply indebted to its first editor, the late Dr. Sisir Kumar Bose. Much of what I know of Netaji's life and times owes largely to Sisir Kumar's work as a historian and archivist."

Ranajit Guha rescued the history of nationalism from its being "hostage to statist interpretation". In a beautifully crafted, eloquent and erudite Netaji Oration, he put ethics back into the study of nationalism and the individual or self, as he put it, back into the study of nationalism. Through a careful reading of *An Indian Pilgrim,* he showed how a process of individuation was inherent in the phenomenon called mass nationalism. The autobiography reveals the young Subhas's search for "a central principle" which he could use as "a peg to hang my whole life on". He found it in Vivekananda's teachings encapsulated in the Sanskrit maxim, *atmano mokshaartham jagaddhitaya [ca]*. "For your own salvation and for the service of humanity—that was to be life's goal," Subhas wrote.

Subhas's letters to Sarat from September 1920 until April 1921 reveal his moral commitments as he prepared to set out on his life as pilgrimage. On April 20, 2021, he lauded his elder brother's "magnanimous spirit". "I know how many hearts I have grieved," he wrote, "how many superiors of mine I have disobeyed. But on the eve of this hazardous undertaking my only prayer is—may it be for the good of our dear country." Having sent in his resignation on April 22, 1921, he told Sarat the following day, "The die is cast, and I earnestly hope that nothing but good will come out of it. He had decided that "compromise is a bad thing—it degrades the man and injures his cause" and was convinced that the moment had come to "wash our hands clean of any connection with the British Government."

In bringing this new edition to readers, I must once more remember those who made certain that future generations would be able to learn from Netaji's book of life. Sisir Kumar Bose never stopped doing Netaji's work from the moment he helped his uncle escape from India in the quest for freedom until he passed away in 2000. He founded the Netaji Research Bureau in 1957 to preserve and disseminate the best traditions of India's freedom movement. He was ably supported throughout by Krishna Bose who helmed the Netaji Research Bureau with utmost grace and dignity as its Chairperson from 2000 until her own passing in 2020. In the early decades the NRB publications department was run by the indefatigable Benode C. Chaudhuri and the archives cared for by the devoted Naga Sundaram of the Indian National Army. In my current responsibility as NRB Chairperson I am very glad to be helped by Sumantra Bose, Director, and Amitava Deshmukh, Treasurer. I would also like to record my gratitude to two senior staff members, Kartik Chakraborty, now retired, and Netai Sundar Thakur, who served for decades. In preparing the materials and manuscript for the current edition, Anirban Bhattacharjee, Anirban Chatterjee, and Manohar Mandal worked tirelessly. Suchetana Ghosh Dostidar read the proofs of this book with care. I would like to thank Nandini Rao, Uday Rao and Nilanjana Majumdar of Orient BlackSwan for their professionalism and dedication in partnering with Netaji Research Bureau in making Netaji's works accessible to the new generation.

EDITORS' INTRODUCTION

Sisir K. Bose and Sugata Bose

'How many selfless sons of the Mother are prepared, in this selfish age,' the fifteen-year-old Subhas asked his mother in 1912, 'to completely give up their personal interests and take the plunge for the Mother? Mother, is this son of yours yet ready?' As he stood on the verge of taking the plunge by resigning from the Indian Civil Service, he wrote to his elder brother Sarat on 6 April 1921: 'I know what this sacrifice means. It means poverty, suffering, hard work and possibly other hardships to which I need not expressly refer but which you can very well understand. But the sacrifice has got to be made—consciously and deliberately. Father says that most of the so-called leaders are not really unselfish. But is that any reason why he should prevent me from being unselfish?' An overpowering sense of mission impelled the young Subhas Chandra Bose to set an early example of leadership as he dedicated himself to a life of selfless service.

Subhas joined the freedom struggle as a lieutenant of Deshbandhu Chittaranjan Das when the non-cooperation movement of 1921 was at its height. After sixteen years of tireless work, several prison terms and long periods of exile he was chosen by Mahatma Gandhi to be the President of the Indian National Congress for 1938. Gandhi's choice became known at the time of the Calcutta meeting of the All India Congress Committee in October 1937. With the Mahatma's blessings Subhas decided to go on a trip to Europe before taking up his duties as Congress President. He spent more than a month from late November 1937 to early January 1938 with Emilie Schenkl at his favourite health resort Badgastein in Austria. There in the course of ten days in December 1937 he wrote ten chapters of his unfinished autobiography.

The handwritten manuscript is now preserved in the archives of the Netaji Research Bureau. This narrative of the first twenty-four years of Bose's life ends with his resignation from the I.C.S. in April 1921. It is not often that remembrances written later in life can be read together with primary source materials, including letters and notes, of the earlier, formative phase. This book is designed to provide the reader with that rare, double first-person perspective. The unfinished autobiography published as Part 1 is complemented in Part 2 with a fascinating collection of seventy letters of his childhood, adolescence and youth. This volume thus supplies the material with which to commence the study of the socio-cultural environment in which Subhas Chandra Bose grew up and the lineaments of his mental and intellectual development. The reader will gain a real insight into the influences—religious, cultural, moral, intellectual and political—that moulded the character and personality of India's foremost radical nationalist. Both the autobiography and the letters are marked by a lucidity and directness which make the basic currents of the author's unorthodox and rebellious life easier to comprehend. Moreover, the letters, which constitute the contemporary material, show an uninhibited play of opinions, emotions and ideas lending greater depth to the conclusions and inferences drawn in the autobiography.

Bose was able to write only the first nine chapters of the chronological narrative of his autobiography in December 1937. He was elected Congress President soon after and could not complete the work in the midst of a hectic and tumultuous public life. However, that he intended to write a complete autobiography is clear from the notes he made on the first page of the original manuscript indicating the plan he had in mind. The notes are as follows:

1. Birth—parentage—family history
2. School Education (a) P. E. School (b) R. C. School
3. College 1913–16—1916–17—1917–19 Scottish C. College 1919—Experimental Psychology
4. 1919–21—Cambridge
5. 1921–23
6. 1924–27 Burma etc.

7. 1927–29
8. 1929–31
9. 1929–31
10. 1932–1933—February
11. 1933–36—March—interlude in India
12. 1936–1937 March
13. 1937 March–December

The significance of this overall plan will be evident to those who turn to Netaji's *Collected Works* published in twelve volumes.[1] Subhas Chandra Bose wrote a separate, analytical account of the independence movement from 1920 to 1942 in two stages—in 1934 and 1942—under the title *The Indian Struggle*.[2] Even though this was not an autobiography, Netaji's personal involvement in the struggle was so complete that the process of his own development can be discerned by the careful reader in his rendering of the history of the nationalist movement.

As he was writing the early part of *An Indian Pilgrim* in Austria, he expressed his intention to write three chapters

---

[1] See Sisir Kumar Bose and Sugata Bose (eds.), *Netaji Collected Works vol 3 In Burmese Prisons* (Calcutta: Netaji Research Bureau and Hyderabad: Orient BlackSwan, 2021); *Netaji Collected Works vol 4 Renunciation and Realization* (Calcutta: Netaji Research Bureau and Ranikhet: Permanent Black, 2016); *Netaji Collected Works vol 5 The Call of the Motherland* (Calcutta: Netaji Research Bureau and Ranikhet: Permanent Black, 2016); *Netaji Collected Works vol 6 Leader of Youth* (Calcutta: Netaji Research Bureau and Ranikhet: Permanent Black, 2016) *Netaji Collected Works vol 7 Letters to Emilie Schenkl* (Calcutta: Netaji Research Bureau and Delhi: Permanent Black, 2004); *Netaji Collected Works vol 8 India's Spokesman Abroad* (Calcutta: Netaji Research Bureau and Ranikhet: Permanent Black, 2012); *Netaji Collected Works vol 9 Congress President* (Calcutta: Netaji Research Bureau and Delhi: Permanent Black, 2004); *Netaji Collected Works vol 10 The Alternative Leadership* (Calcutta: Netaji Research Bureau and Delhi: Permanent Black, 2004); *Netaji Collected Works vol 11 Azad Hind* (Calcutta: Netaji Research Bureau and Hyderabad: Orient BlackSwan, 2021); and *Netaji Collected Works vol 12 Chalo Delhi* (Calcutta: Netaji Research Bureau and Hyderabad: Orient BlackSwan, 2021).

[2] See Sisir Kumar Bose and Sugata Bose (eds.), *Netaji Collected Works vol 2 The Indian Struggle* (Calcutta: Netaji Research Bureau and Hyderabad: Orient BlackSwan, 2022).

on his fundamental beliefs titled 'My Faith (Philosophical)', 'My Faith (Political)' and 'My Faith (Economic)'. These were to form the last three chapters of his complete autobiography. Of these he was able to write only one which forms Chapter 10 of Part 1 of this volume. He attempted to sum up his philosophical ideas in a short article entitled 'My Personal Testament' which he drafted three years later in the Presidency Jail, Calcutta, in November 1940. This we have included in volume 10 of the *Collected Works*.

The tone and trend of the letters in Part 2 of this volume deserve a comment. It has been already said that they are complementary to the autobiography. The very early letters to his mother Prabhabati and his elder brother Sarat Chandra bring to light, as nothing else could, the springs of his idealism and missionary spirit. 'India,' Subhas Chandra Bose wrote to his mother in 1912 when he was only fifteen years old, 'is God's beloved land. He has been born in this great land in every age in the form of the Saviour for the enlightenment of the people, to rid this earth of sin and to establish righteousness and truth in every Indian heart. He has come into being in many countries in human form but not so many times in any other country—that is why I say, India, our motherland, is God's beloved land'.

Subhas's 'discovery of India', unlike Jawaharlal Nehru's, occurred very early in his life when he was barely in his teens. Born on 23 January 1897, he was deeply influenced by the cultural and intellectual milieu of Bengal at the turn of the century and grew up in harmony with the evolution of India's anti-colonial movement. In the course of his school and college career he was in turn a pure humanitarian, a *paribrajaka* and social reformer in the manner and spirit of Vivekananda and eventually a political activist. As the letters to his mother in 1912–13 reveal, his love for the country was at this stage tinged with a religious sensibility and expressed as devotion to the Mother. Yet he was dismayed at the current state of both the country and religion: 'now, wherever religion is practised there is so much bigotry and sin.' He asked his own mother, 'Will the condition of our country continue to go from bad to worse—will not any son of Mother India in distress, in total disregard of his selfish interests, dedicate his whole life to the cause of the Mother?'

The letters to his friends of student days expose the inner struggles of a very sensitive and idealistic adolescent and youth. These need to be read in context and the exaggerated asceticism of his early youth should not lead to a misunderstanding of the values he came to uphold later in life. Bose reflected on this turbulent period of his life in his autobiography with a great deal of wit and detached humour. In his student days he had believed that 'conquest of sex was essential to spiritual progress'. 'As I have turned from a purely spiritual ideal to a life of social service,' he added in a note, 'my views on sex have undergone transformation.'

By the time Subhas graduated from Calcutta University in 1919 and set out to study philosophy in Cambridge and qualify for the Indian Civil Service, he already had a formed personality and his sense of mission was not in doubt. That mission admitted of no compromise. The letters to his elder brother Sarat Chandra Bose during 1921, which he quoted extensively in his unfinished autobiography of 1937, reveal what went through his mind as he moved towards the decision to resign from the I.C.S. These seven remarkable letters were discovered along with eighteen letters from Emilie Schenkl written in 1936–37 in a cigar box in 1980. He had evidently taken these letters to Badgastein in November 1937 and brought them back with him in January 1938. He told his brother of his decision to 'chuck this rotten service' and not to wear 'the emblem of servitude' as 'national and spiritual aspirations' were 'not compatible with obedience to Civil Service conditions'. He was inspired at that time by the ideal of sacrifice set by Aurobindo Ghosh. 'Only on the soil of sacrifice and suffering,' he was convinced, 'can we raise our national edifice.'

In the appendices we have included a number of supporting documentary materials that strengthen the autobiographical text as well as the letters. Apart from the genealogical tables, there is a brief life-sketch of his father Janaki Nath Bose written by Subhas himself and a very old article on Purandar Khan and the Boses of Mahinagar by Nagendra Nath Bose. Subhas drew from the latter article for his chapter on family history. The report of the official enquiry committee on the Oaten incidents and Subhas's own short account of the first Oaten incident should be read with his two chapters in his autobiography on Presidency College. His minutes of the Philosophical Society of Scottish Church College are significant because it is known that his philosophical ideas began to germinate and take shape during his undergraduate studies there. Professor Oaten's poem on his former pupil is included on account of its unusual human interest.

This book in its totality reveals that not only was Subhas's sense of mission fully formed by 1921 but that he had a clear strategic sense of what was needed to win independence even as he began his political life. 'If the members of the services withdraw their allegiance or even show a desire to do so,' he wrote to Sarat Chandra Bose on 6 April 1921, 'then and then only will the bureaucratic machine collapse.' Having himself refused to owe allegiance to the Civil Service in 1921, he embarked on a mighty crusade in 1941 in an attempt to subvert the loyalty of Indians to the armed services and replace it with a new dedication to the cause of India's freedom. As Oaten wrote in 1947:

> Let me recall but this, that while as yet
> The Raj that you once challenged in your land
> Was mighty; Icarus-like your courage planned
> To mount the skies, and storm in battle set
> The ramparts of High Heaven, to claim the debt
> Of freedom owed, on plain and rude demand.
> High Heaven yielded, but in dignity
> Like Icarus, you sped towards the sea.

Part I

AN INDIAN PILGRIM

1. Birth - parentage - family history
2. School Education (a) PS School (b) R.C. School
3. College 1913-16. — 1916-17 — 1917-19 Scottish C. College
   1919 - Experimental Toxicology
4. 1919-21 - Cambridge
5. 1921 - 1923
6. 1923 - 1924
7. 1924 - 1927 Burma tc.
8. 1927 - 1929
9. 1929 - 1931
10. 1932 - 1933 - February
11. 1933 - 1936 — march — interlude in India
12. 1936 — 1937 March
13. 1937 - March - December

Chapter I
Birth Parentage and early Environment

My father had migrated to Orissa in the eighties of the last century and had settled down at Cuttack[2] as a lawyer. There I was born on Saturday, the 23rd January, 1897. My father was descended from Bose of Mahinagar, while my mother, Prabhabati (or rather Prabhavati) belonged to the family of the Duttas of Hatkhola. I was the sixth son and the ninth child of my parents.

// In these days of rapid communication, a night's journey by southwards along the eastern coast takes one from Calcutta to Cuttack and on the way, there is neither adventure nor romance. But things were not quite the same sixty years ago. One had to go either by cart and encounter thieves and robbers en route, or by sea and brave the wrath of the winds and the waves. Since it was safer to trust in God than in brother man, it was more common to travel by boat. Sea-faring vessels would carry passengers up to Chandbali where transhipment would take place and from Chandbali steamers would get to Cuttack through a number of rivers and canals. The description I used to hear from my mother, since childhood, of the rolling and pitching and the accompanying discomfort during the voyage, would leave in me no desire to undergo such an experience. At a time when

The original form in Sanskrit is Basu or rather Vasu. In common parlance you say Bengali; Vasu has become Bose. Cuttack, under the Government of India Act 1935, is the capital of the new province of Orissa. Formerly, till 1905, along with Bihar, it was a part of the Presidency of Bengal. Between 1905 and 1911 when Bengal was partitioned, West Bengal, Bihar and Orissa formed one province while East Bengal and Assam formed another. After 1911 and till quite recently, Bihar and Orissa together formed one province. West and East Bengal have, since 1911, been re-united, while Assam and the Bengali-speaking districts of Sylhet and Cachar have been constituted into a separate province.

CHAPTER I

BIRTH, PARENTAGE AND EARLY ENVIRONMENT

My father, Janakinath Bose, had migrated to Orissa in the eighties of the last century and had settled down at Cuttack as a lawyer. There I was born on Saturday, the 23rd January, 1897. My father was descended from the Boses of Mahinagar, while my mother, Prabhabati (or rather Prabhavati) belonged to the family of the Dutts of Hatkhola. I was the sixth son and the ninth child of my parents.

In these days of rapid communication, a night's journey by train southwards along the eastern coast takes one from Calcutta to Cuttack and on the way there is neither adventure nor romance. But things were not quite the same sixty years ago. One had to go either by cart and encounter thieves and robbers on the road, or by sea and brave the wrath of the winds and the waves. Since it was safer to trust in God than in brother man, it was more common to travel by boat. Sea-going vessels would carry passengers up to Chandbali where transhipment would take place and from Chandbali steamers would get to Cuttack through a number of rivers and canals. The description I used to hear from my mother since childhood of the rolling and pitching and the accompanying discomfort during the voyage would leave no desire in me to undergo such an experience. At a time when distances were long and journey by no means safe, my father must have had plenty of pluck to leave his village home and go far away in search of a career. Fortune favours the brave even in civil life and, by the time I was born, my father had already made a position for himself and was almost at the top of the legal profession in his new domicile.

Though a comparatively small town with a population in the neighbourhood of 20,000, Cuttack[1] had an importance

---

[1] Cuttack, under the Goverment of the India Act, 1935, is the capital of the new province of Orissa. Formerly, till 1905, along with Bihar, it was a part of

of its own owing to a variety of factors. It had an unbroken tradition since the days of the early Hindu Kings of Kalinga. It was de facto capital of Orissa which could boast of such a famous place of pilgrimage as Puri (or Jagannath) and such glorious art-relics as those of Konarak, Bhuvaneswar, and Udaigiri. It was the headquarters not only for the British administration in Orissa, but also for the numerous ruling chiefs in that province. Altogether, Cuttack afforded a healthy environment for the growing child, and it had some of the virtues of both city and country life.

Ours was not a rich but what might be regarded as a well-to-do, middle-class family. Naturally, I had no personal experience of what want and poverty meant and had no occasion to develop those traits of selfishness, greed, and the rest which are sometimes the unwelcome heritage of indigent circumstances in one's early life. At the same time, there was not that luxury and lavishness in our home which has been the ruin of so many promising but pampered young souls or has helped to foster a supercilious, high-brow mentality in them. In fact, considering their worldly means my parents always erred—and, I dare say, rightly too—on the side of simplicity in the upbringing of their children.

The earliest recollection I have of myself is that I used to feel like a thoroughly insignificant being. My parents awed me to a degree. My father usually had a cloak of reserve round him and kept his children at a distance. What with his professional work and what with his public duties, he did not have much time for his family. The time he could spare was naturally divided among his numerous sons and daughters. The youngest child did, of course, come in for an extra dose of fondling, but an addition to the family would soon rob it of its title to special favour. And for the grown-ups it was difficult

---

the Presidency of Bengal. Between 1905 and 1911 when Bengal was partitioned, West Bengal, Bihar and Orissa formed one province, while East Bengal and Assam formed another. After 1911 and till quite recently, Bihar and Orissa together formed one province. West and East Bengal have, since 1911, been re-united, while Assam and the Bengali-speaking districts of Sylhet and Cachar have been constituted into a separate province.

to discern whom father loved more, so strictly impartial he appeared to be, whatever his inner feelings might have been. And my mother? Though she was more humane and it was not impossible at times to detect her bias, she was also held in awe by most of her children. No doubt she ruled the roost and, where family affairs were concerned, hers was usually the last word. She had a strong will, and, when one added to that a keen sense of reality and sound common-sense, it is easy to understand how she could dominate the domestic scene. In spite of all the respect I cherished for my parents since my early years, I did yearn for a more intimate contact with them and could not help envying those children who were lucky to be on friendly terms with their parents. This desire presumably arose out of a sensitive and emotional temperament.

But to be overawed by my parents was not the only tragedy. The presence of so many elder brothers and sisters seemed to relegate me into utter insignificance. That was perhaps all to the good. I started life with a sense of diffidence—with a feeling that I should live up to the level already attained by those who had preceded me. For good or for ill, I was free from over-confidence or cock-sureness. I lacked innate genius but had no tendency to shirk hard work. I had, I believe, a subconscious feeling that for mediocre men industry and good behaviour are the sole passports to success.

To be a member of a large family is, in many ways, a drawback. One does not get the individual attention which is often necessary in childhood. Moreover, one is lost in a crowd as it were, and the growth of personality suffers in consequence. On the other hand, one develops sociability and overcomes self-centredness and angularity. From infancy I was accustomed to living not merely in the midst of a large number of sisters and brothers, but also with uncles and cousins. The denotation of the word 'family' was therefore automatically enlarged. What is more, our house had always an open door for distant relatives hailing from our ancestral village. And, in accordance with a long-standing Indian custom, any visitors to the town of Cuttack who bore the stamp of respectability could—with or without an introduction—drive to our house and expect to be put up there. Where the hotel-system is not so much in vogue and decent hotels are lacking, society has somehow to provide for a social need. The largeness of our household was due not merely to the size of the family, but to the number of dependents and servants as well—and to the representatives of the animal world—cows, horses, goats, sheep, deer, peacock, birds, mongoose, etc. The servants were an institution by themselves and formed an integral part of the household. Most of them had been in service long before I was born and some of them (e.g. the oldest maid-servant) were held in respect by all of us.[2] Commercialism had not then permeated and distorted human relationship; so there was considerable attachment between our servants and ourselves. This early experience shaped my subsequent mental attitude towards servants as a class.

Though the family environment naturally helped to broaden my mind, it could not, nevertheless, rid me of that shy reserve which was to haunt me for years later and which I doubt if I have yet been able to shake off. Perhaps I was and still remain an introvert.

---

[2] Some of them have since retired from service and are enjoying pensions, while others have died.

Chapter II
Family History

The history of our family can be traced back for about 28 generations. The Boses are Kayastha[2] by caste. The founder of the Dakshin-Rārhi[3] clan of the Boses was one Dasaratha Bose, who had two sons, Krishna and Parama. Parama went over to East Bengal and settled there, while Krishna lived in West Bengal. 8th descent in descent from Dasaratha was Mahipati, a man of outstanding ability and intelligence. He attracted the attention of the King of Bengal, who appointed him as minister for Finance and War. In appreciation of his services the King, who was Muslim by religion, conferred on him the title of "Subuddhi Khan".[5] As was the prevailing custom, Mahipati was also given a 'jaigir' (landed property) as a mark of

One of the great-great-grandsons of Dasaratha was Mukti Bose, who resided at Mahinagar, a village about 14 miles to the south of Calcutta, when the family is now known as the Boses of Mahinagar.[4]

1. For some of the facts chronicled here I am indebted to Nagendranath Bose, the reputed antiquarian and historian [vide his article on Purander Khan in Kayastha Patrika (Bengali monthly) for Jaistha, 1335]
2. The Kayasthas claim to be none other than Kshatriyas (i.e. warrior-caste) in origin. According to popular usage, the Kayasthas are classified among the (so-called) higher castes.
3. Dakshin-Rārh probably means South Bengal.
4. From Calcutta Mahinagar can be reached via Chingripota, a station on the Diamond Harbour Railway lines
5. It is interesting to note in this connexion

Mother Prabhabati

CHAPTER II

FAMILY HISTORY[†]

The history of our family can be traced back for about 27 generations. The Boses[1] are Kayastha[2] by caste. The founder of the Dakshin-Rarhi[3] clan of the Boses was one Dasaratha Bose, who had two sons, Krishna and Parama. Parama went over to East Bengal and settled there, while Krishna lived in West Bengal. One of the great-great-grandsons of Dasaratha was Mukti Bose, who resided at Mahinagar, a village about 14 miles to the south of Calcutta, whence the family is now known as the Boses of Mahinagar.[4] Eleventh in descent from Dasaratha was Mahipati, a man of outstanding ability and intelligence. He attracted the attention of the then King of Bengal, who appointed him as Minister for Finance and War. In appreciation of his services, the King who was Muslim by religion, conferred on him the title of 'Subuddhi Khan'.[5] As was the prevailing custom, Mahipati was also given a 'Jaigir' (landed property) as a mark of royal favour and the village of Subuddhipur, not far from Mahinagar, was probably his jaigir. Of Mahipati's ten sons, Ishan Khan, who was the fourth, rose to eminence and maintained his father's position at the Royal Court. Ishan Khan had three sons, all of whom received titles from the King. The second son, Gopinath Bose, possessed extraordinary ability

---

[†] For some of the facts chronicled here I am indebted to Nagendranath Bose, the well-known antiquarian and historian (see his article on Purandar Khan in Kayastha Patrika, Bengali Monthly for Jaistha, 1335).

[1] The original form in Sanskrit is Basu or rather Vasu. In common parlance in Bengali, Vasu has become Bose.

[2] The Kayasthas claim to be none other than Kshatriyas (i.e., warrior-caste) in origin. According to popular usage, the Kayasthas are classified among the (so-called) higher castes.

[3] Dakshin-Rarhi probably means 'South-Bengal'.

[4] From Calcutta Mahinagar can be reached via Chingripota, a station on the Diamond Harbour Railway line.

[5] It is interesting to note in this connection that the Muslim Kings of Bengal used Sanskrit words in their titles. 'Khan' is of course a typically Muslim title.

and prowess and was appointed Finance Minister and Naval Commander by the then King, Sultan Hossain Shah (1493–1519). He was rewarded with the title of Purandar Khan and a jaigir, now known as Purandarpur, not far from his native village of Mahinagar. In Purandarpur there is a tank called 'Khan Pukur' (or Khan's tank) which is a relic of a one-mile long tank excavated by Purandar Khan. The village of Malancha near Mahinagar has grown on the site of Purandar's Garden.

In those days the Hooghly flowed in the vicinity of Mahinagar and it is said that Purandar used to travel by boat to and from Gaud, the then capital of Bengal. He built up a powerful navy which defended the kingdom from external attack and was its commander.

Purandar also made his mark as a social reformer. Before his time, according to the prevailing Ballali custom, the two wings of the Kayastha—Kulin (who were the elite, viz. the Boses, the Ghoses, and the Mitras) and Moulik (the Dutts, the Deys, the Roys, etc.)—did not, as a rule, intermarry. Purandar laid down a new custom[6] to the effect that only the eldest issue of a Kulin need marry into a Kulin family, while the others could marry Mouliks. This custom, which has been generally followed till the present day, saved the Kayastha from impending disaster—the fruit of excessive inbreeding.

Purandar was also a man of letters. His name figures among the composers of Padabali, the devotional songs of the Vaishnavas.

Evidence is afforded by several Bengali poems, like Kavirama's 'Raymangal', that as late as 200 years ago, the Hooghly (called in Bengali—Ganga) flowed by Mahinagar and the neighbouring villages. (Even now, all tanks in the former bed of the 'Ganga' are also called 'Ganga' by courtesy, e.g. Bose's Ganga, meaning thereby Bose's tank.)

---

[6] Intercaste marriage which has been going on for the last 50 years or more has considerably slackened existing caste rules. But in Purandar's time this move was regarded as revolutionary. The outstanding position he had in special and public life enabled him to put through this measure of reform. It is said that he invited over 100,000 Kayasthas to his village to have the new code adopted by them. 'Khan's Pukur' was excavated on this occasion to supply pure drinking water to this assembly.

The shifting of the river-bed struck a death blow at the health and prosperity of these villages. Disturbance of the drainage of the countryside was followed by epidemics, which in turn forced a large section of the population to migrate to other places. One branch of the Bose family—the direct descendants of Purandar Khan—moved to the adjoining village of Kodalia.

After a period of comparative silence, this neighbourhood, containing the village of Kodalia, Chingripota, Harinavi, Malancha, Rajpur, etc. leapt into activity once again. During the early decades of the nineteenth century there was a remarkable cultural upheaval which continued till the end of the century when once again the countryside was devastated by epidemics—malaria carrying off the palm this time. Today one has only to walk through these desolated villages and observe huge mansions overgrown with wild creepers standing in a dilapidated condition, in order to realise the degree of prosperity and culture which the neighbourhood must have enjoyed in the not distant past. The scholars who appeared here about a century ago were mostly men learned in the ancient lore of India, but they were not obscurantists by any means. Some of these Pundits were preceptors of the Brahmo Samaj, then a revolutionary body from the sociocultural point of view, while others were editors of secular journals printed in Bengali which were playing an important part in creating a new Bengali literature and in influencing contemporary public affairs.

Pundit Ananda Chandra Vedantavageesh was the editor of 'Tattwabodhini Patrika', an influential journal of those days and also a preceptor of the Brahmo Samaj. Pundit Dwarakanath Vidyabhusan was the editor of 'Som Prakash', probably the first weekly journal to be printed in the Bengali language. One of his nephews was Pundit Shivanath Shastri, one of the outstanding personalities of the Brahmo Samaj. Bharat Chandra Shiromani was one of the authorities in Hindu Law, especially in the Bengal school of Hindu Law called 'Dayabhag'. Among the artists could be named Kalikumar Chakravarti, a distinguished painter, and among musicians, Aghor Chakravarti and

Kaliprasanna Bose. During the last few decades the locality has played an important part in the nationalist movement. Influential Congressmen like Harikumar Chakravarti and Satkari Banerji (who died in the Deoli Detention Camp in 1936) hail from this quarter, and no less a man than Comrade M. N. Roy, of international fame, was born there.

To come back to our story, the Boses who migrated to Kodalia must have been living there for at least ten generations, for their genealogical tree is available.[7] My father was the thirteenth in descent from Purandar Khan and twenty-sixth from Dasaratha Bose. My grandfather Haranath had four sons, Jadunath, Kedarnath, Devendranath, and Janakinath, my father. Though by tradition our family was Shakta,[8] Haranath was a pious and devoted Vaishnava. The Vaishnavas being generally more nonviolent in temperament, Haranath stopped the practice of goat-sacrifice at the annual Durga Poojah (worship of God as Divine Energy in the form of mother) which used to be celebrated with great pomp every year—Durga Poojah being the most important festival of the Hindus of Bengal. This innovation has been honoured till the present day, though another branch of the Bose family living in the same village still adheres to goat-sacrifice at the annual Poojah.

Haranath's four sons migrated to different places in search of a career. The eldest Jadunath who worked in the Imperial Secretariat had to spend a good portion of his time in Simla. The second, Kedarnath, moved to Calcutta permanently. The third, Devendranath, who joined the educational service of the Government and rose to the rank of Principal, had to move about from place to place and after retirement settled down in Calcutta.

---

[7] See Appendix 1.

[8] The Hindus of Bengal were, broadly speaking, divided into two schools or sects, Shakta and Vaishnava. Shaktas preferred to worship God as Power or Energy in the form of mother. The Vaishnavas worshipped God as Love in the form of father and protector. The difference became manifest at the time of initiation, or 'holy word' which a Shakta received from his 'guru', or preceptor, being different from what a Vaishnava received from his guru. It was customary for a family to follow a particular tradition for generations, though there was nothing to prevent a change from one sect to the other.

My father was born on the 28th May, 1860 and my mother in 1869.[9] After passing the Matriculation (then called Entrance) Examination from the Albert School, Calcutta, he studied for some time at the St. Xavier's College and the General Assembly's Institution (now called Scottish Church College). He then went to Cuttack and graduated from the Ravenshaw College. He returned to Calcutta to take his law degree and during this period came into close contact with the prominent personalities of the Brahmo Samaj, Brahmananda Keshav Chandra Sen, his brother Krishna Vihari Sen, and Umesh Chandra Dutt, Principal of the City College. He worked for a time as Lecturer in the Albert College, of which Krishna Vihari Sen was the Rector. In 1885 he went to Cuttack and joined the bar. The year 1901 saw him as the first non-official elected Chairman of the Cuttack Municipality. By 1905 he became Government Pleader and Public Prosecutor. In 1912 he became a member of the Bengal Legislative Council and received the title of Rai Bahadur. In 1917, following some differences with the District Magistrate, he resigned the post of Government Pleader and Public Prosecutor and thirteen years later, in 1930, he gave up the title of Rai Bahadur as a protest against the repressive policy of the Government.

Besides being connected with public bodies like the Municipality and District Board, he took an active part in educational and social institutions like the Victoria School and Cuttack Union Club. He had extensive charities, and poor students came in for a regular share of them. Though the major portion of his charities went to Orissa, he did not forget his ancestral village, where he founded a charitable dispensary and library, named after his mother and father respectively. He was a regular visitor at the annual session of the Indian National Congress but he did not actively participate in politics, though he was a consistent supporter of Swadeshi.[10] After the commencement of the

---

[9] To be more exact, she was born on the 13th Phalgun, 1275 according to the Bengali year. Phalgun 13th, 1344 is equivalent to February 25th, 1938.

[10] i.e., home-industries.

Non-co-operation Movement in 1921, he interested himself in the constructive activities of the Congress, Khadi[11] and national education. He was all along of a religious bent of mind and received initiation twice, his first guru being a Shakta and the second a Vaishnava. For years he was the President of the local Theosophical Lodge. He had always a soft spot for the poorest of the poor and before his death he made provisions for his old servants and other dependents.

As mentioned in the first chapter, my mother belonged to the family of the Dutts[12] of Hatkhola, a northern quarter of Calcutta. In the early days of British rule, the Dutts were one of those families in Calcutta who attained a great deal of prominence by virtue of their wealth and their ability to adapt themselves to the new political order. As a consequence they played a role among the neo-aristocracy of the day. My mother's grandfather, Kashi Nath Dutt, broke away from the family and moved to Baranagore, a small town about six miles to the north of Calcutta, built a palatial house for himself and settled down there. He was a very well-educated man, a voracious reader and a friend of the students. He held a high administrative post in the firm of Messrs Jardine, Skinner & Co., a British firm doing business in Calcutta. Both my mother's father, Ganganarayan Dutt, and grandfather had a reputation for being wise in selecting their sons-in-law. They were thereby able to make alliances with the leading families among the Calcutta aristocracy of the day. One of Kashi Nath Dutt's sons-in-law was Sir Romesh Chandra Mitter[13] who was the first Indian to be acting Chief Justice of the Calcutta High Court. Another was Rai Bahadur Hari Vallabh Bose who had migrated to Cuttack before my father and as a lawyer had won a unique position for himself throughout the whole of Orissa.

---

[11] Khadi or Khaddar is hand-spun and hand-woven cloth.

[12] The original Sanskrit form of this word is 'Datta' or 'Dutta'. 'Dutt' is an anglicised abbreviation of this word.

[13] This is the same as Mitra. Sir Romesh had three sons—the late Manmatha Nath, Sir Benode, and Sir Pravas Mitter. The late Sir B. C. Mitter was Advocate-General of Bengal and later on, a member of the Judicial Committee of the Privy Council. Sir Pravas Mitter was member of the Executive Council of the Governor of Bengal.

It is said of my maternal grandfather, Ganganarayan Dutt, that before he agreed to give my mother in marriage to my father, he put the latter through an examination and satisfied himself as to his intellectual ability. My mother was the eldest daughter. Her younger sisters were married successively to (the late) Barada Ch. Mitra, I.C.S., District and Sessions Judge, Mr Upendra Nath Bose of Benares City, (the late) Chandra Nath Ghosh, Subordinate Judge and (the late) Dr J. N. Bose, younger brother of the late Rai Bahadur Chuni Lal Bose of Calcutta.

From the point of view of eugenics it is interesting to note that on my father's side, large families were the exception and not the rule. On my mother's side, the contrary seems to have been the case. Thus my maternal grandfather had nine sons and six daughters.[14] Among his children, the daughters generally had large families—including my mother—but not the sons. My parents had eight sons and six daughters,[15] of whom nine—seven sons and two daughters—are still living. Among my sisters and brothers, some—but not the majority—have as many as eight or nine children, but it is not possible to say that the sisters are more prolific than the brothers or vice versa. It would be interesting to know if in a particular family the prolific strain adheres to one sex more than to the other. Perhaps eugenists could answer the question.

---

[14] For the genealogical tree, see Appendix 1.
[15] See Appendix 1.

CHAPTER III

BEFORE MY TIME

It requires a great deal of imagination now to picture the transformation that Indian society underwent as a result of political power passing into the hands of the British since the latter half of the eighteenth century. Yet an understanding of it is essential if we are to view in their proper perspective the kaleidoscopic changes that are going on in India today. Since Bengal was the first province to come under British rule, the resulting changes were more quickly visible there than elsewhere. With the overthrow of the indigenous Government, the feudal aristocracy which was bound up with it naturally lost its importance. Its place was taken by another set of men. The Britishers had come into the country for purposes of trade and had later on found themselves called upon to rule. But it was not possible for a handful of them to carry on their trade or administration without the active co-operation of at least a section of the people. At this juncture those who fell in line with the new political order and had sufficient ability and initiative to make the most of the new situation came to the fore as the aristocracy of the new age.

It is generally thought that for a long time under British rule Muslims[1] did not play an important role, and several theories have been advanced to account for this. It is urged, for instance, that since, in provinces like Bengal, the rulers who were overthrown by the British were Muslims by religion, the Muslim community maintained for a long time an attitude of sullen animosity and non-cooperation towards the new rulers, their culture and their administration. On the other hand it is said that, prior to the establishment of British rule in India, the Muslim aristocracy had already grown thoroughly effete

---

[1] Also called Mohammedans.

Chapter III
Before my time   changes that are going
                    on in India today

It requires a great deal of imagination *now* to picture the transformation that Indian Society underwent as a result of political power passing into the hands of the British since the latter half of the eighteenth century. Yet an understanding of it is essential if we are to view in their proper perspective the kaleidoscopic Since Bengal was the first province to come under British rule, the resulting changes were more quickly visible there than elsewhere. With the overthrow of the indigenous government, the feudal aristocracy which was bound up with it, naturally lost its importance. Its place was taken by another set of men. The Britishers had come into the country for purposes of trade and had later on found themselves called upon to rule. But it was not possible for a handful of them to carry on either trade or administration without the active cooperation of at least a section of of the people. At this juncture, those who fell in line with the new political order and had sufficient ability and initiative to make the most of the new situation, came to the fore as the aristocracy of the new age.

It is generally thought that for a long time under British rule, ⟶ Muslims[1] did not play an important role. And several theories have been advanced to account for

[1] Also called Mohammedans.

Father Janakinath

and worn out and that Islam did not at first take kindly to modern science and civilization. Consequently, it was but natural that under British rule the Muslims should suffer from a serious handicap and go under for the time being. I am inclined, however, to think that in proportion to their numbers,[2] and considering India as a whole, the Muslims have never ceased to play an important role in the public life of the country, whether before or under British rule—and that the distinction between Hindu and Muslim of which we hear so much nowadays is largely an artificial creation, a kind of Catholic–Protestant controversy in Ireland, in which our present-day rulers have had a hand. History will bear me out when I say that it is a misnomer to talk of Muslim rule when describing the political order in India prior to the advent of the British. Whether we talk of the Moghul Emperors at Delhi, or of the Muslim Kings of Bengal, we shall find that in either case the administration was run by Hindus and Muslims together, many of the prominent Cabinet Ministers and Generals being Hindus. Further, the consolidation of the Moghul Empire in India was effected with the help of Hindu commanders-in-chief. The Commander-in-chief of Nawab Sirajudowla, whom the British fought at Plassey in 1757 and defeated, was a Hindu, and the rebellion of 1857 against the British, in which Hindus and Muslims were found side by side, was fought under the flag of a Muslim, Bahadur Shah.

Be that as it may, it is a fact so far as Bengal is concerned, whatever the causes may be, most of the prominent personalities that arose soon after the British conquest were Hindus. The most outstanding of them was Raja Ram Mohan Roy (1772–1833) who founded the Brahmo Samaj[3] in 1828. The dawn of the nineteenth century saw a new

---

[2] According to the 1931 census, the Muslims are roughtly 24.7 per cent of the total population of British India which is about 271.4 millions; roughly 13.5 per cent of the total population of the Indian states which is 79 millions and roughly 22 per cent of the total population of India, which is 350.5 millions.

[3] The Brahmo Samaj can best be described as a reformist movement within Hindu society, standing for the religious principles of the Vedanta in their pristine form and discarding later accretions like image-worship and the caste-system. Originally the Brahmos tended to break away from Hindu Society, but their present attitude is to regard themselves as a integral part of it.

awakening in the land. This awakening was cultural and religious in character and the Brahmo Samaj was its spearhead. It could be likened to a combination of the Renaissance and Reformation. One aspect of it was national and conservative— standing for a revival of India's culture and a reform of India's religions. The other aspect of it was cosmopolitan and eclectic—seeking to assimilate what was good and useful in other cultures and religions. Ram Mohan was the visible embodiment of the new awakening and the herald of a new era in India's history. His mantle fell successively on 'Maharshi' Devendranath Tagore (1818–1905), father of the poet Rabindranath Tagore, and Brahmananda Keshav Chandra Sen (1838–1884) and the influence of the Brahmo Samaj grew from day to day.

There is no doubt that at one time the Brahmo Samaj focussed within itself all the progressive movements and tendencies in the country. From the very beginning the Samaj was influenced in its cultural outlook by Western science and thought, and when the newly established British Government was in doubt as to what its educational policy should be—whether it should promote indigenous culture exclusively or introduce Western culture—Raja Ram Mohan Roy took an unequivocal stand as the champion of Western culture. His ideas influenced Thomas Babington Macaulay when he wrote his famous Minute on Education[4] and ultimately became the policy of the Government. With his prophetic vision, Ram Mohan had realised, long before any of his countrymen did, that India would have to assimilate Western science and thought if she wanted to come into her own once again.

The cultural awakening was not confined to the Brahmo Samaj, however. Even those who regarded the Brahmos as

---

[4] Macaulay came to Calcutta as Law Member of the Governor General's Council in the autumn of 1834. He was appointed President of the Committee of Public Instruction which he found divided into the Orientalist and English parties. On February 2, 1835, he submitted a Minute to the Governor General, Bentinck, supporting the English party which was adopted by the Government.

too heretical, revolutionary, or iconoclastic were keen about the revival of the indigenous culture of India. While the Brahmos and other progressive sections of the people replied to the challenge of the West by trying to assimilate all that was good in Western culture, the more orthodox circles responded by justifying whatever there was to be found in Hindu society and by trying to prove that all the discoveries and inventions of the West were known to the ancient sages of India. Thus the impact of the West roused even the orthodox circles from their self-complacency. There was a great deal of literary activity among them and they produced able men like Sasadhar Tarkachuramani—but much of their energy was directed towards meeting the terrible onslaughts on Hindu religion coming from the Christian missionaries. In this there was common ground between the Brahmos and the orthodox Pundits, though in other matters there was no love lost between them. Out of the conflict between the old and the new, between the conservatives and the radicals, between the Brahmos and the Pundits, there emerged a new type—the noblest embodiment of which was Pundit Iswar Chandra Vidyasagar. This new type of Indian stood for progress and for a synthesis of Eastern and Western culture and accepted generally the spirit of reform which was abroad, but refused to break away from Hindu society or to go too far in emulating the West, as the Brahmos were inclined to do at first. Iswar Chandra Vidyasagar, for instance, was brought up as an orthodox Pundit, became the father of modern Bengali prose and a protagonist of Western science and culture, and was a great social reformer and philanthropist[5]—but till the last, he stuck to the simple and austere life of an orthodox Pundit. He boldly advocated the remarriage of Hindu widows and incurred the wrath of the conservatives in doing so—but he based his arguments mainly on the fact that the ancient

---

[5] Speaking of the Pundit, the poet Madhusudan Dutt, the originator of blank verse in Bengali, once wrote... "You are not merely the ocean of knowledge (Vidyasagar means literally 'the ocean of knowledge') as people know you in India, but also the ocean of generosity."

scriptures approved of such a custom. The type which
Iswar Chandra represented ultimately found its religious
and philosophical expression in Ramakrishna Paramahansa
(1834–1886) and his worthy disciple, Swami Vivekananda
(1863–1902). Swami Vivekananda died in 1902 and the
religio-philosophical movement was continued through the
personality of Arabindo Ghose (or Ghosh). Arabindo did
not keep aloof from politics. On the contrary, he plunged
into the thick of it, and by 1908 became one of the foremost
political leaders. In him, spirituality was wedded to politics.
Arabindo retired from politics in 1909 to devote himself
exclusively to religion; but spirituality and politics continued
to be associated together in the life of Lokamanya B. G. Tilak
(1856–1920) and Mahatma Gandhi (1869).

This brief narrative will serve as a rough background to
the contents of this book and will give some idea of the social
environment which existed when my father was a student of
the Albert School[6] in Calcutta. Society was then dominated by
a new aristocracy, which had grown up alongside of British
rule, whom we should now call, in socialist parlance, the allies
of British 'Imperialism'. This aristocracy was composed roughly
of three classes or professions—(1) landlords, (2) lawyers and
civil servants and (3) merchant-princes. All of them were the
creation of the British, their assistance being necessary for
carrying out the policy of administration-cum-exploitation.

The landlords who came into prominence under British
rule were not the semi-independent or autonomous chiefs of
the feudal age, but mere tax-collectors who were useful to a
foreign Government in the matter of collecting land-revenue
and who had to be rewarded for their loyalty during the
Rebellion of 1857, when the existence of British rule hung
by a thread.

Though the new aristocracy dominated contemporary
society and, as a consequence, men like Maharaja Jatindra
Mohan Tagore and Raja Benoy Krishna Deb Bahadur were

---

[6] Here he was a class-fellow of Sir P. C. Ray, the well-known chemist and
philanthropist.

regarded by the Government as the leaders of society, they had little in the way of intellectual or moral appeal. That appeal was exercised in my father's youth by men like Keshav Chandra Sen and to some extent, Iswar Chandra Vidyasagar. Wherever the former went, crowds followed him. He was, indeed, the hero of the hour. The spiritual fervour of his powerful orations raised the moral tone of society as a whole and of the rising generations in particular. Like other students, my father, too, came under his magic influence, and there was a time when he even thought of a formal conversion to Brahmoism. In any case, Keshav Chandra undoubtedly had an abiding influence on my father's life and character. Years later, in far-off Cuttack, portraits of this great man would still adorn the walls of his house, and his relations with the local Brahmo Samaj continued to be cordial throughout his life.

Though there was a profound moral awakening among the people during the formative period of my father's life, I am inclined to think that politically the country was still dead. It is significant that his heroes—Keshav Chandra and Iswar Chandra[7]—though they were men of the highest moral stature, were by no means anti-Government or anti-British. The former used to state openly that he regarded the advent of the British as a divine dispensation. And the latter did not shun contact with the Government or with Britishers as a 'non-co-operator' today would, though the keynote of his character was an acute sense of independence and self-respect. My father, likewise, though he had a high standard of morality, and influenced his family to that end, was not anti-Government. That was why he could accept the position of Government Pleader and Public Prosecutor, as well as a title from the Government. My father's elder brother, Principal Devendra Nath Bose, belonged to the same type. He was a man of unimpeachable character, greatly loved and respected by his students

---

[7] Both of them were educationists and, largely, under their inspiration, a new type of teachers, possessing a high moral character, was produced. My father was also a teacher for some time and might have taken up teaching as a profession.

for his intellectual and moral attainments, but he was a Government servant in the Education Department. Likewise, before my father's time it was possible for Bankim Chandra Chatterji[8] (1838–1894) to compose the 'Bande Mataram'[9] song and still continue in Government service. And D. L. Roy[10] could be a magistrate in the service of the Government and yet compose national songs which inspired the people. All this could happen some decades ago, because that was an age of transition, probably an age of political immaturity. Since 1905, when the partition of Bengal was effected in the teeth of popular opposition and indignation, a sharpening of political consciousness has taken place, leading to inevitable friction between the people and the Government. People are nowadays more resentful of what the Government does and the Government in its turn is more suspicious of what the people say or write. The old order has changed, yielding place to new, and today it is no longer possible to separate morality from politics—to obey the dictates of morality and not land oneself in political trouble. The individual has to go through the experience of his race within the brief span of his own life, and I remember quite clearly that I too passed through the stage of what I may call non-political morality, when I thought that moral development was possible while steering clear of politics—while complacently giving unto Caesar what is Caesar's. But now I am convinced that life is one whole. If we accept an idea, we have to give ourselves wholly to it and to allow it to transform our entire life. A light brought into a dark room will necessarily illuminate every portion of it.

---

[8] One of the fathers of modern Bengali Literature.

[9] 'Bande Mataram' literally means 'I salute the mother' (i.e., motherland). It is the nearest approach to India's national anthem.

[10] One of the foremost Bengali dramatists and composer of national songs—father of Dilip Kumar Roy. He died in 1913.

Chapter IV
At School (1)

I was nearing my fifth birth-day (January, 1902) when I was told that I would be sent to school. I do not know how other children have felt in similar circumstances, but I was delighted. To see your elder brothers and sisters dress and go to school day after day and be left behind at home simply because you are not big enough — not old enough — is a galling experience. At least, so I had felt and that is why I was overjoyed. It was to be a red-letter day for me. At last I was going to join the grown-up respectable folks who did not stay at home except on holidays. We had to start at about 10 A.M. because the classes commenced exactly at 10.30. A.M. Two uncles of about the same age as myself were also to be admitted along with myself. When we were all ready, we began to run towards the carriage which was to take us to school. Just then, as ill-luck would have it, I slipped and fell. I was hurt and with a bandage round my head, I was ordered to bed.

The rumbling of the carriage-wheels grew fainter in the distance. The lucky ones had gone,

Family photograph at Cuttack—Netaji then a schoolboy, standing on extreme right

CHAPTER IV

AT SCHOOL (1)

I was nearing my fifth birthday (January, 1902) when I was told I would be sent to school. I do not know how other children have felt in similar circumstances, but I was delighted. To see your elder brothers and sisters dress and go to school day after day and be left behind at home simply because you are not big enough—not old enough—is a galling experience. At least, so I had felt, and that is why I was overjoyed.

It was to be a red-letter day for me. At long last I was going to join the grown-up respectable folks who did not stay at home except on holidays. We had to start at about 10 a.m. because the classes commenced exactly at 10 a.m. Two uncles of about the same age as myself were also to be admitted along with myself. When we were all ready, we began to run towards the carriage which was to take us to school. Just then, as ill-luck would have it, I slipped and fell. I was hurt and, with a bandage round my head, I was ordered to bed. The rumbling of the carriage wheels grew fainter in the distance. The lucky ones had gone, but there I lay with darkness staring me in the face and my fond hopes dashed to the ground.

Twenty-four hours later I found solace.

Ours was a missionary school[1] meant primarily for European and Anglo-Indian boys and girls with a limited number of seats (about 15 per cent) for Indians. All our brothers and sisters had joined this school, and so I did. I do not know why our parents had selected this school, but I presume it was because we would master the English language better and sooner there than elsewhere, and knowledge of English had a premium in those days. I still remember that when I went to school I had just learnt the

---

[1] Protestant European School (P. E. School) run by the Baptist Mission.

English alphabet and no more. How I managed to get along without being able to speak a word of English beats me now. I have not yet forgotten one of my first attempts at English. We had been given slate pencils and told to sharpen them before trying to write. Mine was done better than that of my uncle; so I pointed that out to our teacher by saying, 'Ranendra mot[2] I shor'[3]—and thought that I had talked in English.

Our teachers were Anglo-Indians (and mostly ladies) with the exception of the headmaster and headmistress, Mr and Mrs Young, who had come out from England. Most of our teachers we did not fancy. Some like Mr Young we feared, though we respected, for he was too liberal with his cane. Some like Miss Cadogan we tolerated. Others like Miss S. we positively hated and would cry 'Hurrah' if she ever absented herself. Mrs Young we liked, but Miss Sarah Lawrence who was our first teacher in the Infant Class we loved. She had such a sympathetic understanding of the child's mind that we were irresistibly drawn towards her. But for her, I doubt if I would have got on so easily at a time when I was unable to express myself in English.

Though the majority of the teachers and pupils were Anglo-Indians, the school was based on the English model and run on English lines, as far as Indian conditions would permit. There were certain things we did learn there which we would have missed in an Indian school. There was not that unhealthy emphasis on studies which obtains in Indian schools. Outside studies, more attention was given to deportment, neatness, and punctuality than is done in an Indian school. In the matter of studies, the students received more individual attention at the hands of their teachers and the daily work was done more regularly and systematically than is possible in an Indian school. The result was that practically no preparation was needed when an examination had to be faced. Moreover, the

---

[2] 'Mota' in Bengali means 'thick' and 'mot' was a distortion of it.
[3] 'Shoroo' in Bengali means 'thin' and 'shor' was a distortion of it.

standard of English taught was much higher than that of Indian schools. But after giving due consideration and credit to all this, I doubt if I should today advise an Indian boy to go to such a school. Though there was order and system in the education that was imparted, the education itself was hardly adapted to the needs of Indian students. Too much importance was attached to the teaching of the Bible, and the method of teaching it was as unscientific as it was uninteresting. We had to learn our Bible lessons by heart whether we understood anything or not, as if we were so many priests memorizing the sacred texts. It would be no exaggeration for me to say that though we were taught the Bible day in day out and for seven long years, I came to like the Bible for the first time several years later when I was in College.

There is no doubt that the curriculum was so framed as to make us as English in our mental make-up as possible. We learnt much about the geography and history of Great Britain but proportionally little about India—and when we had to negotiate Indian names, we did so as if we were foreigners. We started our Latin declensions—'bonus, bona, bonum'—rather early and did not have to be bothered about our Sanskrit declensions—'Gajah, Gajow, Gajah'—till we had left the P. E. School. When it came to music, we had to train our ears to 'Do, Ray, Me, Fah' and not to 'Sah, Ray, Gah, Mah'. The readers contained stories and anecdotes from English history or fairy tales which are current in Europe and there was not a word in them of Indian origin. Needless to add, no Indian language was taught[4] and so we neglected our mother-tongue altogether until we joined an Indian school.

It would be wrong to conclude from the above that we were not happy at school. On the contrary. During the first few years we were not conscious at all that the education imparted was not suited to Indian conditions. We eagerly learnt whatever came our way and fell completely in line with the school-system, as the other pupils did. The school

---

[4] I believe there has been a change for the better in recent years.

had a reputation for turning out well-behaved boys and girls, and we tried to live up to it. Our parents, I think, were on the whole satisfied with our progress. With the school authorities our stock was high, because the members of our family were generally at the top in whichever class they happened to be.

Sports naturally came in for some amount of attention, but not as much as one would expect in a school run on English lines. That was probably due to the fact that our headmaster was not much of a sportsman himself. He was a unique personality in many ways and strong-willed—and the stamp of his character was visible everywhere within the precincts of the school. He was a stern disciplinarian and a great stickler for good behaviour. In the Progress Report marks were given not only for the different subjects but also for (1) Conduct, (2) Deportment, (3) Neatness, (4) Punctuality. No wonder therefore that the boys and girls turned out were well-mannered. For misbehaviour or indiscipline, boys were liable to be flogged[5] with a cane, but only two of the teachers had this authority—the headmaster and his worthy spouse.

Mr Young had several idiosyncrasies, however, and many were the jokes we would have at his expense. He had an elder brother, a bachelor and a missionary with a venerable beard, who was exceedingly fond of children and would love to play with them. To distinguish our headmaster from his elder brother, we nicknamed him 'Young Young', the latter being called 'Old Young'. Mr Young Young was very sensitive to cold and even on a warm day he would shut the windows lest the draught should come in. He would frequently warn us about the risk of catching cold and getting cholera therefrom. If he ever felt out of sorts, he would take such a stiff dose of quinine as would make him almost deaf. After he had lived twenty years in the country, he could speak hardly a word in

---

[5] Nobody seemed to mind the caning which Mrs Young administered, for the boys usually came smiling out of her room. But the headmaster's flogging was a different story altogether and there was hardly any boy who would not turn pale as he growled, "Go into my room, Sir".

the local dialect and never cared to go in for sight-seeing or touring. If the caretaker forgot to put something on his table, Mr Young would ring for him, point to the thing wanted, but, unable to scold him in the local dialect, would content himself with glaring at him and then muttering, "All this ought to have been done before". If a messenger brought in a letter and Mr Young wanted to ask him to wait, he would run up to his wife, get the correct words from her, and go on repeating them till he was able to come out and throw them at the man.

With all this our headmaster was a man who bore himself with dignity and poise and commanded our respect, though it was tinged with fear. Our headmistress was a motherly lady who was universally liked. And I must say that there was never any attempt to influence unduly our social and religious ideas. Things went on smoothly for some years and we seemed to have fitted into our *milieu* splendidly, but gradually there appeared a rift within the lute. Something happened which tended to differentiate us from our environment. Was it the effect of local causes or was it the echo of larger socio-political disturbances? That is a poser I shall not answer for the present.

To some extent this differentiation was inevitable, but what was not inevitable was the conflict that arose out of it. We had been living in two distinct worlds and as our consciousness developed we began to realise slowly that these two worlds did not always match. There was, on the one hand, the influence of family and society which was India. There was, on the other, another world, another atmosphere, where we spent most of our working days, which was not England, of course, but a near approach to it. We were told that, because we were Indians, we could not sit for scholarship examinations[6], like Primary School and Middle School Examinations though in our annual examinations many of us were topping the class. Anglo-Indian boys could join the Volunteer Corps and shoulder a rifle, but we could not. Small incidents like these began to open our eyes to the fact that as Indians we were a

---

[6] This was because Indian boys would carry away the scholarships.

class apart, though we belonged to the same institution. Then there would be occasional quarrels between English (or Anglo-Indian) and Indian boys which would finish up with a boxing bout[7], in which sympathies would be mobilized along racial lines. The son of a very high Indian official who was a fellow student would organise matches between Indians and Europeans at his place, and those of us who could play well would join either side. I can also remember that we Indian boys talking among ourselves would sometimes say that we were fed up with the Bible and that for nothing in the world would we ever change our religion. Then there came the new regulations of the Calcutta University making Bengali a compulsory subject for the Matriculation, Intermediate and Degree Examinations and introducing other changes in Matriculation curriculum. We were soon made to realise that the curriculum of the P. E. School did not suit us and that, unlike the other boys, we would have to begin anew the study of Bengali and Sanskrit when we joined an Indian school in order to prepare for the Matriculation Examination. Last but not least, there was the influence of my elder brothers who had already left our school and were preparing for the Matriculation, Intermediate and Degree Examinations and who spoke to us at home of a different world in which they moved about.

It would be wrong to infer from the above that I was in revolt against my school environment after I had been there some years. I was there for seven years, from 1902 to 1908, and was to all intents and purposes satisfied with my surroundings. The disturbing factors referred to above were passing incidents which did not affect the even tenor of our life. Only towards the end did I have a vague feeling of unhappiness, of maladaptation[8] to my environment and a strong desire to join an Indian school where, so I thought, I would feel more at home. And strangely

---

[7] In these bouts my uncles and some of my brothers always gave a good account of themselves.

[8] It is possible that this feeling grew within me because I was too much of an introvert, as I have remarked at the end of the first chapter.

enough, when in January, 1909, I shook hands with our headmaster and said good-bye to the school, the teachers and the students, I did so without any regret, without a momentary pang. At the time, it was quite impossible for me to understand what had gone wrong with me. Only from this distance of time and with the help of an adult mind can I now analyse some of the factors that had been at work.

So far as studies were concerned my record during this period was satisfactory, because I was usually at the top. But as I did badly in sports and did not play any part in the bouts that took place, and as studies did not have the importance which they have usually in an Indian school, I came to cherish a poor opinion of myself.[9] The feeling of insignificance—of diffidence—to which I have referred before, continued to haunt me. Having joined the lowest standard I had probably got into the habit of looking up to others and of looking down upon myself.

Considering everything, I should not send an Indian boy or girl to such a school now. The child will certainly suffer from a sense of maladaptation and from consequent unhappiness, especially if he or she is of a sensitive nature. I should say the same of the practice of sending Indian boys to public schools in England which prevailed and still prevails[10] in certain aristocratic circles in India. For the same reason, I strongly condemn the move taken by certain Indians to start Indian schools run by English teachers on the lines of English public schools. It is possible that some boys, for example those who are mentally extrovert, may not suffer from a feeling of maladaptation and may feel quite happy in such an environment. But introvert children are bound to suffer, and in that event the reaction against the system and all that it stands for is bound to be hostile. Apart from this psychological consideration, a system of education which ignores Indian conditions, Indian requirements, and Indian history and

---

[9] Perhaps this was responsible to some extent for the feeling of unhappiness to which I have referred in the preceding paragraph.

[10] I am fortified in this view by what I saw of the Indian products of English public schools when I was a student at Cambridge.

sociology is too unscientific to commend itself to any rational support. The proper psychological approach for a cultural rapprochement between the East and the West is not to force 'English' education on Indian boys when they are young, but to bring them into close personal contact with the West when they are developed, so that they can judge for themselves what is good and what is bad in the East and in the West.

Chapter V
At School (2)

It is strange how your own opinion of yourself can be influenced by what others think of you. In January 1909, when I joined the Ravenshaw Collegiate School, Cuttack, a sudden change came over me. Among European and Anglo-Indian boys, my parentage had not counted for anything, but among our own people, it was different. ————→ Further, my knowledge of English was above the ordinary level and that gave me an added estimation in the eyes of my new class-mates. Even the teachers treated me with undue consideration, because they expected me to stand first and in an Indian school, studies, and not sports, brought credit and reward. At the first quarterly examination, I did justify the hopes placed in me. ————————→ The new atmosphere in which I lived and moved forced me to think better of myself — viz. that I was worth something and was not an insignificant creature. It was not a feeling of pride that crept into me but of self-confidence, which till then I had been lacking and which is the sine qua non of all success in life.

This time it was not the infant class which I joined but the fourth class — so I did not have to

† In our time the numbering was different from what obtains now. The first class was the topmost class in a high school.

শ্রীশ্রীঈশ্বর সহায়

কইঞে
শনিবার।

পরম পূজনীয়া শ্রীমতী মাতাসম্পুন্নী—
শ্রী চরণকমলেষু——

মা,

আজ নবমী; সুতরাং আপনি এখন দেশে—— দেবীর আরাধনায় নিমগ্ন আছেন।

৭ ভুস্ত? তেই হু- পূজা—
বেশী জাঁকজমক সম্পন্ন হইলে। কিন্তু মা জাঁকজমকে প্রয়োজন কি? যাঁহাকে আমরা ভক্তি করি—তাঁহাকে যদি প্রাণ খুলিয়া সদ, সদ, চন্দ- ভাবিতে পারা?- তাহা হইলে যথেষ্ট- হইল; আর গাঁঠীক কি প্রয়োজন? যে পূজায়- আমরা ভক্তি- চন্দন ও প্রেম- পুষ্প- গুণহার লইব তাহাই এস্থলে প্রকৃত সর্ব্বশ্রেষ্ঠ - পূজা—। জাঁকজমকে সম্মুখে ভক্তি পলায়ন করে।

A page from a letter to his mother (1912)

CHAPTER V

AT SCHOOL (2)

It is strange how your opinion of yourself can be influenced by what others think of you. In January, 1909, when I joined the Ravenshaw Collegiate School, Cuttack, a sudden change came over me. Among European and Anglo-Indian boys my parentage had counted for nothing, but among our own people it was different. Further, my knowledge of English was above the ordinary level and that gave me an added estimation in the eyes of my new class-mates. Even the teachers treated me with undue consideration, because they expected me to stand first, and in an Indian school studies, and not sports, brought credit and reward. At the first quarterly examination I did justify the hopes placed in me. The new atmosphere in which I lived and moved forced me to think better of myself—that I was worth something and was not an insignificant creature. It was not a feeling of pride that crept into me but of self-confidence which till then had been lacking and which is the *sine qua non* of all success in life.

This time it was not the infant class which I joined but the fourth[1] class—so I did not have to look up all the time. Boys of the fourth class considered themselves as belonging to one of the higher classes and moved about with an air of importance. So did I. But in one respect I was seriously handicapped in spite of all the other advantages I enjoyed. I had read hardly a word of Bengali—my mother-tongue—before I joined this school, while the other boys had already reached a high standard. I remember that the first day I had to write an essay on 'Cow' (or was it 'Horse'?), I was made the laughing-stock of all my class-mates. I knew nothing of grammar and

---

[1] In our time the numbering was different from what obtains now. For instance, formerly the first class was the top class in a High School.

precious little of spelling and when the teacher read out
my composition to the whole class with running comments,
punctuated with laughter, flowing in from all sides, I felt
humbled to the dust. I had never had this experience before—
to be laughed at for deficiency in studies—and on top of it,
I had lately developed a species of self-consciousness which
had made me ultrasensitive. For weeks and months the
Bengali lessons would give me the creeps. But for the time
being, however acute the mental torture, there was nothing
I could do but put up with the humiliation and secretly resolve
to make good. Slowly and steadily I began to gain ground and
at the annual examination I had the satisfaction of getting the
highest marks in that subject.

I enjoyed my new surroundings, the more so as I had
longed for the change. At the other school, though I had
been there for seven years, I had not left behind any friends.
Here it looked as if I would enter into lasting friendship
with at least some of my classmates. My friends were not
of the sporting type because I did not take kindly to sports
and only the drill lessons interested me. Apart from my own
lukewarmness, there was another obstacle to my taking
to sports enthusiastically. It was customary for the boys to
return home after school-hours, have a light tiffin, and
then go out for games. My parents did not like us to do
that. Either they thought that sports would interfere with
our studies or they did not regard the atmosphere of the
playground as congenial to our mental health. Possibly the
latter consideration weighed more with them. Be that as it
may, the domestic situation was such that if we wanted to
go out for games, we had to do it on the sly. Some of my
brothers and uncles did do so and occasionally, when they
were caught, were given a talking-to. But, knowing my
parents' habits, it was generally possible to dodge them,
especially as they were in the habit of going out for a drive
and walk. If I had had a strong desire like the others, I could
easily have joined them at the games. But I did not. Moreover,
I was then of a goody-goody nature and was busy devouring

ethical verses in Sanskrit. Some of these verses taught that the highest virtue consisted in obeying one's father—that when one's father was satisfied all the gods were satisfied[2]—that one's mother was even greater than one's father etc., etc. I therefore thought it better not to do what would displease my parents. So I would take to gardening along with those who did not go out for games. We had a fairly big kitchen and flower garden adjoining our house and in company with the gardener we would water and tend the plants or do some digging or help lay out the beds. Gardening I found absorbingly interesting. It served, among other things, to open my eyes to the beauties of nature, about which I shall have something to say later on. Besides gardening, we would also go in for physical exercise and gymnastics for which there were arrangements at home.

Looking back on my past life I feel inclined to think that I should not have neglected sports. By doing so, I probably developed precocity and accentuated my introvert tendencies. To ripen too early is not good, either for a tree or for a human being and one has to pay for it in the long run. There is nothing to beat nature's law of gradual development, and however much prodigies may interest us at first they generally fail to fulfil their early promise.

For two years life rolled on in much the same way. Among the teachers and students there were both Bengalees and Oriyas and the relations between them were quite cordial. One did not hear in those days—at least we students did not hear—of any ill-feeling or misunderstanding between the people of the two sister provinces. So far as the members of our family were concerned, we could never think or feel in terms of narrow parochialism or provincialism. For that we have to thank our parents. My father had extensive contacts with the people of Orissa, and intimate personal relations with many distinguished Oriya families. His outlook was consequently broad and

---

[2] Pitah Swargah, Pitah Dharma, Pitahi Paramantapah, etc.

his sympathies wide and they unconsciously influenced the rest of his family. I cannot remember ever to have heard from his lips one single disparaging remark about the people of Orissa—or for the matter of that about the people of any other province. Though he was never effusive in his emotions and was inclined to be reserved, he could endear himself to all those who came into contact with him wherever he happened to be at the time. Such parental influences work unobtrusively and only in later life can the children discover by a process of analysis what helped to mould their character or give their life a definite direction.

Of the teachers there was one who left a permanent impression on my youthful mind. That was our headmaster, Babu Beni Madhav Das. The very first day I saw him taking his rounds—and I was then just over twelve—I felt what I should now call an irresistible moral appeal in his personality. Up till then I had never experienced what it was to respect a man. But for me, to see Beni Madhav Das was to adore him. I was not old enough then to realise what it was that I adored. I could only feel that here was a man who was not an ordinary teacher, who stood apart from, and above, the rest of his tribe. And I secretly said to myself that if I wanted an ideal for my life, it should be to emulate him.

Talking of an ideal, I am reminded of an experience I had when I was at the P. E. School. I was then about ten. Our teachers asked us to write an essay on what we would like to be when we were grown up. My eldest brother was in the habit of giving us talks on the respective virtues of a judge, magistrate, commissioner, barrister, doctor, engineer, and so forth, and I had picked up odd things from what I had heard him say. I jumbled up as many of these as I still remembered, and wound up by saying that I would be a magistrate. The teacher remarked that to be a magistrate after being a commissioner would be an anti-climax, but I was too young to understand the status of the different professions and designations. After that I had no occasion to be worried by the thought of what I should aspire to be in later life. I only remember hearing in talks within the family circle that the highest position one could get to was the Indian Civil Service.[3]

The headmaster did not usually give any regular lessons till the boys reached the second class. So I began to long for the day when I would reach the second class and be entitled to listen to his lectures. That day did arrive,[4] but my good fortune did not last long. After a few months orders for his transfer came. However, before he left us he had succeeded in rousing in me a vague perception of moral values—an inchoate feeling that in human life moral values should count more than anything else. In other words he had made me feel the truth of what we had read in our Poetry-Book:

The rank is but the guinea's stamp
The man is the gold for all that.

And it was well that I had, for about this time the usual mental changes—best described in scientific terminology as sex-consciousness—which are incidental to approaching puberty, began to overtake me.

I remember vividly the parting scene when headmaster Beni Madhav took leave of his devoted and admiring pupils. He entered the class-room visibly moved and, in a voice ringing with emotion, said, 'I have nothing more to say but invoke the blessings of God on you....' I could not listen any more. Tears rushed to my eyes and I cried out within myself. But a hundred eyes were on the alert and I managed to restrain myself. The classes were then dismissed and the boys began to file off. Passing near his room I suddenly saw him standing in the verandah watching the boys depart. Our eyes met. The tears which I had managed to restrain within the class-room now began to flow. He saw them and was also moved. I stood paralysed

---

[3] In those days it was nicknamed the heaven-born service.
[4] I was then fourteen.

for a moment and he came up to say that we would meet
again. This was, I believe, the first time in my life that I had
to weep at the time of parting and the first time I realised
that only when we are forced to part do we discover how
much we love.[5]

The next day there was a public meeting organised by the
staff and students to accord him a farewell. I was one of those
who had to speak. How I got through my part I do not know,
for internally I was all in tears. I was, however, painfully
surprised to find that there were many among the staff and
the students who did not realise at all what a sorrowful event
it was. When the headmaster spoke in reply, his words seemed
to pierce through my soul. I could hear only his opening
words saying that he had never expected, when he first came
to Cuttack, that there would be so much affection in store
for him. Then I ceased to listen but continued to gaze at his
impassioned countenance, which spoke volumes to me. There
was an expression, a glow, therein—which I had seen in the
portraits of Keshav Chandra Sen. And no wonder, since he
was Keshav Chandra's ardent disciple and devotee.[6]

It was now a different school altogether—so dull,
uninteresting, and uninspiring—for a light that had hitherto
shone there had vanished. But there was no help, the classes
had to be attended, the lessons learnt, and the examinations
taken. The wheel of life grinds on regardless of our joys and
sorrows.

It is interesting how you can sometimes come nearer to a
person when you have parted from him. This happened in the
present case. I started a correspondence with Headmaster Beni
Madhav which went on for some years. One thing I now learnt
from him—how to love nature and be inspired by her, not merely
aesthetically, but ethically as well. Following his instructions,
I took to what, in the absence of anything better, might be
described as a species of nature-worship. I would choose a

---

[5] I have had repeated demonstrations of this principle in later life.
[6] There is a saying in Sanskrit—'As you think, so you become'.

beauty-spot on the river-bank or on a hill or in a lonely meadow in the midst of an enchanting sunset-glow, and practise contemplation. 'Surrender yourself completely to nature', he would write, 'and let Nature speak to you through her Protean mask'. This sort of contemplation had given him peace of mind, joy, and strength of will.

How far I profited ethically from this effort I cannot say. But it certainly opened my eyes to the hidden and neglected beauties of nature and also helped me to concentrate my mind. In the garden, among flowers, sprouting leaves and growing plants, I would find an indescribable joy and I would love to ramble, alone or in the company of friends, amid the wild beauties of nature with which the countryside was so plentifully supplied. I could realise the truth of what the poet had said:

> A primrose by the river's brim,
> A yellow primrose is to him,
> And it is something more.

Wordsworth's poems now had an added significance for me and I would simply revel in the descriptions of natural scenery in Kalidas's[7] poetry and in the Mahabharata[8] which, thanks to my Pundit, I could enjoy in the original Sanskrit.

I was at this time entering on one of the stormiest periods in my psychical life which was to last for five or six years. It was a period of acute mental conflict causing untold suffering and agony, which could not be shared by any friends and was not visible to any outsider. I doubt if a growing boy normally goes through this experience—at least I hope he does not. But I had in some respects a touch of the abnormal in my mental make-up. Not only was I too much of an introvert, but I was in some respects precocious. The result was that at an age

---

[7] The greatest poet and dramatist of ancient India who wrote in Sanskrit.

[8] The Mahabharata and Ramayana are the two greatest epics of ancient India.

when I should have been tiring myself out on the football field, I was brooding over problems which should rather have been left to a more mature age. The mental conflict, as I view it from this distance, was a two-fold one. Firstly, there was the natural attraction of a worldly life and of worldly pursuits in general, against which my higher self was beginning to revolt. Secondly, there was the growth of sex-consciousness, quite natural at that age, but which I considered unnatural and immoral and which I was struggling to suppress or transcend.

Nature-worship, as described above, was elevating and therefore helpful to a certain point, but it was not enough. What I required—and what I was unconsciously groping after—was a central principle, which I could use as a peg to hang my whole life on, and a firm resolve to have no other distractions in life. It was no easy job to discover this principle or idea and then consecrate my life to it. My agony could have been terminated, or at least considerably mitigated, if I had either given in at the outset as so many have done, or had with one bold effort of the will fixed on an idea and heroically brushed aside all other allurements. But I would not give in—there was something within which would not let me do so. I had therefore to fight on. And a stiff fight it was, because I was weak. For me the difficulty was not about the determination of life's goal so much as about concentrating my entire will to that single goal. Even after I had decided what was the most desirable object in life, it took me a long time to establish peace and harmony within myself by bringing under control contrary or rebellious tendencies, for though the spirit was willing the flesh was weak. A stronger will than mine would undoubtedly have managed things more easily.

One day by sheer accident I stumbled upon what turned out to be my greatest help in this crisis. A relative of mine,[9] who was a new-comer to the town, was living next door and I had to visit him. Glancing over his books,

[9] S. C. M.

I came across the works of Swami Vivekananda. I had hardly turned over a few pages when I realised that here was something which I had been longing for. I borrowed the books from him, brought them home, and devoured them. I was thrilled to the marrow of my bones. My headmaster had roused my aesthetic and moral sense—had given a new impetus to my life—but he had not given me an ideal to which I could give my whole being. That Vivekananda gave me.

For days, weeks, months I poured over his works. His letters as well as his speeches from Colombo to Almora, replete as they were with practical advice to his countrymen, inspired me most. From this study I emerged with a vivid idea of the essence of his teachings. 'Atmano Mokshartham Jagaddhitaya,'—for your own salvation and for the service of humanity—that was to be life's goal. Neither the selfish monasticism of the middle ages, nor the modern utilitarianism of Bentham and Mill, could be a perfect ideal. And the service of humanity included, of course, the service of one's country—for, as his biographer and chief disciple, Sister Nivedita, pointed out,[10] 'The queen of his adoration was his motherland. There was not a cry within her shores that did not find in him a responsive echo.' The Swami himself in one of his passionate utterances had said, 'Say brothers at the top of your voice—the naked Indian, the illiterate Indian, the Brahman Indian, the Pariah Indian is my brother.' Talking of the future, he had remarked that the Brahman (religious caste), the Kshatriya (warrior caste) and the Vaisya (trader caste) each had had their day and now came the turn of the Sudras, the down-trodden masses. To the ancient scriptures he had given a modern interpretation. Strength, strength, is what the Upanishads[11] say, he had often declared; have faith (shraddha) in yourselves as Nachiketa[12] of old had. To some idle monks he had turned round

---

[10] See her book, *The Master as I Saw Him.*

[11] The Upanishads are the philosophical portion of the ancient scriptures, the Vedas.

[12] The son of one of the ancient sages of India.

and said, 'Salvation will come through football and not through the Gita.'[13]
I was barely fifteen when Vivekananda entered my life. Then there followed a revolution within and everything was turned upside down. It was, of course, a long time before I could appreciate the full significance of his teachings or the greatness of his personality, but certain impressions were stamped indelibly on my mind from the outset. Both from his portraits as well as from his teachings, Vivekananda appeared before me as a full-blown personality. Many of the questions which vaguely stirred my mind, and of which I was to become conscious later on, found in him a satisfactory solution. My headmaster's personality ceased to be big enough to serve as my ideal. I had previously thought of studying philosophy as he had done and of emulating him. Now I thought of the path which Vivekananda had indicated.

From Vivekananda I turned gradually to his master, Ramakrishna Paramahansa. Vivekananda had made speeches, written letters, and published books which were available to the layman. But Ramakrishna, who was almost an illiterate man, had done nothing of the kind. He had lived his life and had left it to others to explain it. Nevertheless, there were books or diaries published by his disciples which gave the essence of his teachings as learnt from conversations with him. The most valuable element in these books was his practical direction regarding character-building in general and spiritual uplift in particular. He would repeat unceasingly that only through renunciation was realisation possible—that without complete self-abnegation spiritual development was impossible to acquire. There was nothing new in his teaching, which is as old as Indian civilisation itself, the Upanishads having taught thousands of years ago that through abandonment of worldly desires alone can immortal life be attained. The effectiveness of Ramakrishna's appeal lay, however, in the fact that he had practised what he preached

---

[13] *The Gita* or *Bhagavad Gita* contains the essence of Hindu philosophy and may be regarded as the Bible of the Hindus.

and that, according to his disciples, he had reached the acme of spiritual progress.

The burden of Ramakrishna's precepts was—renounce lust and gold. This two-fold renunciation was for him the test of a man's fitness for spiritual life. The complete conquest of lust involved the sublimation of the sex-instinct, whereby to a man every woman would appear as mother.

I was soon able to get together a group of friends (besides my relative S. C. M.) who became interested in Ramakrishna and Vivekananda. At school and outside, whenever we had a chance, we would talk of nothing else but this topic. Gradually we took to long walks and excursions which would give us greater opportunities for meeting and discussion. Our numbers began to swell and we had a welcome acquisition in a young student[14] with a spiritual bent of mind who could sing devotional songs with deep fervour.

At home and abroad we began to attract attention. That was inevitable because of our eccentricities. Students did not, however, venture to ridicule us, because our prestige was high, as some of us occupied the top places at school. But such was not the case at home. My parents noticed before long that I was going out frequently in the company of other boys. I was questioned, warned in a friendly manner, and ultimately rebuked. But all to no purpose. I was rapidly changing and was no longer the goody-goody boy afraid of displeasing his parents. I had a new ideal before me now which had inflamed my soul—to effect my own salvation and to serve humanity by abandoning all worldly desires and breaking away from all undue restraints. I no longer recited Sanskrit verses inculcating obedience to one's parents; on the contrary, I took to verses which preached defiance.[15]

I doubt if I have passed through a more trying period in my life than now. Ramakrishna's example of renunciation

---

[14] H. M. S.
[15] 'You, Divine Mother, are my only refuge—neither father nor mother; neither friend nor brother', etc.

and purity entailed a battle royale with all the forces of the lower self. And Vivekananda's ideal brought me into conflict with the existing family and social order. I was weak, the fight was a long-drawn one in which success was not easy to obtain, hence tension and unhappiness with occasional fits of depression.

It is difficult to say which aspect of the conflict was more painful—the external or the internal. A stronger or less sensitive mind than mine would have come out successful more quickly or suffered much less acutely than I did. But there was no help, I had to go through what was in store for me. The more my parents endeavoured to restrain me, the more rebellious I became. When all other attempts failed, my mother took to tears. But even that had no effect on me. I was becoming callous, perhaps eccentric, and more determined to go my own way, though all the time I was feeling inwardly unhappy. To defy my parents in this way was contrary to my nature and to cause them pain was disagreeable, but I was swept onwards as by an irresistible current. There was very little appreciation or understanding at home of what I was dreaming at the time, and that added to my misery. The only solace was to be found in the company of friends and I began to feel more at home when away from home.

Studies began to lose their importance for me and, but for the fact that for years I had studied hard, I would have gone under. The only thing that now mattered to me was mental or spiritual exercise. I had no proper guide at the time and turned to books for such help as they could afford me. Only later did I realise that not all of these were written by reliable or experienced men. There were books on Brahmacharya or sex-control, which were readily made use of. Then there were books on meditation which were greedily devoured. Books on Yoga and especially Hatha-Yoga[16] were eagerly hunted after

---

[16] Yoga means literally 'Union' (with Godhead). The word 'Yoga' is used, however, to indicate not merely the goal but also the means. Yogic practice has two branches... 'Raja-Yoga' and 'Hatha-Yoga'. 'Raja-Yoga' is concerned with the control of the mind and 'Hatha-Yoga' with that of the body.

and utilised. And over and above this, all kinds of experiments were made. A faithful narration of all that I went through would suffice to make a first-class entertainment. Small wonder that some thought that I was on the verge of lunacy.

The first time I resolved to sit down in the Yogic fashion, the problem was how to do it without being seen and how to face ridicule should I be discovered during the act. The best thing was to attempt it in the dark after sunset, and so I did. But I was ultimately seen one day and there was a titter. One night while I was meditating in secret, the maid happened to come in to make the bed and bumped against me in the dark. Imagine her surprise when she found that she had knocked against a lump of flesh.

Concentration was practised in many ways. A black circle was made in the centre of a white background and the eyes were brought to stare fixedly at it till the mind became a perfect blank. Gazing at the blue sky was occasionally practised, and what beat everything was staring at the scorching mid-day sun with eyes wide open. Self-mortification of various kinds was also resorted to—for instance, eating simple vegetarian food, getting up in the early hours of the morning, hardening the body to heat and cold, etc.

Much of this had to be done with as little publicity as possible, whether at home or outside. One of Ramakrishna's favourite maxims was: practise contemplation in a forest or in a quiet corner, in your house or in your own mind, so that none may observe you. The only people who may know of it are fellow-devotees or fellow-Yogis. After we had practised for some time what we considered to be Yoga, we began to compare notes. Ramakrishna had often referred to the inner psychic experiences, including extraordinary powers, which would come one's way as he progressed along the spiritual path and had warned his disciples against feeling elated over them or indulging in self-advertisement or self-enjoyment of any sort. These psychic experiences and powers had to be transcended if one wanted to reach the higher regions of spiritual consciousness. Even after some months' effort I found that I could not lay claim to any such experience. I had a feeling of confidence, and more peace of mind and self-control than before, but that was about all. Perhaps this is due to the want of a Guru (Preceptor), thought I, since people say that Yoga cannot be practised without a Guru. So began my search for a Guru.

In India those who have given up the world and consecrated their whole life to spiritual effort sometimes adopt the life of a traveller (Paribrajak) or undertake an all-India pilgrimage. It is therefore not difficult to find them in the vicinity of holy places like Hardwar, Benares, Puri (or Jagannath) or Rameshwaram. Owing to its proximity to Puri, Cuttack also attracted a large number of them. These monks[17] are of two classes—those who belong to some organisation, 'Ashrama' or 'Muth', and those who are entirely free, have no organisation behind them, and hate to get entangled in any way. Our group—for by now we had a definite group—became interested in all the Sadhus who happened to visit the town, and if any member got information about any such visitor, he would pass it at once to the rest. Various were the types whom we visited, but I must say that those of the hermit type were more likable. They would not care to have any disciples and would spurn money in any form. If they wanted to instruct anybody in Yoga, they would prefer those who like themselves had no worldly attachment at all. The Sadhus who belonged to an organisation or were themselves married men did not appeal to me. They would generally search for disciples among men of wealth and

---

[17] Also called Sannyasis, Sadhus or fakirs, though fakirs are generally Mohammedans by religion. These must be distinguished from priests. Among the Hindus, priests are an integral part of society. They are Brahmans and are generally married. They perform religious and social ceremonies for the ordinary householder. Sadhus, on the other hand, renounce caste and all their family relationship when they take to holy orders. They do not as a rule perform religious or social ceremonies for householders. Their sole function is to show to others the path of spiritual progress. They may be regarded as outside the pale of social conventions.

position who, when recruited, would be an acquisition to their organisation.

Once there came an old Sannyasi, more than ninety years old, the head of a well-known Ashrama of all-India repute, one of whose disciples was a leading medical practitioner of the town. It soon became the rage to visit him and we too joined the crowd. After doing obeisance to him we took our seats. He was very kind to us—in fact, affectionate—and we were drawn towards him. Some hymns were recited by his disciples to which we respectfully listened. At the end we were given printed copies of his teachings and were advised to follow them. We inwardly resolved to do so—at least I did. The first item was—eat neither fish nor flesh nor eggs. Our family diet was non-vegetarian, and it was not possible to adhere to vegetarian food without coming in for criticism and perhaps opposition. Nevertheless, I obeyed the mandate despite all obstruction. The second item was daily recitation of certain hymns. That was easy. But the next item was formidable—the practice of submissiveness to one's parents. We had to begin the day by doing obeisance (pranam) to our parents. The difficulty about doing this was a two-fold one. Firstly, there was never any practice to do daily obeisance to our parents. Secondly, I had passed the stage when I believed that obedience to one's parents was in itself a virtue. I was rather in a mood to defy every obstacle to my goal, no matter from what source it came. However, with a supreme effort of the will, I mastered myself and marching straight to my father in the morning, I made obeisance as instructed by my preceptor.[18] I can still recall the scene—how my father was taken aback at this unexpected sight. He asked me what was the matter, but without uttering a word I marched back after doing my duty. Up till now I have not the faintest notion of what he or my mother (who also had to undergo the same experience) thought of me at that time. It was nothing less than torture every morning to muster

---

[18] Another friend of mine, H. M. S., kept me company in this.

sufficient strength of mind to go up to my parents and do obeisance to them. Members of the family or even servants must have wondered what had made the rebellious boy suddenly so submissive. Little did they know perhaps that behind this phenomenon was the hand of a Sadhu.

After some weeks, perhaps months, I began to question myself as to what I had gained from the above practice and, not being satisfied with the reply, I gave it up. I went back to the teachings of Ramakrishna and Vivekananda. No realisation without renunciation—I told myself again.

It would be a mistake to conclude that my conception of a religious life was restricted to the practice of individualistic Yoga. Though for some time I went crazy over Yogic exercise, it slowly dawned on me that for spiritual development social service was necessary. The idea came probably from Vivekananda for, as I have indicated above, he had preached the ideal of the service of humanity which included the service of one's country. But he had further enjoined on everyone to serve the poor, for according to him God often comes to us in the form of the poor and to serve the poor is to worship God. I remember that I became very liberal with beggars, fakirs, and Sadhus, and whenever any of them appeared before our house, I helped them with whatever came within my reach. I derived a peculiar satisfaction from the act of giving.

Before I was sixteen I had my first experience of what may be glorified with the appellation of village reconstruction work. We went to a village in the outskirts of the town with the object of attempting some service. We entered the village primary school and did some teaching. By the teachers and the villagers in general we were warmly welcomed and we felt greatly encouraged. We then proceeded to another village but met with a sad experience there. When we entered the village, the villagers who had seen us from a distance collected in a body and as we advanced, they began to retreat. It was difficult to get at them or to talk to them as friends. We were shocked to find that we were regarded not only as strangers but as suspicious characters or enemies, and it did not take us long to understand that whenever well-dressed men had come into the village they must have done so as tax-collectors or in some similar capacity, and had behaved in such a manner as to create this gulf between the villagers and ourselves. A few years later, I was to have a similar experience in some other villages in Orissa.

It would be correct to say that, as long as I was at school, I did not mature politically, though in other matters I was inclined to be precocious. This was due partly to my innate proclivity which pointed in a different direction, partly to the fact that Orissa was a political backwater, and partly to lack of inspiration within the family circle. Occasionally I did hear about the affairs of the Congress from my elder brothers, but that did not make any impression on me. The first bomb thrown in 1908 created a stir everywhere and we too were momentarily interested. At the P. E. School where I then was, our headmistress condemned the throwing of bombs. The matter was soon forgotten however. About the same time processions used to be brought out in the town to condemn the partition of Bengal and to propagate the cause of Swadeshi (Home-industry). They occasioned a mild interest, but politics was tabooed in our house—so we could not take part in any political activity. Our interest sometimes found expression in peculiar ways such as cutting out pictures of revolutionaries from the papers and hanging them up in our study. One day we had a visitor, a relative of ours and a police officer, who saw these pictures and complained to my father, with the result that before we returned from school the pictures were all removed, much to our chagrin.

Up till December 1911 I was politically so undeveloped that I sat for an essay competition on the King's (George V) Coronation. Though I generally stood first in English composition, I did not get the prize on this occasion. During the Christmas vacation I went to Calcutta with the rest of the family when King George V visited that city, and I returned in an enthusiastic frame of mind.

The first political impetus I received was in 1912 from a student[19] about the same age as myself. He came to Cuttack and Puri on a tour and was introduced to us by Headmaster Beni Madhav Das. Before he came, he was connected with a certain group[20] in Calcutta which had as its ideal—spiritual uplift and national service along constructive lines. His visit to Cuttack came off at a time when my mind was beginning to turn towards social and national problems. In our group there was a friend who was more interested in national service than in Yoga. Another friend was always dreaming of the Bengali soldier, Suresh Biswas, who had migrated to South America (I think it was Brazil) and had made a name for himself there. And as a stepping stone to such a career, this friend was practising wrestling while some of us were busy with Yoga. At a psychologically opportune moment, the visitor talked to us passionately about our duty to our country and about his group in Calcutta, and I was greatly impressed. It was good to be linked up with an organisation in the metropolis and we heartily welcomed his visit. On his return to Calcutta, he made a report about us and not long after we received a communication from the head of the group. Thus began a connection which was to last several years.

As I approached the end of my school career, my religious impulse began to grow in intensity. Studies were no longer of primary importance. The members of our group would meet as frequently as possible and go out on excursions. We could thereby keep away from home and enjoy one another's company longer. As a rule, the teachers failed to inspire us—with the exception of one or two who were followers of Ramakrishna and Vivekananda. My parents' Guru[21] visited Cuttack about this time and, while he was there, was able to rouse my religious interest still further.

[19] H. K. S.

[20] The head of this group was one S. C. B. who was studying medicine.

[21] This was their first Guru. After his death they received initiation from another Guru.

But his inspiration did not go very far because he was not a 'Sannyasi'. Among the teachers there was only one who was politically minded and, when we were about to leave school, he congratulated me on deciding to go to Calcutta where I would meet people who could inspire me politically.

I believe that impressions received in early life linger long and, for good or for ill, have a potent influence on the mind of the growing child. I remember that in infancy I often used to hear stories of ghosts, either from servants or from older members of the family. One particular tree was pointed out as being the favourite abode of ghosts. These stories when narrated at night had a most chilling effect. On a moonlit night after hearing such a story it was easy to conjure up a ghost on a tree out of the play of light and shade. One of our servants—a Mohammedan cook—must have done as much, for one night he declared that he was possessed by some spirit. A sorcerer had to be called and the spirit exorcised. Such experiences were reinforced from other quarters. For instance, we had a Mohammedan coachman who would tell us how skilled he was in the art of exorcising spirits and how often his services were requisitioned for that purpose. According to him, he had to slit his forearm near the wrist and offer the spirit some blood as a parting drink. One could question his veracity, but the fact remains that we did see sometimes fresh incisions on his wrist as well as marks of old ones. He was also a bit of a Hakim[22] and would prepare quack remedies for various ailments like indigestion, diarrhoea, etc. I must say that such experience in infancy did not have a particular wholesome effect on my mind and it required an effort to overthrow such influences when I grew into boyhood.

---

[22] There are two indigenous systems of medicine in India which are still in vogue—Ayurveda and Unani. Those who practise the former are called Kavirajes or Vaids, while those who practise the latter are called Hakims. The Ayurvedic system comes down from the very ancient times, while the Unani system came into vogue at the time of the Moghul Emperors. Though there are many quacks practising these systems, there is no doubt that Kavirajes and Hakims sometimes effect wonderful cures where Western doctors fail.

In this task of freeing my mind of superstitions, Vivekananda was of great help to me. The religion that he preached—including his conception of Yoga—was based on a rational philosophy, on the Vedanta,[23] and his conception of Vedanta was not antagonistic to, but was based on, scientific principles.[24] One of his missions in life was to bring about a reconciliation between science and religion, and this, he held, was possible through the Vedanta.

Those who tackle the problem of child education in India will have to consider the uncongenial influences which mould the child's mind at the present day. Of allied interest is the question of the lullaby songs which are sung by the mother, the aunt, or the nurse to rock the child to sleep or of the means adopted to induce an unwilling child to take its food. Too often the child is frightened into doing both. In Bengal one of the most popular lullaby songs describes the 'Bargis' (or the Pindari hordes) raiding the countryside after nightfall. Certainly not a congenial song for a sleepy child.

One will also have to consider the dreams which sometimes disturb the child's sleep and leave an effect on its waking life as well. A knowledge of the psychology and mechanism of dreams will enable the guardian or the tutor to understand the child's mind and thereby help it to overcome unwholesome influences preying on its mind. I say this because I myself was troubled greatly by frightful dreams about snakes, tigers, monkeys, and the like in my early years. Only when I began experimenting with Yoga in an empirical fashion later on, did I hit upon a mental exercise which relieved me of such unpleasant dreams[25] once for all.

---

[23] Vedanta is a general term for the philosophical portion of the Hindu Scriptures.

[24] It should be remembered that Vivekananda was trained in Western logic and philosophy and was inclined to be a sceptic and agnostic before he came under the influence of Ramakrishna. Since he had an emancipated mind, he could extract the essence of religion out of a mass of superstitions and mystical accretions in which it is sometimes found embedded in India.

[25] I shall have occasion to refer later on to other dreams which disturbed me from time to time, e.g. sex-dreams, dreams of university examination, dreams of arrest and imprisonment, etc.

It is possible in a country like India and especially in families where conservative, parochial, sectarian, or caste influences reign supreme, to grow into maturity and even obtain high University degrees without being really emancipated. It often happens, therefore, that at some stage or other one has to revolt against social or family conventions. I was lucky, however, that the environment in which I grew up was on the whole conducive to the broadening of my mind. In my infancy I was brought into touch with English people, English education, and English culture. After that I went back to our culture—both classical and modern—and even while I was at school I had inter-provincial contacts and friendship which I would have been deprived of, if I had been living in Bengal. Lastly, my mental attitude towards Muslims in general was largely, though unconsciously, influenced by my early contacts. The quarter in which we lived was a predominantly Muslim one and our neighbours were mostly Muslims. They all looked up to father as ordinary villagers do to a patriarch. We took part in their festivals, like the Moharrum, for instance, and enjoyed their akhara[26]. Among our servants were Muslims who were as devoted to us as the others. At school I had Muslim teachers and Muslim classmates with whom my relations—as also the relations of other students—were perfectly cordial. In fact, I cannot remember ever to have looked upon Muslims as different from ourselves in any way, except that they go to pray in a mosque. And friction or conflict between Hindus and Muslims was unknown in my early days.

Though the atmosphere in which I grew up was on the whole liberalizing, there were occasions when I was forced into a clash with social or family conventions. I remember one incident when I was about fourteen or fifteen. A class friend[27] of mine who was also a neighbour of ours invited some of us to dinner. My mother came to

---

[26] Physical sports which Muslims indulge in on the occasion of the Moharrum festival.
[27] D. N. D.

know of it and gave instructions that no one was to go. It might have been because his social status was lower than ours, or because he belonged to a lower caste, or simply because on medical grounds it was considered inadvisable to dine out. And it is true that very rarely did we go anywhere for dinner. However, I regarded my mother's orders as unjustified and felt a peculiar pleasure in defying them. When I took to religion and Yoga seriously and wanted freedom to go where I liked and meet whomsoever I wished, I frequently came up against parental instructions. But I had no hesitation in disobeying them because by that time I believed, under the inspiration of Vivekananda, that revolt is necessary for self-fulfilment—that when a child is born, its very cry is a revolt against the bondage in which it finds itself.

Looking back on my school days I have no doubt that I must have appeared to others as wayward, eccentric, and obstinate. I was expected to do well at the Matriculation Examination and raise the prestige of the school and great must have been the disappointment of my teachers when they found me neglecting my studies and running after ash-laden Sadhus. What my parents must have thought and felt over a promising boy going off his head can best be imagined. But nothing mattered to me except my inner dreams, and the more resistance I met, the more obstinate I became. My parents then thought that a change of environment would perhaps do me good and that in the realistic atmosphere of Calcutta I would shed my eccentricities and take to a normal life like the rest of my tribe.

I sat for the Matriculation Examination in March, 1913 and came out second in the whole University. My parents were delighted and I was packed off to Calcutta.

Chapter VI

Presidency College (1)

Little did my people know what Calcutta had in store for me. I was separated from a small group of eccentric school-boys whom I had gathered 'round myself in Cuttack, but in Calcutta I found crowds of them. No wonder that I soon became the despair of my parents. To resume my story, I joined the Presidency College, then regarded as the premier College of the Calcutta University. I had three months holiday before the colleges were to reopen after the Summer Vacation. But I lost no time in getting → into touch with that group, an emissary of which I had met a year ago in Cuttack. A lad of sixteen usually feels lost in a big city like Calcutta, but such was not the case with me. Before the College opened, I had made myself at home in Calcutta and found a number of friends of my choice.

The first few days of college life were interesting to a degree. The standard of the Matriculation Examination being lower in Indian (than in British) Universities, Indian matriculates enter college earlier than British boys do. I was barely sixteen and a half years old when I walked into the precincts of Presidency College; nevertheless, like so many others, I felt as if I was suddenly entering into man's estate. That was indeed a pleasurable feeling. We had ceased to be boys and we

As a High School student

PRESIDENCY COLLEGE (1)

Little did my people know what Calcutta had in store for me. I was separated from a small group of eccentric school-boys whom I had gathered round myself in Cuttack. But in Calcutta I found crowds of them. No wonder that I soon became the despair of my parents.

This was not my first visit to Calcutta. I had been there several times since my infancy, but every time this great city had intrigued me, bewildered me beyond measure. I had loved to roam about its wide streets and among its gardens and museums and I had felt that one could not see enough of it. It was like a leviathan which one could look at from outside and go on admiring unceasingly. But this time I came to settle down there and to mix with its inner life. I did not, of course, know then that this was the beginning of a connection which would perhaps last all my life.

Life in Calcutta, like life in any other modern metropolis, is not good for everybody and it has been the ruin of many promising souls. It might have proved disastrous in my case, had not I come there with certain definite ideas and principles fixed in my mind. Though I was passing through a period of stormy transition when I left school, I had by then made certain definite decisions for myself—I was not going to follow the beaten track, come what may; I was going to lead a life conducive to my spiritual welfare and the uplift of humanity; I was going to make a profound study of philosophy so that I could solve the fundamental problems of life; in practical life I was going to emulate Ramakrishna and Vivekananda as far as possible and, in any case, I was not going in for a worldly career. This was the outlook with which I faced a new chapter in my life.

These decisions were not the offspring of one night's

thought or the dictation of any one personality. It had taken me months and years of groping to arrive at them. I had looked into so many books and sat at the feet of so many persons in order to discover how my life should be shaped and what the highest ideals were that I could hold up before myself. The discovery would have been easy and the task of translating it into action still easier if I had not been pulled by my lower self in one direction and by family influence in another. Owing to this double tension the latter portion of my school life was a period of intense mental conflict and of consequent unhappiness. The conflict itself was nothing new. Everybody who sets up an ideal before himself or endeavours to strike out a new path has to go through it. But my suffering was unusually acute for two reasons. Firstly, the struggle overtook me too early in life. Secondly, the two conflicts came upon me simultaneously. If I had encountered them consecutively, the agony would have been greatly alleviated. But man is not always the architect of his fate, he is sometimes the creature of his circumstances.

The strain of a fight on two fronts was so great for a highly-strung lad like myself that it was quite on the cards that I would have ended in a breakdown or in some mental aberration. That I did not do so was due either to sheer luck or to some higher destiny, if one believes in it. Now that I have come out of the ordeal comparatively unscathed, I do not regret what I have been through. I have this consolation to offer myself that the struggle made a man of me. I gained self-confidence, which I had lacked before and I succeeded in determining some of the fundamental principles of my life. From my experience, I may, however, warn parents and guardians that they should be circumspect in dealing with children possessing an emotional and sensitive nature. It is no use trying to force them into a particular groove, for the more they are suppressed, the more rebellious they become and this rebelliousness may ultimately develop into rank waywardness. On the other hand, sympathetic understanding combined with a certain amount of latitude may cure them of angularities and idiosyncrasies. And when they are drawn towards an idea which militates against worldly notions, parents and guardians should not attempt to thwart or ridicule them, but endeavour to understand them and through understanding to influence them, should the need arise.

What may be the ultimate truth about such notions as God, soul and religion, from the purely pragmatic point of view I may say that I was greatly benefited by my early interest in religions and my dabbling in Yoga. I learnt to take life seriously. Standing on the threshold of my college career, I felt convinced that life had a meaning and a purpose. To fulfil that purpose, a regular schooling of the body and the mind was necessary. But for this self-imposed schooling during my school-life, I doubt if I would have succeeded in facing the trials and tribulations of my later years, in view of the delicate constitution with which I had been endowed from my birth.

I have indicated before that up to a certain stage in my life I had fitted into my environment splendidly and accepted all the social and moral values imposed from without. This happens in the life of every human being. Then there comes a stage of doubt—not merely intellectual doubt like that of Descartes—but doubt embracing the whole of life. Man begins to question his very existence—why he was born, for what purpose he lives, and what his ultimate goal is. If he comes to a definite conclusion, whether of a permanent or of a temporary nature, on such problems, it often happens that his outlook on life changes—he begins to view everything from a different perspective and goes in for a revaluation of existing social and moral values. He builds up a new world of thought and morality within himself and, armed with it, he faces the external world. Thereafter, he either succeeds in moulding his environment in the direction of his ideal or fails in the struggle and succumbs to reality as he finds it.

It depends entirely on a man's psychic constitution how far his doubt will extend and to what extent he would like to reconstruct his inner life, as a stepping stone towards the reconstruction of reality. In this respect, each individual is a law unto himself (or herself). But in one matter we stand on common ground. No great achievement, whether internal or external, is possible without a revolution in one's life. And this revolution has two stages—the stage of doubt or scepticism and the stage of reconstruction. It is not absolutely necessary for revolutionising our practical life—whether individual or collective—that we should tackle the more fundamental problems, in relation to which we may very well have an agnostic attitude. From the very ancient times, both in the East and in the West, there have been schools of philosophy and ethics based on materialism or agnosticism. In my own case, however, the religious pursuit was a pragmatic necessity. The intellectual doubt which assailed me needed satisfaction and, constituted as I then was, that satisfaction would not have been possible without some rational philosophy. The philosophy which I found in Vivekananda and in Ramakrishna came nearest to meeting my requirements and offered a basis on which to reconstruct my moral and practical life. It equipped me with certain principles with which to determine my conduct or line of action whenever any problem or crisis arose before my eyes.

That does not mean that all my doubts were set at rest once for all. Unfortunately, I am not so unsophisticated as that. Moreover, progress in life means a series of doubts followed by a series of attempts at resolving them.

Perhaps the most bitter struggle I had with myself was in the domain of sex-instinct. It required practically no effort on my part to decide that I should not adopt a career of self-preferment, but should devote my life to some noble cause. It required some effort to school myself, physically and mentally, for a life of service and unavoidable hardship. But it required an unceasing effort, which continues till today, to suppress or sublimate the sex-instinct.

Avoidance of sexual indulgence and even control of

active sex-desire is, I believe, comparatively easy to attain. But for one's spiritual development, as understood by Indian Yogis and Saints, that is not enough. The mental background—the life of instinct and impulse—out of which sex-desire arises has to be transformed. When this is achieved, a man or woman loses all sex-appeal and becomes impervious to the sex-appeal of others; he transcends sex altogether. But is it possible or is it only mid-summer madness? According to Ramakrishna it is possible, and until one attains this level of chastity, the highest reaches of spiritual consciousness remain inaccessible to him. Ramakrishna, we are told, was often put to the test by people who doubted his spirituality and mental purity, but on every occasion that he was thrown in the midst of attractive women, his reactions were non-sexual. In the company of women, he could feel as an innocent child feels in the presence of its mother. Ramakrishna used always to say that gold and sex are the two greatest obstacles in the path of spiritual development and I took his words as gospel truth.

In actual practice the difficulty was that the more I concentrated on the suppression or sublimation of the sex-instinct, the stronger it seemed to become, at least in the initial stages. Certain psycho-physical exercises, including certain forms of meditation, were helpful in acquiring sex-control. Though I gradually made progress, the degree of purity which Ramakrishna had insisted on, seemed impossible to reach. I persisted in spite of temporary fits of depression and remorse, little knowing at the time how natural the sex-instinct was to the human mind. As I desired to continue the struggle for the attainment of perfect purity, it followed that I had to visualise the future in terms of a celibate life.

It is now a moot question whether we should spend so much of our time and energy in trying to eradicate or sublimate an instinct which is as inherent in human nature as in animal life. Purity and continence in boyhood and in youth are of course necessary, but what Ramakrishna and Vivekananda demanded was much more than that, nothing less than complete transcending of sex-consciousness. Our stock of physical and psychic energy is, after all, limited. Is it worthwhile expending so much of it in an endeavour to conquer sex? Firstly, is complete conquest of sex—that is, a complete transcending or sublimation of the sex-instinct, indispensable to spiritual advancement? Secondly, even if it is, what is the relative importance of sex-control[1] in a life which is devoted not so much to spiritual development as to social service—the greatest good of the greatest number? Whatever the answer to these two questions may be, in the year 1913 when I joined College, it was almost a fixed idea with me that conquest of sex was essential to spiritual progress, and that without spiritual uplift human life had little or no value. But though I was at grips with the demon of sex-instinct, I was still far from getting it under control.

If I could live my life over again, I should not in all probability give sex the exaggerated importance which I did in my boyhood and youth. That does not mean that I regret what I did. If I did err in overemphasising the importance of sex-control, I probably erred on the right side, for certain benefits did accrue therefrom—though perhaps incidentally. For instance, it made me prepare myself for a life which did not follow the beaten track and in which there was no room for ease, comfort, and self-aggrandisement.

To resume my story, I joined the Presidency College, then regarded as the premier College of the Calcutta University. I had three months' holiday before the colleges were to reopen after the summer vacation. But I lost no time in getting into touch with that group, an emissary of which I had met a year ago in Cuttack. A lad of sixteen usually feels lost in a big city like Calcutta, but such was not the case with me. Before the College opened I had made myself at home in Calcutta and found a number of friends of my choice.

The first few days of College life were interesting to

---

[1] As I have gradually turned from a purely spiritual ideal to a life of social service, my views on sex have undergone transformation.

a degree. The standard of the Matriculation Examination being lower in Indian than in British Universities, Indian Matriculates enter College earlier than British boys do. I was barely sixteen and a half years old when I walked into the precincts of Presidency College; nevertheless, like so many others, I felt as if I was suddenly entering into man's estate. That was indeed a pleasurable feeling. We had ceased to be boys and were now men. The first few days were spent in taking stock of our class-mates and sizing them up. Everybody seemed to be anxious to have a look at those who had come out at the top. Hailing from a district town I was inclined to be shy and reserved at first. Some of the students coming from Calcutta schools, like the Hindu and Hare Schools, had a tendency to be snobbish and give themselves airs. But they could not carry on like that, because the majority of the higher places at the Matriculation Examination had been captured by boys from other schools and, moreover, we were soon able to hold our own against the metropolitans.

Before long I began to look out for men of my own way of thinking among my class-mates. Birds of a feather flock together—so I managed to get such a group. It was unavoidable that we should attract a certain amount of attention because we consciously wore a puritanic exterior; but we did not care. In those days one could observe several groups[2] among the College students, each with a distinctive character. There was firstly a group consisting of the sons of Rajas and rich folks and those who preferred to hobnob with them. They dressed well and took a dilettante interest in studies. Then there was a group of bookworms—well-meaning, goody-goody boys with sallow faces and thick glasses. Thirdly, there was a group similar to ours consisting of earnest boys who considered themselves the spiritual heirs of Ramakrishna and Vivekananda. Last but not least, there existed a secret group of revolutionaries about whose existence most of the students were quite unaware. The character of

---

[2] Sometimes these groups ran into one another.

Presidency College itself was different from what it is now.[3] Though it was a Government institution, the students as a rule were anything but loyalist. This was due to the fact that the best students were admitted into the College without any additional recommendations and regardless of their parentage. In the councils of the C.I.D.,[4] the Presidency College students had a bad name—so ran the rumour. The main hostel of the College, known as the Eden Hindu Hostel, was looked upon as a hot-bed of sedition, a rendezvous of revolutionaries, and was frequently searched by the police.

For the first two years of my College life I was greatly under the influence of the group referred to above and I developed intellectually during this period. The group consisted mainly of students, the leaders being two students of the Medical College.[5] It followed generally the teachings of Ramakrishna and Vivekananda but emphasised service as a means to spiritual development. It interpreted social service not in terms of building hospitals and charitable dispensaries, as the followers of Vivekananda were inclined to do, but as national reconstruction, mainly in the educational sphere.[6] Vivekananda's teachings had been neglected by his own followers—by the Ramakrishna Mission which he had founded—and we were going to give effect to them. We could therefore be called the neo-Vivekananda group, and our main object was to bring about a synthesis between religion and nationalism, not merely in the theoretical sphere but in practical life as well. The emphasis on nationalism was inevitable in the political atmosphere of Calcutta of those days.

When I left Cuttack in 1913 my ideas were altogether nebulous. I had a spiritual urge and a vague idea of social service of some sort. In Calcutta I learnt that social service

---

[3] The presence of men like the late Sir J. C. Bose and Sir P. C. Ray among the professorial staff also had some effect.

[4] India's Scotland Yard (Criminal Investigation Department).

[5] S. C. B. and J. K. A.

[6] Possibly the example of the Christian Missionaries had some influence.

was an integral part of Yoga and it meant not merely relief to the halt, the maimed and the blind, but national reconstruction on modern lines. Beyond this stage, the group did not travel for a long time, because like myself it was groping for more light and for a clarification of its practical ideals. There was one thing highly creditable about the group—its members were exceedingly alert and active, many of them being brilliant scholars. The activity of the group manifested itself in three directions. There was a thirst for new ideas; so new books on philosophy, history, and nationalism were greedily devoured and the information thus acquired was passed on to others. Members of the group were also active in recruiting new members from different institutions in various cities, with the result that before long the group had wide contacts. Thirdly, the members were active in making contacts with the prominent personalities of the day. Holidays would be utilised for visiting the holy cities like Benares or Hardwar with the hope of meeting men who could give spiritual light and inspiration, while those interested in national history would visit places of historical importance and study history on the spot. I once joined a touring party who journeyed for seven days, book in hand, in the environs of Murshidabad, the pre-British capital of Bengal, and we thereby acquired more insight into the previous history of Bengal than we would have done if we had studied at home or at school for months.

On some important questions the ideas of the group were in a state of flux, such was the question of our relations with our respective families. The name, constitution, plan of work, etc. of the group were not settled either. But our ideas slowly moved in the direction of a first-class educational institution which would turn out real men and would have branches in different places. Some members of the group interested themselves in the study of existing educational institutions like Tagore's Santi-Niketan and the Gurukul University in Upper India. In recruiting new members, attention was given to enlisting brilliant students studying different subjects, so that we would have trained professors in all the subjects when the time came for us to launch our scheme. The group stood for celibacy and the leaders held that a breach with one's family was inevitable at some stage or other. But the members were not given any clear direction to break with their families, though the way they moved about made it inevitable that their families would be estranged. Most of the weekends were spent away from home, often without permission. Sometimes institutions like the Ramakrishna Mission's Muth at Belur would be visited. Sometimes important personalities,[7] generally religious people, would be interviewed. Sometimes our own members in different places would invite us and we would spend a day or two with them. Outside college hours most of my time would be spent in the company of members of the group. Home had no attraction for me—for it was a world quite different from that of my dreams. The dualism in my life continued and it was a source of unhappiness. This was accentuated whenever unfavourable comments were made at home about my ideas or activities.

Politically, the group was against terroristic activity and secret conspiracy of every sort. The group was therefore not so popular among the students, for in those days the terrorist-revolutionary movement had a peculiar fascination for the students of Bengal. Even those who would keep at a safe distance from such an organisation would not withhold their sympathy and admiration, so long as they did not land themselves in trouble. Occasionally there would be friction between members of our group and members of some terrorist-revolutionary organisations engaged in recruiting. Once a very interesting incident took place. Since our group was very active, the C.I.D. became very suspicious about its real character, wondering if there was anything hidden behind a religious exterior. Steps were taken to arrest a member whom they

---

[7] We visited the poet Rabindranath Tagore and he gave a discourse on village reconstruction. This was in 1914, years before the Congress took up this work.

considered to be the leader of the group. At this juncture the police intercepted some correspondence passing between members of a terrorist-revolutionary organisation, in which there was a proposal to liquidate the above leader of our group for luring away some of its members into the path of non-violence. The correspondence revealed our real character to the police and thereby not only prevented the arrest but saved us from police persecution which would otherwise have been unavoidable. In the winter of 1913 we had a camp at Santipur, a place 50 miles from Calcutta on the river Hooghly, where we lived as monks wearing orange-coloured clothes. We were raided by the police and all our names and addresses were taken down, but no serious trouble followed beyond an enquiry into our antecedents.

In my undergraduate days Arabindo Ghose was easily the most popular leader in Bengal, despite his voluntary exile and absence since 1909. His was a name to conjure with. He had sacrificed a lucrative career in order to devote himself to politics. On the Congress platform he had stood up as a champion of left-wing thought and a fearless advocate of independence at a time when most of the leaders, with their tongues in their cheeks, would talk only of colonial self-government. He had undergone incarceration with perfect equanimity. His close association with Lokamanya B. G. Tilak[8] had given him an all-India popularity, while rumour and official allegation had given him an added prestige in the eyes of the generation by connecting him with his younger brother Barindra Kumar Ghose, admittedly the pioneer of the terrorist movement. Last but not least, a mixture of spirituality and politics had given him a halo of mysticism and made his personality more fascinating to those who were religiously inclined. When I came to Calcutta in 1913, Arabindo was already a legendary figure. Rarely have I seen people speak of a leader with such rapturous enthusiasm and many were

---

[8] Lokamanya Tilak was popularly known as 'Bardada' or Elder brother and Arabindo as 'Chotdada' or Younger brother. Tilak was the leader of the left-wing or 'extremist' party in the Congress.

the anecdotes of this great man, some of them probably true, which travelled from mouth to mouth. I heard, for instance, that Arabindo had been in the habit of indulging in something like automatic writing. In a state of semi-trance, pencil in hand, he would have a written dialogue with his own self, giving him the name of 'Manik'. During his trial, the police came across some of the papers in which the 'conversations' with 'Manik' were recorded, and one day the police prosecutor, who was excited over the discovery, stood up before the Court and gravely asked for a warrant against a new conspirator, 'Manik', to the hilarious amusement of the gentlemen in the dock.

In those days it was freely rumoured that Arabindo had retired to Pondicherry for twelve years' meditation. At the end of that period he would return to active life as an "enlightened" man, like Gautama Buddha of old, to effect the political salvation of his country. Many people seriously believed this, especially those who felt that it was well nigh impossible to successfully contend with the British people on the physical plane without the aid of some supernatural force. It is highly interesting to observe how the human mind resorts to spiritual nostrums when it is confronted with physical difficulties of an insurmountable character. When the big agitation started after the Partition of Bengal in 1905, several mystic stories were in circulation. It was said, for instance, that on the final day of reckoning with the British there would be a "march of the blanketeers" into Fort William in Calcutta. Sannyasis or fakirs with blankets on their shoulders would enter the Fort. The British troops would stand stock-still, unable to move or fight, and power would pass into the hands of people. Wish is father to the thought and we loved to hear and to believe such stories in our boyhood.

As a College student it was not the mysticism surrounding Arabindo's name which attracted me, but his writings and also his letters. Arabindo was then editing a monthly journal called *Arya* in which he expounded his philosophy. He used also to write to certain select people in Bengal. Such letters would pass rapidly from hand to hand, especially in circles interested in spirituality-cum-politics. In our circle somebody would read the letter aloud and the rest of us would enthuse over it. In one such letter Arabindo wrote, "We must be dynamos of the divine electricity so that when each of us stands up, thousands around may be full of the light—full of bliss and Ananda." We felt convinced that spiritual enlightenment was necessary for effective national service.

But what made a lasting appeal to me was not such flashy utterances. I was impressed by his deeper philosophy. Shankara's doctrine of Maya was like a thorn in my flesh. I could not accommodate my life to it nor could I easily get rid of it. I required another philosophy to take its place. The reconciliation between the One and the Many, between God and Creation, which Ramakrishna and Vivekananda had preached, had indeed impressed me but had not till then succeeded in liberating me from the cobwebs of Maya. In this task of emancipation, Arabindo came as an additional help. He worked out a reconciliation between Spirit and Matter, between God and Creation, on the metaphysical side and supplemented it with a synthesis of the methods of attaining the truth—a synthesis of Yoga, as he called it. Thousands of years ago the Bhagavad Gita had spoken about the different Yogas—Jnana Yoga or the attainment of truth through knowledge; Bhakti Yoga or the attainment of truth through devotion and love; Karma Yoga or the attainment of truth through selfless action. To this, other schools of Yoga had been added later—Hatha Yoga aiming at control over the body and Raja Yoga aiming at control over the mind through control of the breathing apparatus. Vivekananda had no doubt spoken of the need of Jnana (knowledge), Bhakti (devotion and love) and Karma (selfless action) in developing an all-round character, but there was something original and unique in Arabindo's conception of a synthesis of Yoga. He tried to show how by a proper use of the different Yogas one could rise step by step to the highest truth. It was so refreshing, so inspiring, to read Arabindo's writings as a contrast to the denunciation of knowledge and action by the later-day Bengal Vaishnavas. All that was needed in my eyes to make Arabindo an ideal guru for mankind was his return to active life.

Of quite a different type from Arabindo was Surendra Nath Banerji, once the hero of Bengal and certainly one of the makers of the Indian National Congress. I saw him for the first time at a meeting of the Calcutta Town Hall[9] in connection with Mahatma Gandhi's Satyagraha[10] campaign in South Africa. Surendra Nath was still in good form and with his modulated voice and rolling periods he was able to collect a large sum of money at the meeting. But despite his flowery rhetoric and consummate oratory, he lacked that deeper passion which one could find in such simple words of Arabindo: "I should like to see some of you becoming great; great not for your own sake, but to make India great, so that she may stand up with head erect amongst the free nations of the world. Those of you who are poor and obscure—I should like to see your poverty and obscurity devoted to the service of the motherland. Work that she might prosper, suffer that she might rejoice."[11]

So long as politics did not interest me, my attention was directed towards two things—meeting as many religious teachers as possible and qualifying for social service. I doubt if there was any religious group or sect in or near Calcutta with whom we did not come into contact. With regard to social service, I had some novel and interesting experience. When I became eager to do some practical work, I found out a society for giving aid to the poor. This society[12] used to collect money and foodstuffs every Sunday by begging from door to door. The begging used to be done by student-volunteers and I became one of them.

---

[9] This was probably towards the end of 1913 or the beginning of 1914.

[10] This may be paraphrased as 'passive resistance' or 'civil disobedience'.

[11] An extract from a political speech of Arabindo which my eldest brother was fond of repeating.

[12] The Anath Bhandar of South Calcutta.

The collections used to consist mainly of rice, and each volunteer had to bring in between 80 and 160 lbs. of rice at the end of his round. The first day I went out sack in hand for collecting rice, I had to overcome forcibly a strong sense of shame, not having been accustomed to this sort of work. Up to this day I do not know if the members of our family were ever aware of this activity of mine. The sense of shame troubled me for a long time and, whenever there was any fear of coming across a known face, I simply did not look to the right or to the left but jogged along with sack in my hand or over my shoulders.

At college I began to neglect my studies. Most of the lectures were uninteresting[13] and the professors still more so. I would sit absent-minded and go on philosophizing about the why and wherefore of such futile studies. Most boring of all was the professor of mathematics whose formulae would bring me to the verge of desperation. To make life more interesting and purposeful, I engaged in various public activities of the student community, barring sports of course. I also went out of my way to get acquainted with such professors as Sir P. C. Ray the eminent chemist and philanthropist, who did not belong to out department but was extremely popular with the students. Organising debates, collecting funds for flood and famine relief, representing the students before the authorities, going out on excursions with fellow-students—such activities were most congenial to me. Very slowly I was shedding my introvert tendencies and social service was gaining ground on the individualistic Yoga.

I sometimes wonder how at a particular psychological moment a small incident can exert a far-reaching influence on our life. In front of our house in Calcutta, an old, decrepit beggar woman used to sit every day and beg for alms. Every time I went out or came in, I could not help seeing her. Her sorrowful countenance and her tattered clothes pained me whenever I looked at her or even thought of her.

---

[13] This impression must have been due partly to the fact that my interest in studies had flagged.

By contrast, I appeared to be so well off and comfortable that I used to feel like a criminal. What right had I—I used to think—to be so fortunate to live in a three-storied house when this miserable beggar woman had hardly a roof over her head and practically no food or clothing? What was the value of Yoga if so much misery was to continue in the world? Thoughts like these made me rebel against the existing social system.

But what could I do? A social system could not be demolished or transformed in a day. Something had to be done for this beggar woman in the meantime and that too unobtrusively. I used to get money from home for going to and returning from College by tramcar. This I resolved to save and spend in charity. I would often walk back from College—a distance of over three miles—and sometimes even walk to it when there was sufficient time. This lightened my guilty conscience to some extent.

During the first year in College I returned to Cuttack to spend the vacations there with my parents. My Calcutta record was much worse than my Cuttack record, so there was no harm in letting me return to my friends there. At Cuttack, though I had regularly roamed about with my friends, I had never absented myself from home at night. But in Calcutta I would often be absent for days without obtaining permission. On returning to Cuttack, I got into my old set again. Once, when my parents were out of town, I was invited to join a party of friends who were going into the interior on a nursing expedition in a locality which was stricken with cholera. There was no medical man in the party. We had only a half-doctor, whose belongings consisted of a book on homœopathy, a box of homœopathic medicines, and plenty of common sense. We were to be the nurses in the party. I readily agreed and took leave of my uncle, who was then doing duty for my father, saying that I would be away a few days. He did not object, not knowing at the time that I was going out to nurse cholera patients. I was out for only a week, as my uncle came to know of our real plans a few days after I had left and sent another uncle posthaste after me to bring me back. The searching party had to scour the countryside before they could spot us.

In those days cholera was regarded as a fatal disease and it was not easy to get people to attend cholera patients. Our party was absolutely fearless in that respect. In fact, we took hardly any precautions against infection and we all lived and dined together. In the way of actual medical relief, I do not think we could give much. Many had died before we arrived there and, among the patients we found and nursed, the majority did not recover. Nevertheless, a week's experience opened a new world before my eyes and unfolded a picture of real India, the India of the villages—where poverty stalks over the land, men die like flies, and illiteracy is the prevailing order. We had very little with us in the way of bedding and clothing, because we had to travel light in order to be able to cover long distances on foot. We ate what we could get in the way of food and slept where we could. For me, one of the most astonishing things was the surprise with which we were greeted when we first arrived on the scene of our humanitarian efforts. It intrigued the poor villagers to know why we had come there. Were we Government officials? Officials had never come to nurse them before. Neither had well-to-do people from the town bothered about them. They therefore concluded that we must have undertaken this tour in order to acquire reputation or merit. It was virtually impossible to knock this idea out of their heads.

When I was back in Calcutta the craze for 'sadhu'-hunting continued. About sixty miles from the city, on the bank of a river near a district town, there lived a young ascetic hailing from the Punjab. Along with a friend of mine[14] I would visit him frequently whenever I could get away from Calcutta. This ascetic would never take shelter under a roof, for the ideal which he practised evidently was:

"The sky thy roof, the grass thy bed,
And food what chance may bring."

---

[14] H. K. S.

I was greatly impressed by this man—his complete renunciation of worldly desires, his utter indifference to heat, cold[15] etc., his mental purity and loving temperament. He would never ask for anything, but, as often happens in India, crowds[16] would come to him and offer food, clothing, etc. and he would take only his minimum requirements. If only he had been more intellectually developed, he could have lured me from my worldly moorings.

After I came into contact with this ascetic, the desire to find a guru grew stronger and stronger within me and in the summer vacation of 1914, I quietly left on a pilgrimage with another friend[17] of mine. I borrowed some money from a class friend who was getting a scholarship and repaid him later from my scholarship. Of course, I did not inform anybody at home and simply wrote a postcard when I was far away. We visited some of the well-known places of pilgrimage in Upper India—Lachman-Jhola, Hrishikesh, Hardwar, Muttra, Brindaban, Benares, Gaya. At Hardwar we were joined by another friend. In between we also visited places of historical interest like Delhi and Agra. At all these places we looked up as many Sadhus as we could and visited several 'Ashramas'[18] as well as educational institutions like Gurukul and Rishikul.[19] At one of the Ashramas in Hardwar they felt uncomfortable when we went there, not knowing if we were really spiritually minded youths or were revolutionaries appearing in that cloak. This tour which lasted nearly two months brought us in touch not only with a number of holy men, but also with some of the patent

---

[15] When it was about midday, he would light five fires (Panchagni) and sitting in the middle, would practise meditation in the scorching sun. He told me that snakes would often crawl over his body at night but that did not disturb his sleep.

[16] Among his visitors were the C.I.D. Police who wanted to know if he was merely a harmless ascetic.

[17] H. P. C.

[18] These are homes for ascetics. Nowadays there are also Ashramas for political workers.

[19] These are institutions based on ancient Hindu ideals. The Gurukul being connected with the Arya Samaj is naturally more reformist in outlook than the Rishikul, especially in the matter of caste.

shortcomings of Hindu society, and I returned home a wiser man, having lost much of my admiration for ascetics and anchorites. It was well that I had this experience off my own bat, for in life there are certain things which we have to learn for ourselves.

The first shock that I received was when, at an eating-house in Hardwar, they refused to serve us food. Bengalees, they said, were unclean like Christians because they ate fish. We could bring our plates and they would pour out the food, but we have to go back to our lodging and eat there. Though one of my friends was a Brahman, he too had to eat the humble pie. At Buddha-Gaya we had a similar experience. We were guests at a Muth to which we had been introduced by the head of the Ramakrishna Mission at Benares. When we were to take our food we were asked if we would not like to sit separately, because all of us were not of the same caste. I expressed my surprise at this question because they were followers of Shankaracharya, and I quoted a verse[20] of his in which he had advised to give up all sense of difference. They could not challenge my statement because I was on strong ground. The next day when we went for a bath we were told by some men there not to draw the water from the well because we were not Brahmans. Fortunately, my Brahman friend, who was in the habit of hanging his sacred thread on a peg, had it on him at the moment. With a flourish he pulled it out from under his chaddar and just to defy them he began to draw the water and pass it on to us, much to their discomfiture.[21]

At Muttra we lived in the house of a Panda[22] and visited a hermit who was living in an underground room on the other bank of the river. He strongly advised us to return home and to give up all ideas of renouncing the world. I remember I was greatly annoyed at a hermit speaking

---

[20] Sarvatotsrija Bheda-Jnanam.

[21] All this happened in 1914. But India is now a changed country.

[22] A Panda is a Brahman priest attached to one of the temples. He runs a boarding-house where pilgrims visiting the place come and stay. Many of them are regular blood suckers and make the life of the pilgrims miserable from the time they reach the railway station.

in that fashion. While we were at Muttra we became very friendly with an Arya Samajist[23] living next door. This was too much for our Panda who gave us a warning that these Arya Samajists were dangerous men since they denounced image-worship.

The monkeys at Muttra who could not be kept down in any way were a regular pest. If any door or window was left ajar for any brief moment they would force their way in and carry away what they found or tear it into bits. We were not sorry to leave Muttra and from there we proceeded to Brindaban where on arrival we were surrounded by several Pandas who offered us board and lodging. To get out of their clutches we said that we wanted to go to the Gurukul institution. At once they put their fingers to their ears and said that no Hindu should go there. However, they were good enough to spare us their company.

Several miles away from Brindaban at a place called Kusum Sarobar, a number of Vaishnava asceties were living in single-roomed cottages amid groves where deer and peacocks were roaming. It was indeed a beautiful spot—'meet nurse' for a religious mind. We visited them and were given a warm welcome and spent several days in their company. In that brotherhood was one Mouni Baba who had not spoken a word for ten years. The leader or guru of this colony was one Ramakrishnadas Babaji who was well-versed in Hindu philosophy. In his talks he maintained the position that the Vaishnavic doctrine of Dwaitadwaita[24] represented a further progress beyond the Adwaita doctrine of Monism of Shankaracharya. At that time Shankaracharya's doctrine represented to me the quintessence of Hindu philosophy—though I could not adapt my life to it and found the teaching of Ramakrishna

---

[23] The Arya Samaj was founded by Dayananda Saraswati. It aimed at a purification of Hindu religion and Hindu society by reverting to the pristine purity of the ancient times and of the original scriptures—the Vedas. The Arya Samaj does not believe in image-worship or in the caste system. In this respect it is similar to the Brahmo Samaj. The Arya Samaj has a large following in the Punjab and also in the United Provinces.

[24] This could perhaps be translated as 'Dualism beyond Monism'.

and Vivekananda to be more practical—and I did not relish hearing Shankaracharya assailed by anyone. On the whole, I enjoyed my stay at Kusum Sarobar and we left with a very high opinion of the ascetics there.

Coming to Benares we were welcomed at the Ramakrishna Mission's Muth by the late Swami Brahmananda who knew my father and our family quite well. While I was there, a great deal of commotion was talking place at home. My parents who had waited long for my return were now feeling desperate. Something had to be done by my brothers and uncles. But what could they do? To inform the police did not appeal to them, for they were afraid that the police might harass more than they might help. So they betook themselves to a fortune-teller who had a reputation for honesty. This gentleman after taking counsel with the spirits announced that I was hale and hearty and was then at a place to the north-west of Calcutta, the name of which began with the letter B. It was immediately decided that that place must be Baidyanath[25] for there was an Ashrama there at the head of which was a well-known yogi. No sooner was this decision made than one of my uncles was packed off there to get hold of me. But it proved to be a wild-goose chase for I was then at Benares.

After an exciting experience I turned up one fine morning quite unexpectedly. I was not repentant for having taken French leave, but I was somewhat crestfallen, not having found the guru I had wanted so much. A few days later I was in bed, down with typhoid—the price of pilgrimage and guru-hunting. Not even the soul can make the body defy the laws of health with impunity.

While I lay in bed the Great War broke out.

---

[25] Or rather Vaidyanath; in Bengali the pronunciation would be the same.

PRESIDENCY COLLEGE (2)

In spite of the political atmosphere of Calcutta and the propaganda carried on among the students by the terrorist revolutionaries, I wonder how I would have developed politically, but for certain fortuitous circumstances. I often met, either in College or in the Hostel, several of those who—I learnt afterwards—were important men in the terrorist-revolutionary movement and who later were on the run. But I was never drawn towards them, not because I believed in non-violence as Mahatma Gandhi does, but because I was then living in a world of my own and held that the ultimate salvation of our people would come through the process of national reconstruction. I must confess that the ideas of our group as to how we would be ultimately liberated were far from clear. In fact, it was sometimes seriously discussed whether it would not be a feasible plan to let the British manage the defence of India and reserve the civil administration to ourselves. But two things forced me to develop politically and to strike out an independent line for myself—the behaviour of Britishers in Calcutta and the Great War.

Since I left the P. E. School in January, 1909, I had had very little to do with Britishers. Between 1909 and 1913, only occasionally did I see a Britisher—perhaps some official visiting the school. In the town of Cuttack, too, I saw little of them, for they were few and lived in a remote part. But in Calcutta it was different. Every day while going to or returning from College, I had to pass through the quarter inhabited by them. Incidents in tram-cars occurred not infrequently. Brishers using these cars would be purposely rude and offensive to Indians in various ways. Sometimes they would put their feet up on the front-seats if they happened to be occupied by Indians, so that their shoes would touch the bodies of

chapter VII.

Presidency College (II)

Go to pp. 86 and 87 - Book III

Since I left the P. E. School in January, 1909, I had very little to do with Britishers. Between 1909 and 1913, only occasionally did I see a Britisher — perhaps some official visiting the school. In the town of Cuttack, too, I saw little of them, for they were few and lived in a remote part. But in Calcutta it was different. Every day while going to or returning from college, I had to pass through the quarter inhabited by them. ~~and I had to~~ ~~~~. Incidents in tram-cars occurred not infrequently. Britishers in various ways using these cars would be purposely rude and offensive to Indians. Sometimes they would put their feet up on the front seats if they happened to be occupied by Indians, so that their shoes would touch the bodies of the latter. Many Indians — ~~poor~~ clerks going to office — would put up with the insult but it was difficult for others to do so. I was not only sensitive by temperament but had been accustomed to a different treatment from my infancy. Often hot words would pass between Britishers & myself in the tram-cars. On rare occasions some Indian passengers would come to realization of God? Where is their unification with the Supreme soul, of which we now simply talk of. All is gone! Hushed is their Vedic strain! No more are the songs of the Sama Veda to be heard resounding on the banks of the sacred Ganges! But there is hope yet – I think there is hope yet – the angel of hope has appeared in our midst to put fire in our souls and to shake off our dull sloth. It is the saintly Vivekananda. There stands he, with his angelic appearance, his large and piercing eyes and his sacred dress to preach to the whole world, the sacred truths lying embedded in Hinduism!

A page from a letter to brother Sarat Chandra then in England (1913)

the latter. Many Indians—poor clerks going to office—would put up with the insult, but it was difficult for others to do so. I was not only sensitive by temperament but had been accustomed to a different treatment from my infancy. Often hot words would pass between Britishers and myself in the tram-cars. On rare occasions some Indian passengers would come to blows with them. On the streets the same thing happened. Britishers expected Indians to make way for them and if the latter did not do so, they were pushed aside by force or had their ears boxed. British Tommies were worse than civilians in this matter and among them the Gordon Highlanders had the worst reputation. In the railway trains it was sometimes difficult for an Indian to travel with self-respect, unless he was prepared to fight. The railway authorities or the police would not give the Indian passengers any legitimate protection, either because they were Britishers (or Anglo-Indians) themselves or because they were afraid of reporting against Britishers to the higher authorities. I remember an incident at Cuttack when I was a mere boy. One of my uncles had to return from the railway station because Britishers occupying the higher class compartments would not allow an Indian to come in. Occasionally we would hear stories of Indians in high position, including High Court Judges, coming into conflict with Britishers in railway trains. Such stories had a knack of travelling far and wide.

Whenever I came across such an incident my dreams would suffer a rude shock, and Shankaracharya's Doctrine of Maya would be shaken to its very foundations. It was quite impossible to persuade myself that to be insulted by a foreigner was an illusion that could be ignored. The situation would be aggravated if any Britishers on the College staff were rude or offensive to us. Unfortunately such instances were not rare.[1] I had some personal experience of them during my first year in College but they

---

[1] Before my time on several occasions English professors had been thrashed by the students. These stories were carefully chronicled and handed down from generation to generation.

were not of a serious nature, though they were enough to stir up bitterness.

In conflicts of an inter-racial character the law was of no avail to Indians. The result was that after some time Indians, failing to secure any other remedy, began to hit back. On the streets, in the tram-cars, in the railway trains, Indians would no longer take things lying down.[2] The effect was instantaneous. Everywhere the Indian began to be treated with consideration. Then the word went round that Englishman understands and respects physical force and nothing else. This phenomenon was the psychological basis of the terrorist-revolutionary movement—at least in Bengal.

Such experience as related above naturally roused my political consciousness but it was not enough to give a definite turn to my mental attitude. For that the shock of the Great War was necessary. As I lay in bed in July, 1914, glancing through the papers and somewhat disillusioned about Yogis and ascetics, I began to re-examine all my ideas to revalue all the hitherto accepted values. Was it possible to divide a nation's life into two compartments and hand over one of them to the foreigner, reserving the other to ourselves? Or was it incumbent on us to accept or reject life in its entirety? The answer that I gave myself was a perfectly clear one. If India was to be a modern civilised nation, she would have to pay the price and she would not by any means shirk the physical, the military, problem. Those who worked for the country's emancipation would have to be prepared to take charge of both the civil and military administration. Political freedom was indivisible and meant complete independence of foreign control and tutelage. The war had shown that a nation that did not possess military strength could not hope to preserve its independence.

After my recovery I resumed my usual activities and spent most of my time with my friends, but inwardly I had

---

[2] I knew a student in College, a good boxer, who would go out for his constitutional to the British quarter of the city and invite quarrels with Tommies.

changed a great deal. Our group was developing rapidly, in number and in quality. One of the leading members, a promising doctor,[3] was sent to England for further studies so that on his return he could be of greater assistance to the group and greater service to the country. Everyone who could afford it contributed his mite towards his expenses and I gave a portion of my scholarship. Following this, another leading member accepted a commission in the Indian Medical Service, and it was hoped that he would thereby gain valuable experience and also lay by some money for future work.

After two years' hectic life my studies were in a hopeless condition. At the Intermediate Examination in 1915, though I was placed in the first division (which, by the way, was an easy affair), I was low down in the list. I had a momentary feeling of remorse and then resolved to make good at the degree examination.

For my degree, I took the honours course in philosophy—a long cherished desire. I threw myself heart and soul into this work. For the first time in my College career I found interest in studies. But what I gained from this was quite different from what I had expected in my boyhood. At school I had expected that a study of philosophy would give me wisdom—knowledge about the fundamental questions of life and the world. I had possibly looked upon the study of philosophy as some sort of Yogic exercise and I was bound to be disappointed. I actually acquired not wisdom but intellectual discipline and a critical frame of mind. Western philosophy begins with doubt (some say it ends with doubt also). It regards everything with a critical eye, takes nothing on trust, and teaches us to argue logically and to detect fallacies. In other words, it emancipates the mind from preconceived notions. My first reaction to this was to question the truth of the Vedanta on which I had taken my stand so long. I began to write essays in defence of materialism, purely as an intellectual exercise. I soon came into conflict with the

[3] This experiment ended in failure for he married a French lady and settled in England and never returned to India.

atmosphere of our group. It struck me for the first time that they were dogmatic in their views, taking certain things for granted, whereas a truly emancipated man should accept nothing without evidence and argument.

I was proceeding merrily with my studies when a sudden occurrence broke into my life. One morning in January, 1916, when I was in the College library I heard that a certain English professor had manhandled some students belonging to our year. On enquiry it appeared that some of our class-mates were walking along the corridor adjoining Mr O.'s lecture-room, when Mr O., feeling annoyed at the disturbance, rushed out of the room and violently pushed back a number of students who were in the front row. We had a system of class-representatives whom the Principal[4] consulted on general matters and I was the representative of my class. I immediately took the matter up with the Principal and suggested among other things that Mr O. should apologise to the students whom he had insulted. The Principal said that since Mr O. was a member of the Indian Educational Service, he could not coerce him into doing that. He said further that Mr O. had not manhandled any students or used force against them—but had simply 'taken them by the arm' which did not amount to an insult. We were naturally not satisfied and the next day there was a general strike of all the students. The Principal resorted to all sorts of coercive and diplomatic measures in order to break the strike, but to no avail. Even the Moulvi Sahib's efforts to wean away the Muslim students ended in failure. Likewise the appeals of popular professors like Sir P. C. Ray and Dr D. N. Mullick fell flat. Among other disciplinary measures, the Principal levied a general fine on all the absentee students.

A successful strike in the Presidency College was a source of great excitement throughout the city. The strike contagion began to spread, and the authorities began to get nervous. One of my professors who was fond of me

---

[4] Mr H. R. J. (deceased).

was afraid that I would land myself in trouble being one of the strike-leaders. He took me aside and quietly asked me if I realised what I was in for. I said that I was—whereupon he said that he would say nothing more. However, at the end of the second day's strike pressure was brought to bear on Mr O. He sent for the students' representatives and settled the dispute amicably with them, a formula honourable to both parties having been devised in the meantime.

The next day the lectures were held and the students assembled in an atmosphere of 'forgive and forget'. It was naturally expected that after the settlement the Principal would withdraw the penal measures he had adopted during the strike, but they were disappointed. He would not budge an inch—the fine would have to be paid unless a student pleaded poverty. All appeals made by the students as well as by the professors proved to be unavailing. The fine rankled in the minds of the students, but nothing could be done.

About a month later a similar incident came like a bolt from the blue. The report went out that Mr O. had again manhandled a student—but this time it was a student of the first year. What were the students to do? Constitutional protests like strikes would simply provoke disciplinary measures and appeals to the Principal would be futile. Some students therefore decided to take the law into their own hands. The result was that Mr O. was subjected to the argument of force and in the process was beaten black and blue. From the newspaper office to Government House everywhere there was wild commotion.

It was alleged at the time that the students had attacked Mr O. from behind and thrown him down the stairs. This allegation is entirely false. Mr O. did receive one solitary stroke from behind, but that was of no account. His assailants—those who felled him—were all in front of him and on the same level with him. Being an eye witness myself I can assert this without fear of contradiction. It is necessary that this point should be made clear in fairness to the students.

Immediately after this the Government of Bengal issued a communique ordering the College to be closed and appointing a Committee of Enquiry to go into continued disturbances in that institution. The temper of the Government was naturally very high and it was freely rumoured that the Government would not hesitate to close down the College for good. No doubt the Government would have given the fullest support to the staff as against the students. But as ill-luck would have it, the Principal fell out with the Government over the official communique. As the Government orders were issued over his head, he felt that his amour propre had been hurt and his prestige damaged. He called on the Honourable Member in charge of Education and made a scene at his place. The next day another official communique was issued saying that the Principal[5] was placed under suspension for 'gross personal insult' to the Honourable Member.

But before power could slip out of his hands the Principal acted. He sent for all those students who were in his black list including myself. To me he said—or rather snarled—in unforgettable words, 'Bose, you are the most troublesome man in the College. I suspend you'. I said 'Thank you', and went home. Shankaracharya's Maya lay dead as a door nail.

Soon after the Governing Body met and confirmed the Principal's order. I was expelled from the Presidency College. I appealed to the University for permission to study in some other college. That was refused. So I was virtually rusticated from the University.

What was to be done? Some politicians comforted me by saying that the Principal's orders were ultra vires since the Committee of Enquiry had taken over all his powers. All eyes were turned to the Committee.

---

[5] Subsequently, the Principal was reinstated, probably after he had made amends and he retired for good. Here I must say in fairness to him that he was very popular with the students for protecting them against police prosecution on several occasions. On the present occasion he probably lost his head and could not decide whether he should side entirely with the authorities or with the students. If he had done either, he would have had at least one party to side with him.

The Committee was presided over by Sir Asutosh Mukherji, former Vice-Chancellor and Judge of the High Court. Naturally we expected justice. I was one of those who had to represent the students' case. I was asked a straight question—whether I considered the assault on Mr O. to be justified. My reply was that though the assault was not justified, the students had acted under great provocation. And I then proceeded to narrate seriatim the misdeeds of the Britishers in Presidency College during the last few years. It was a heavy indictment, but wiseacres thought that by not unconditionally condemning the assault on Mr O. I had ruined my own case. I felt, however, that I had done the right thing regardless of its effect on me.

I lingered on in Calcutta hoping against hope that something favourable would turn up. The Committee submitted its report and there was hardly a word in favour of the students. Mine was the only name singled out for mention—so my fate was sealed.

Meanwhile the political atmosphere in Calcutta grew from bad to worse. Wholesale arrests were made, and among the latest victims were some expelled students of the Presidency College. My elder brothers were alarmed and held a hurried consultation. The consensus of opinion was that to stay in Calcutta without any ostensible vocation was extremely risky. I should, therefore, be packed off to a quiet corner like Cuttack where there was comparative safety.

Lying on the bunk in the train at night I reviewed the events of the last few months. My educational career was at an end, and my future was dark and uncertain. But I was not sorry—there was not a trace of regret in my mind for what I had done. I had rather a feeling of supreme satisfaction, of joy that I had done the right thing, that I had stood up for our honour and self-respect and had sacrificed myself for a noble cause. After all, what is life without renunciation, I told myself. And I went to sleep.

Little did I then realise the inner significance of the

tragic events of 1916. My Principal had expelled me, but he had made my future career. I had established a precedent for myself from which I could not easily depart in future. I had stood up with courage and composure in a crisis and fulfilled my duty. I had developed self-confidence as well as initiative, which was to stand me in good stead in future. I had a foretaste of leadership—though in a very restricted sphere—and of the martyrdom that it involves. In short, I had acquired character and could face the future with equanimity.

(133)

Chapter VIII
My studies resumed

It was the end of March, 1916, when I came down to Cuttack as a rusticated student. Fortunately, no stigma attached to that appellation. By students everywhere I was regarded with sympathy tinged with respect, because I had stood up for their cause. There was no change whatsoever in the attitude of my parents and strange to say, my father never put one question to me about the events in college, or my part therein. My elder brother in Calcutta had sympathised with me in my tribulation, believing that I had done the right thing in the circumstances I had to face. My parents' attitude, as far as I could judge from their behaviour in spite of their reserve, seemed to be that I had to suffer for being the spokesman of the students. It was a great relief to know that I had the sympathy of those with whom I had to spend my days and nights and that they did not think ill of me because I had sent down.

Thus my relations with my family did not suffer a set-back, but rather improved. The same could not be said of the group. Throughout the exciting events of January and February I had not taken counsel with them and had acted entirely on my own initiative. Later on I gathered that they did not quite approve of what I had done and

The University Unit of India Defence Force (1917), Netaji standing second from right

MY STUDIES RESUMED

It was the end of March, 1916, when I came down to Cuttack as a rusticated student. Fortunately, no stigma attached to that appellation. By students everywhere I was regarded with sympathy tinged with respect, because I had stood up for their cause. There was no change whatsoever in the attitude of my parents and, strange to say, my father never put one question to me about the events in College or my part therein. My elder brothers in Calcutta had sympathised with me in my tribulations believing that I had done the right thing in the circumstances that I had to face. My parents' attitude, as far as I could judge from their behaviour in spite of their reserve, seemed to be that I had to suffer for being the spokesman of the students. It was a great relief to know that I had the sympathy of those with whom I had to spend my days and nights and that they did not think ill of me because I had been sent down.

Thus my relations with my family did not suffer a set-back, but rather improved. The same could not be said of the group. Throughout the exciting events of January and February I had not taken counsel with them and had acted entirely on my own initiative. Later on I gathered that they did not quite approve of what I had done and would have liked to see me avoid a direct conflict with the powers that be. When I decided to leave Calcutta I did not so much as inform them, though previously I had spent days and nights in their company, joining in their plans for the future. By this time the group had become a well-knit organisation. Most of the important members in Calcutta belonging to different institutions used to live in one boarding-house, where every afternoon those living at home or in other hostels would assemble for discussion and exchange of ideas. The group

was bringing out for private circulation a manuscript journal
as its organ. Regular lessons used to be given to educate
the members in different subjects, and since emphasis was
laid on moral and religious training it was but natural that
'Gita' classes should form a regular feature of the afternoon
gatherings.

It will be easily realised that after the recent happenings,
mentally I was not the same man as when I left home and
comfort two years ago to find a guru for myself. The change
came somewhat suddenly—like a storm—and turned
everything upside down. But long before the storm broke,
a silent change had been going on within me of which
I was unconscious at the time. Firstly, I was being pulled in
the direction of social service. Secondly, in spite of all my
eccentricities, I was acquiring moral stamina. Consequently,
when I was faced with a sudden crisis which put to the test
my sense of social duty, I was not found wanting. Without a
tremor I took my stand and gladly faced the consequences.
Shyness and diffidence vanished into thin air.

What was I to do now? I could not continue my studies
because I did not know where and when I would have to
begin again. The expulsion being for an indefinite period
amounted to a sentence for life, and there was no certainty
that the University authorities would relent after a time and
permit me to resume my studies. I sounded my parents as to
whether they would send me abroad to study, but my father
set his face against the idea. He was definitely of opinion
that I should have the blot on my escutcheon removed before
I could think of going abroad. That meant taking my degree
from the Calcutta University first.

I had therefore to hold my soul in patience till the
University authorities would think of reconsidering their
orders, and meanwhile I had to fill my time somehow.
Putting my books aside, I took to social service with
passionate zeal. In those days epidemics like cholera and
smallpox were of frequent occurrence in Orissa. Most
people were too poor to afford a doctor and, even when

they could do so, there was the further difficulty of finding nurses. It would sometimes happen that if cholera broke out in a hostel or boarding-house, the inmates would clear off bag and baggage, leaving the victims to their fate. There is no reason to be surprised at this, because prior to the introduction of saline injection treatment following the researches of Leonard Rogers, cholera was a most fatal disease, and in addition highly contagious. Fortunately, there was a group among the students, consisting partly of my old friends, who would go out to different parts of the city and do voluntary nursing. I readily joined them. We concentrated on such fell diseases as cholera and smallpox, but our services were available for other diseases as well. We also did duty in the cholera ward of the local Civil Hospital, for there were no trained nurses there and nursing was left in the hands of ignorant and dirty sweepers. In spite of the dire lack of adequate nursing, the cholera mortality in the hospital was much lower than in the village we had visited two years ago with a box of homoeopathic medicine and under the leadership of a halfdoctor. The fact is that saline injections worked like magic and, when they were administered at an early stage of the disease, there was eighty per cent chance of recovery.

Nursing cholera patients we enjoyed greatly, especially when we found that several patients were thereby saved from the jaws of death. But in the matter of taking precautions, I was criminally negligent. I never cared to disinfect my clothes when I returned home and, of course, I did not volunteer information to anybody as to where I had been. I wonder that during all the months that I had been doing nursing I did not carry infection to other people or get infected myself.

With cholera patients I never had a feeling of repulsion even when I had to handle soiled clothes, but I could not say the same of smallpox in an advanced stage of suppuration. It required all my strength of mind to force me to attend such a patient. However, as a schooling, this sort of voluntary work had its value and I did not shirk it.

Nursing brought in other allied problems. What about those who died in spite of doctoring and nursing? There was no association for taking charge of the dead bodies and cremating them in the proper manner. In the case of unclaimed bodies, the municipal sweepers would come and dispose of them as they liked. But who would relish the idea of having his body labelled as unclaimed after death? The nurses, therefore, were often called upon to function as undertakers. According to the Indian custom we would have to carry the dead body ourselves to the cremation ground and perform the funeral rites. The problem was comparatively simple when the dead person had well-to-do relatives and only needed volunteers. But there were cases when there was no money available and we had to send the hat round for meeting the expenses of cremation. Apart from cases which volunteers had nursed, there were other cases where outside physical help was needed to perform the funeral rites and we had to minister in such cases as well.

Interesting and useful though nursing was, it could not fill all my time. Moreover, nursing was but an expedient; it was not a permanent remedy for any of our national ills. In our group we had always criticised the Ramakrishna Mission for concentrating on hospitals and flood and famine relief and neglecting nation-building work of a permanent nature, and I had no desire to repeat their mistake. Consequently, I tried my hand at youth organisation. I got together a large number of youths and we started an organisation with different departments for their physical, intellectual, and moral advancement. This work went on pretty well while I was there. About this time I was brought face to face with the problem of untouchability. In a students' hostel which was one of our favourite haunts there was a Santal student called Majhi. The Santals are generally looked upon as an inferior caste, but the students who were broadminded did not mind that, and Majhi was welcomed as a boarder. Things went on all right for a time. One day a personal servant of one of the boarders somehow came to know that Majhi was a Santal and he tried to stir up trouble by calling upon the other servants to refuse to work in the hostel if Majhi did not leave. Fortunately nobody was in a mood to listen to his demand and the trouble was nipped in the bud. What struck me at the time was that the really higher castes, who could have objected, never so much as thought of the case of the Santal student—whereas the servant who himself belonged to a comparatively low caste appeared highly indignant. Soon after this incident Majhi fell ill with typhoid and we made it a point to nurse him with extra care and consideration. In this, to my surprise and joy, my mother joined me.

To fill the gaps in my time I went out on excursions with friends to different places of religious or historical interest. Life in the open with plenty of walking was good for the health and it gave opportunities for that intimate communion with other souls which is never possible within the four walls of a room. Moreover, it helped me to keep away from home where I had nothing particular to do, because individualistic Yoga had no longer any attraction for me and the study of text-books did not interest me. I now tried an experiment in using our religious festivals for developing our group life. From the earliest times the important religious ceremonies have been festivals in which the whole of society participates. Take the Durga Poojah in a village in Bengal. Though the religious part of the Poojah lasts only five days, work in connection with it lasts several weeks. During this period practically every caste or profession in the village is needed for some work or other in connection with the Poojah. Thus, though the Poojah may be performed in one home, the whole village participates in the festivity and also profits financially from it. In my infancy in our village home a drama used to be staged at the end of the Poojah which the whole village would enjoy. During the last fifty years, owing to the gradual impoverishment of the country and migration from the villages, these religious festivals have been considerably reduced and in some cases have ceased altogether. This has affected the circulation of money within the village economy and on the social side has made life dull and drab.

There is another form of religious festivity in which the community participates even more directly. In such cases the Poojah is performed not in a home but in some public hall and the expenses are borne not by one family, but by the community. These festivals, called Baroari Poojah,[1] have also been gradually going out of existence. So in 1917 we decided to organise such a Poojah. On the social side it was a great success and it was therefore repeated in the following years.

During this period, on the mental side I remember to have made a distinct progress in one respect, that of the practice of self-analysis.[2] This is a practice which I have regularly indulged in ever since and have benefited greatly thereby. It consists of throwing a powerful searchlight on your own mind with a view to knowing yourself better. Usually before going to sleep or in the early morning I would spend some time over this. This analysis would be of two kinds—analysis of myself as I was at that time and analysis of my whole life. From the former I would get to know more about my hidden desires and impulses, ideals and aspirations. From the latter I would begin to comprehend my life better, to view it from the evolutionary standpoint, to understand how in the past I had been struggling to fulfil myself, to realise my errors of the past and thereby draw conclusions for the future.

I had not practised self-analysis long before I made two discoveries, both important for myself. Firstly, I knew very little about my own mind till then, that there were ignoble impulses within me which masqueraded under a more presentable exterior. Secondly, the moment I put my finger on something ignoble or unworthy within me, I half-conquered it. Weaknesses of the mind, unlike

---

[1] During the last ten years Baroari Poojah has once again become extremely popular in Calcutta. Physical display, exhibitions, etc. are organised in connection with these Poojahs.

[2] I hit upon this method quite empirically in my effort to master my own mind. At that time I did not know anything about psycho-analysis.

diseases of the body, flourished only when they were not detected. When they were found out, they had a tendency to take to their heels.[3]

One of the immediate uses I made of self-analysis was in ridding myself of certain disturbing dreams. I had fought against such dreams in my earlier life with some measure of success, but as I gradually improved my method of analysis, I got even better results. The earliest dreams of an unpleasant character were those of snakes, wild animals, etc. In order to rid myself of snake-dreams, I would sit down at night before going to sleep and picture myself in a closed room full of poisonous snakes and repeat to myself—'I am not afraid of being bitten; I am not afraid of death'. While thinking hard in this way I would doze off to sleep. After I practised in this way for a few days I noticed a change. At first the snakes appeared in my dreams but without frightening me. Then they dropped off altogether. Dreams of other wild animals were similarly dealt with. Since then I have had no trouble at all.

About the time I was expelled from College I began to have dreams of house-searches and arrests. Undoubtedly they were a reflection of my subconscious thoughts and hidden anxieties. But a few days' exercise cured me altogether. I had only to picture to myself house-searches and arrests going on without disturbing me and to repeat to myself that I was not upset in any way. Another class of dreams which occasionally disturbed me, though not to the same extent, was about examinations for which I was not prepared or in which I fared badly. To tackle such dreams I had to repeat to myself that I was fully prepared for the examination and was sure of doing well. I know of people who are troubled by such dreams till late in life, and sometimes get into an awful fright in their dreams. For such people a more prolonged exercise may be necessary, but relief is sure to come if

---

[3] Later on when I took up the study of psychology I learnt that a mental conflict was cured immediately the sufferer understood its origin or cause through psycho-analysis.

they persist. If a particular class of dreams appears to be persistent, a closer analysis should be made of them with a view to discovering their composition.

The dreams most difficult to get rid of are those about sex. This is because sex is one of the most powerful instincts in man and because there is a periodicity in sex-urge which occasions such dreams at certain intervals. Nevertheless, it is possible to obtain at least partial relief. That, at any rate, has been my experience. The method would be to picture before the mind the particular form that excites one in his dreams and to repeat to himself that it does not excite him any longer—that he has conquered lust. For instance, if it is the case of a man being excited by a woman, the best course would be for him to picture that form before his mind as the form of his mother or sister. One is likely to get discouraged in his fight with sex-dreams unless he remembers that there is a periodicity in sex-urge which does not apply to other instincts and that the sex-instinct can be conquered or sublimated only gradually.

To continue our narrative, I returned to Calcutta after a year's absence in order to try my luck with the University authorities once again. It was a difficult job, but the key to the situation was with Sir Asutosh Mukherji, the virtual dictator of the University. If he willed it, the penal order could be withdrawn. While waiting for the matter to come up, I grew restless and looked out for a suitable outlet for my energy. Just then the campaign for recruitment to the 49th Bengalees was going on. I attended a recruiting meeting at the University Institute and felt greatly interested. The next day I quietly went to the office in Beadon Street where recruits were medically examined and offered myself for recruitment. Army medical examinations are always nasty and they show no consideration for any sense of shame. I went through it without flinching. I was sure that I would pass all the other tests, but I was nervous about my eyesight which was defective. I implored the I. M. S. officer, who happened to be an Indian, to pass me as fit, but he regretted that for an eye examination I would have to go to another officer. There is a saying in Bengali—'it gets dark just where there is a fear of a tiger appearing'—and so it happened in this case. This officer, one Major Cook I think, happened to be very particular about eye-sight and, though I had passed every other test, he disqualified me. Heartbroken I returned home.

I was informed that the University authorities would probably be amenable, but that I would have to find a College where I could be admitted if the University had no objection. The Bangabasi College offered to take me in, but there was no provision there for the honours course in philosophy. So I decided to approach the Scottish Church College. One fine morning without any introduction whatsoever I went straight to the Principal of that College, Dr Urquhart, and told him that I was an expelled student, but that the University was going to lift the ban, and I wanted to study for the honours course in philosophy in his College. He was evidently favourably impressed, for he agreed to admit me, provided the Principal of the Presidency College did not stand in the way. I would have to get a note from him to the effect that he had no objection to my admission into the Scottish Church College. That was not an easy task for me. My second brother, Sjt. Sarat Chandra Bose, who was my guardian in Calcutta, however, offered to do this for me and he interviewed the new Principal.[4] Mr W., he told me, was quite tractable on this point but he wanted me to call on him once. I went and was put through a searching cross examination about the events of the previous year. At the end he wound up by saying he was concerned more with the future than the past and would not object to my going to some other institution. That was all that I wanted. I had no desire to go back to the Presidency College.

Once admitted, I took to my studies with zeal and devotion. I had lost two years and when I joined the third year class again in July, 1917, my class-mates had taken

---

[4] Mr W.

their B.A. and were studying for their M.A. degree. At college I led a quiet life. There was no possibility of any friction with the authorities with such a tactful and considerate man as Dr Urquhart as Principal. He was himself a philosophy man and lectured on that subject, besides giving Bible lessons. His Bible lessons were very interesting and, for the first time, the Bible did not bore me. It was such a welcome change from the Bible lessons in the P. E. School. Life was humdrum in College except for the fact that I took part in the activities of the College Societies, especially the Philosophical Society. But I soon found something to add some spice to my daily life.

The Government had agreed to start a University unit in the India Defence Force—India's Territorial Army—and recruiting was going on for this unit, a double company. The physical tests would not be so stiff as in the regular army tests, especially in the matter of vision. So there was a chance of my getting in. This experiment was being sponsored on the Indian side by the late Dr Suresh Chandra Sarvadhikari,[5] the famous Calcutta surgeon, whose zeal for providing military training for Bengalees was unbounded. I was not disappointed this time. Our training began at the Calcutta Maidan in mufti and the officers and instructors were provided by the Lincolns Regiment in Fort William. It was a motley crowd that assembled there the first day to answer the roll-call. Some in dhoti (Bengalee style), some in shorts (semi-military style), some in trousers (civilian style), some bareheaded,

---

[5] Dr Sarvadhikari, Dr S. K. Mullick (now dead) and some others were pioneers of the movement to persuade the Government to admit Bengalees into the Army. During the war, when the Government was hard up in the matter of man-power, they were successful. Bengalees were first allowed to join the Ambulance Corps and were sent to Mesopotamia. As they had a very good record there, they were admitted into the regular army and the 49th Bengalees was then started. Bengalees were also admitted into the Indian Territorial Force and the University Infantry was the university section of that force. The University Infantry is now a permanent corps but the Bengalee units in the regular army were disbanded at the end of the war. In 1916 I met a demobilised officer of the Bengal Ambulance Corps who had been present at the siege of Kut-el-Amara and thereafter was a prisoner of war in Turkey. I was greatly excited by his tales of adventure and wanted to join the army.

some in turbans, some with hats, and so on. It did not look as if soldiers could be made out of them. But the entire aspect changed when two months later we shifted to the vicinity of the Fort, got into military uniform, pitched our tents, and began drilling with our rifles. We had camp life for four months and enjoyed it thoroughly. Part of it was spent at Belghurriah about twelve miles from Calcutta where we had our musketry practice at the rifle range. What a change it was from sitting at the feet of anchorites to obtain knowledge about God, to standing with a rifle on my shoulder taking orders from a British army officer!

We did not see any active service nor did we have any real adventure. Neverthless we were enthusiastic over our camp-life. There is no doubt that it engendered real esprit de corps, though we had never experienced anything like military life before. Besides our parade we had recreation of all sorts—official and unofficial—and sports as well. Towards the end of our training we had mock-fights in the dark which were interesting and exciting to a degree. The company had its comic figures and many were the jokes we would have at their expense. At an early stage they were put in a separate squad, called the 'Awkward Squad'. But as they improved, they were drafted into the regular platoons. Jack Johnson,[6] however, refused to change and till the last he stood out as a unique personality and had to be tolerated even by the Officer Commanding.

Our O. C., Captain Gray, was a character. He was a ranker, which meant much, considering the conservative traditions of the British Army. It would be difficult to find a better instructor than he. A rough Scotsman with a gruff voice, on the parade-ground he always wore a scowl on his face. But he had a heart of gold. He always meant well and his men knew it and therefore liked him, despite his brusque manners. For Captain Gray we will do anything—that is how we felt at the time. When he

---

[6] That was his nickname.

joined our Company, the staff officers in Fort William were of opinion that we would be utter failures as soldiers. Captain Gray showed that their estimate was wrong. The fact is that, being all educated men, we picked up very soon. What ordinary soldiers would take months to learn we would master in so many weeks. After three weeks' musketry training there was a shooting competition between our men and our instructors, and the latter were beaten hollow. Our instructors refused to believe at first that our men had never handled rifles before. I remember asking our platoon-instructor one day to tell me frankly what he thought of us as soldiers. He said that on parade we were smart but that our fighting stamina could be tested only during active service. Our O. C. was satisfied with our turn-out, at least he said so when we broke up, and he felt proud when the military secretary to the Governor complimented us on our parade the day we furnished the guard-of-honour to His Excellency at the Calcutta University Convocation. His satisfaction was even greater when we did well at the Proclamation Parade on New Year's Day.

I wonder how much I must have changed from those days when I could find pleasure in soldiering. Not only was there no sign of maladaptation to my new environment but I found a positive pleasure in it. This training gave me something which I needed or which I lacked. The feeling of strength and of self-confidence grew still further. As soldiers we had certain rights which as Indians we did not possess. To us as Indians, Fort William was out of bounds, but as soldiers we had right of entry there, and as a matter of fact the first day we marched into Fort William to bring our rifles, we experienced a queer feeling of satisfaction, as if we were taking possession of something to which we had an inherent right but of which we had been unjustly deprived. The route-marches in the city and elsewhere we enjoyed, probably because it gave us a sense of importance. We could snap our fingers at the police and other agents of the Government by whom we were in the habit of being harassed or terrorised.

The third year in College was given up to soldiering and the excitement connected therewith. Only in my fourth year[7] did I commence my studies in right earnest. At the B.A. Examination in 1919 I did well, but not up to my expectations. I got first-class honours in philosophy but was placed second in order of merit. For my M.A. course I did not want to continue philosophy. As I have remarked before, I was to some extent disillusioned about philosophy. While it developed the critical faculty, provoked scepticism, and fostered intellectual discipline, it did not solve any of the fundamental problems for me. My problems could be solved only by myself. Besides this consideration there was another factor at work. I myself had changed considerably during the last three years. I decided therefore to study experimental psychology for my M.A. examination. It was a comparatively new science I found absorbing, but I was not destined to continue it for more than a few months.

One evening, when my father was in Calcutta, he suddenly sent for me. I found him closeted with my second brother, Sarat. He asked me if I would like to go to England to study for the Indian Civil Service. If I agreed I should start as soon as possible. I was given twenty-four hours to make up my mind.

It was an utter surprise to me. I took counsel with myself and, within a few hours, made up my mind to go. All my plans about researches in psychology were put aside. How often, I wondered, were my carefully laid plans going to be shattered by the superior force of circumstances. I was not so sorry to part company with psychology, but what about joining the Indian Civil Service and accepting a job under the British Government? I had not thought of that even in my dreams. I persuaded myself, however, that I could never pass the I.C.S. examination

---

[7] In the Indian Universities after the 1st and 2nd year comes the Intermediate Examination. After the 3rd and 4th year comes the B.A. or B.Sc. Examination and after the 5th and 6th year comes the M.A. or M.Sc. Examination.

at such short notice, for by the time I reached England and settled down to study, barely eight months would be left and I had but one chance, in view of my age. If, however, I managed to get through, there would be plenty of time to consider what I should do.

I had to leave at a week's notice. A berth was somehow secured in a boat going all the way by sea. But the difficulty was about my passport. There one was left to the tender mercies of the C.I.D., especially in a province like Bengal. And from the police point of view, my antecedents were certainly not irreproachable. Through the good offices of a high police official who was a distant relative of mine, I was introduced to police headquarters and within six days my passport was forthcoming. A marvel indeed!

Once again I had done things off my own bat. When I consulted the group regarding my proposed journey to England, they threw cold water on the project. One of the most promising members who had been to England had married and settled down there and did not think of returning. It was dangerous to try another experiment. But I was adamant. What did it matter if one member had gone astray? It did not follow that others would do the same—so I argued. My relations with the group had been growing increasingly lukewarm for some time past, and I had joined the University infantry without consulting them. But this was the limit. Though we did not say so, we felt that we had come to the parting of the ways, since I was determined to strike out a line for myself.

Then I visited the Provincial Adviser for studies in England, himself a product of Cambridge and a Professor of the Presidency College. He knew me by sight and naturally did not have a high opinion of an expelled student. As soon as he heard that I intended to sit for the I.C.S. examination the next year, he summoned up all his powers of dissuasion. I had no chance whatsoever against the 'tip-toppers' from Oxford and Cambridge; why was I going to throw away ten thousand rupees? That was the burden of his homily. Realising the force of his argument and unable to find an answer to his question, I simply said, "My father wants me to throw away the ten thousand rupees". Then seeing that he would do nothing to help me secure admission to Cambridge, I left him.

Relying entirely on my own resources and determined to try my luck in England, I set sail on the 15th September, 1919.

CHAPTER IX

AT CAMBRIDGE

When I left India the Jallianwalla Bagh massacre at Amritsar had already taken place. But hardly any news of it had travelled outside the Punjab. Punjab was under martial law and there was a strict censorship on all news sent out from that province. As a consequence, we had heard only vague rumours of some terrible happenings at Lahore and Amritsar. One of my brothers who was then working at Simla brought us some news—or rather rumours—about the Punjab happenings and about the Anglo-Afghan war in which the Afghans had got the better of the British. But on the whole the public were ignorant of what had been going on in the north-west, and I sailed for Europe in a complacent mood.

On the boat we found quite a number of Indian passengers, mostly students. Accordingly we considered it advisable to take a separate table where we would feel more at home. Our table was presided over by an elderly and estimable lady, the wife of a deceased Indian Civil Servant. The majority of the passengers were Britishers of the sun-burnt snobbish type. Association with them was hardly possible—so we Indians kept mostly to ourselves. Occasionally there would be friction between an Indian passenger and a Britisher over some thing or other, and though nothing very serious took place by the time we reached England, we all had a feeling of resentment at the supercilious attitude of the Britisher towards Indians. One interesting discovery I made during the voyage—Anglo-Indians develop a love for India and the Indian people when they are out of India. In the boat there were a few Anglo-Indian passengers. The nearer we came to Europe, the more home-sick—I mean 'India-sick'—they became. In England Anglo-Indians cannot pass themselves off as Englishmen. They have, moreover, no home there, no

Chapter IV

At Cambridge

When I left India, the Jallianwalla Bagh massacre at Amritsar had already taken place. But hardly any news of it had travelled outside the Punjab. Punjab was under martial law and there was a strict censorship on all news sent out from that province. As a consequence we had heard only vague rumours of some terrible happenings at Lahore and Amritsar. One of my brothers who was then working at Simla brought us some news — or rather rumours — about the Punjab happenings and also about the Anglo-Afghan war in which the Afghans had got the better of the British. But on the whole the public were ignorant of what had been going on in the north-west and I sailed for Europe in a complacent mood.

On the boat we found quite a number of Indian passengers - mostly students. Accordingly we considered it advisable to take a separate table where we would feel more at home. Our table was presided over by an elderly and estimable lady, the wife of a deceased Indian Civil Servant. The majority of the passengers were Britishers of the sun-burnt snobbish type. Association with them

As a student in England (1920)

associations, no contacts. It is, therefore, inevitable that the farther they go from India, the closer they should feel drawn towards her.

I do not think that we could have chosen a slower boat than the City of Calcutta. She was scheduled to reach Tilbury in 30 days but actually took a week more. That was because she was held up at Suez for want of coal, owing to the coal-strike in England. Our only consolation was that we called at a number of ports on our way. To make life on board for five weeks somewhat bearable, we had to fall back on that spice of life, humour. One fellow-passenger had been ordered by his wife not to touch beef. By another passenger he was tricked into taking 'copta curry' of beef—which he thoroughly enjoyed—under the impression that it was mutton 'copta curry'. Great was his remorse when he discovered his mistake after twelve hours. Another passenger had orders from his fiancée to write a letter every day. He spent his time reciting love-poems and talking about her. Whether we liked it or not, we had to listen. He was beside himself with joy when one day I remarked in reply to his importunity that his fiancée had Grecian features.

Even the longest day has its end; so we did reach Tilbury after all. It was wet and cloudy—typical London weather. But there was plenty of excitement to make us oblivious of outside nature. When I first went down into a tube-station, I enjoyed the experience, for it was some-thing new.

The next morning I began exploring. I called at the office of the Adviser to Indian students at Cromwell Road. He was very nice to me, gave me plenty of advice, but added that so far as admission to Cambridge was concerned, there was nothing doing. There by chance I met some Indian students from Cambridge. One of them strongly advised me to proceed straight to Cambridge and try my luck there, instead of wasting my time at Cromwell Road. I agreed, and the next day I was at Cambridge. Some students from Orissa, whom I had known slightly before,

lent me a helping hand. One[1] of them who belonged to
Fitzwilliam Hall took me to Mr Reddaway, the Censor, and
introduced me to him. Mr Reddaway was exceedingly kind
and sympathetic, gave me a patient hearing, and at the end
wound up by saying that he would admit me straightaway.
The problem of admission settled, the next question was about
the current term which had begun two weeks ago. If I lost that
term then I would probably have to spend nearly a year more
in order to qualify for a degree. Otherwise, I would take my
degree by June, 1921. On this point also Mr Reddaway was
accommodating beyond my expectation. He made use of the
coal-strike and of my military service in order to persuade
the University authorities to stretch a point in my favour. He
succeeded, and the result was that I did not lose that term.
Without Mr Reddaway I do not know what I would have done
in England.

I reached London about the 25th October and it was the
first week of November before I could settle down to work
at Cambridge. I had an unusually large number of lectures
to attend—part of them for the Mental and Moral Sciences
Tripos and the rest for the Civil Service Examination. Outside
my lecture hours I had to study as hard as I could. There was
no question of any enjoyment for me, besides what I could get
from hard work. I was to appear under the old Civil Service
Regulations which necessitated my taking up eight or nine
different subjects, some of which I had to study for the first
time. My subjects were as follows: English Composition,
Sanskrit, Philosophy, English Law, Political Science, Modern
European History, English History, Economics, Geography.
Over and above studying these subjects, I had to do surveying
and map-making (Cartography) for the Geography paper and
to learn something of French in connection with the Modern
History paper.

The work for the Mental and Moral Sciences Tripos
was more interesting but I could not devote much time to

---

[1] S. M. D.

it, beyond attending the lectures. Among my lecturers were Prof. Sorley (Ethics), Prof. Myers (Psychology), and Prof. McTaggart (Metaphysics). During the first three terms I devoted practically my whole time to preparing for the Civil Service Examination. In the way of recreation, I attended the meetings of the Indian Majlis and the Union Society.

Cambridge after the war was conservative. Oxford was much the same but was beginning to go liberal. One could judge of the prevailing atmosphere from the fact that pacifists, socialists, conscientious objectors, and the like could not easily address a public meeting at Cambridge. The undergraduates would generally come and break up the meetings and 'rag' the lecturer by throwing bags of flour at him or giving him a ducking in the river. 'Ragging' was of course a legitimate recreation for the undergraduates there and I heartily approved of it. But breaking up meetings simply because the speaker represented a different ideology did not appeal to me.

What greatly impressed an outsider like myself was the measure of freedom allowed to the students, and the general esteem in which they were held by all and sundry. This undoubtedly had a very wholesome effect on their character. What a change, I thought, from a police-ridden city like Calcutta where every student was looked upon as a potential revolutionary and suspect! And living in the atmosphere of Cambridge, it was difficult to imagine the incidents in the Calcutta Presidency College—professors maltreating students—for there it was the professors who ran the risk of being maltreated by the undergraduates. In fact, unpopular dons were occasionally 'ragged' by the undergrads and their rooms raided by the latter though in a friendly way, for later on they were compensated for any damage done. Even when a ragging was going on in the streets of Cambridge, causing damage to public property, the police would behave with remarkable restraint, a thing quite impossible in India.

Apart from the measure of freedom enjoyed by the students, which would naturally appeal more to me than to British students born and brought up in a free atmosphere, the consideration and esteem with which they were treated everywhere was very striking. Even a fresher coming up for the first time would at once get the impression that a high standard of character and behaviour was expected of him, and he would be bound to react favourably. This consideration shown towards the undergraduates was not confined to Cambridge but existed to some extent all over the country. In the trains when one was questioned and replied that he was at Cambridge (or Oxford), the attitude of the questioner would change at once. He would become friendly—or shall I say more respectful? This was my personal experience. If there is an element of snobbishness in those who go up to Cambridge or Oxford, I certainly do not hold a brief for it. But having been brought up in a police-ridden atmosphere, it is my firm conviction that there is a lot to be said in favour of allowing students and young men more freedom and treating them with consideration as if they were responsible citizens.

I remember an incident when I was a College student in Calcutta. I was then awfully fond of buying new books. If I set my heart on a book in a shop-window, I would not rest till I possessed it. I would feel so restless till I got the book that I had to buy it before I returned home. One day I went to one of the biggest shops in College Street and asked for a book on philosophy, on which I was very keen at the time. The price was announced and I found that I was short by a few rupees. I requested the manager to let me have the book and promised to bring the balance the next day. He replied that that was not possible, I would have to pay the full price down first. I was not only disappointed at failing to get the book but was extremely hurt because I was distrusted in this way.[2] It was therefore such a relief to find that you could walk into any shop in Cambridge and order anything you liked without having to bother about payment on the spot.

There is another thing which drew my admiration—

---

[2] I know that things have changed now.

the debates at the Union Society's meetings. The whole atmosphere was so exhilarating. There was perfect freedom to talk what you liked or attack whomsoever you wished. Prominent members of Parliament and sometimes members of the Cabinet took part in these debates in a spirit of perfect equality and would, of course, come in for slashing criticism not unmixed with invective at times. Once Horatio Bottomley, M. P. was taking part in a debate. He was warned by an oppositionist speaker—'There are more things in heaven and earth, Horatio, than your John Bull dreams of.'

Sparkling bits of humour would enliven the proceedings. During the course of a debate on Ireland a pro-Irish speaker, while exposing the real character of the Government, referred to the 'forces of law and order on one side and of Bonar Law and disorder on the other.'

Among the guests at these debates, besides well-known parliamentary figures, there were also those who were on the threshold of a public career. I remember, for instance, that Dr Hugh Dalton was often present at these debates. He was a prospective M. P. nursing some constituency at the time. Sir Oswald Mosely, then a Left Wing Liberal (or Labourite) participated in a debate on India. He vehemently denounced[3] the policy of Dyer and O'Dwyer and raised a storm in British circles by his remark that the events in Amritsar in 1919 were the expression of racial hatred. Sir John Simon and Mr Clynes once came to plead the miners' cause before the Cambridge public at Guildhall. The undergrads turned up with the object of giving them a hot time. Sir John Simon had to run the gauntlet, but when Mr Clynes got up (I think he had been a miner himself) he spoke with such sincerity and passion that those who had come to scoff remained to pray.

During the six terms that I was in Cambridge the relations between British and Indian students were on the whole quite cordial, but in few cases did they ripen into

---

[3] What a change now.

real friendship. I say this not from my personal experience alone but from general observation as well. Many factors were responsible for this. The war undoubtedly had its effect. One could detect in the average Britisher a feeling of superiority beneath a veneer of bon-homie which was not agreeable to others. On our side, after the post-war events in India and particularly the tragedy at Amritsar, we could not but be sensitive (perhaps ultrasensitive) with regard to our self-respect and national honour. It also pained us to find that among middle-class Englishmen there was a great deal of sympathy for General Dyer. It is probable that speaking generally the basis for a friendship between Britishers and Indians did not exist. We were politically more conscious and more sensitive than we had been before. Consequently friendship with an Indian presupposed sympathy, or at least toleration, for his political ideas. That was not always easy to find. Among the political parties only Labour expressed sympathy for Indian aspirations. It followed that there was greater possibility of friendship with Labourites or people having pro-Labour views and sentiments.

The above remarks are of a general nature, and must provide for exceptions. I myself made friends with people, students and non-students, holding conservative views regarding British politics, which continues till the present day in spite of all that I have been through. That was possible because they had sufficient toleration for my ideas. The intelligentsia of Great Britain has been passing through something like an intellectual revolution during the last decade, and specially during the last five years, and I daresay that that is reflected in the atmosphere of Cambridge, Oxford, London, and other places. The experience of today may not therefore tally with that of 1919 and 1920.

That I have not misjudged British mentality as I found it soon after the war can be demonstrated from one or two incidents. It is generally claimed that the average Briton has a sense of fairplay, a sportsmanlike spirit. During my time at Cambridge we Indians wanted more proof of it. The tennis champion for the year was an Indian student, Sunder Dass, who naturally got the blue. We expected that he would be called upon to captain the team in the inter-varsity matches. But in order to frustrate that, an old blue who had already gone down was sent for and made to stay on for another year. On paper it was all right. The senior blue had the priority in the matter of captaining the team, but everybody knew what had passed behind the scenes and there was silent resentment in the ranks of the Indian students.

Another instance. One day we saw a notice inviting applications from undergraduates for enlistment in the University Officers' Training Corps. Some of us went up and applied. We were told that the question would have to be referred to the higher authorities. After some time came the reply that the India Office objected to our enlisting in the O. T. C. The matter was brought before the Indian Majlis and it was decided to take the matter up with the Secretary of State for India, and Mr K. L. Gauba and I were authorised to interview him if necessary. The then Secretary, Mr E. S. Montague, referred us to the Under-Secretary of State for India, the Earl of Lytton, who received us cordially and gave us a patient hearing. He assured us that the India Office had no objection at all and that the opposition came from the War Office. The War Office was informed that the enlistment of Indians in the O. T. C. would be resented by British students. Further, the War Office was afraid that since members of the O. T. C., when fully qualified, were entitled to commissions in the British Army, a difficult situation would arise if Indian students after qualifying in the O. T. C. demanded commissions in the British Army. Lord Lytton added that personally he thought it was inevitable that in future Indian officers should be in charge of mixed regiments, but the prejudice against Indians unfortunately persisted in certain circles and could not be ignored. We replied that in order to obviate the difficulty we were prepared to give an assurance that we would not ask for commissions in the British Army. We added that we were more interested in getting the training than in joining the army as a profession. On returning to Cambridge we again tackled the O. T. C. staff, and we were again told that the War Office was not objecting to the proposal but the India Office. Whatever the truth, no doubt that there was prejudice against Indians in certain British circles. As long as I was there, our demands were not met by the authorities and I daresay the position is the same today as it was seventeen years ago.

Indian students at Cambridge at that time had, on the whole, a satisfactory record, especially in the matter of studies. In sports, too, they did not do badly at all. We would only have liked to see them doing well in boating. Now that boating is becoming popular in India, it is to be hoped that in future they will figure conspicuously in boating also.

The question is often raised as to whether it is desirable to send Indian students abroad and if so at what age. In 1920 an official committee was appointed, presided over by Lord Lytton, to consider the affairs of Indian students in Great Britain, and this point was also discussed in connection therewith. My considered opinion was and still is that Indian students should go abroad only when they have attained a certain level of maturity. In other words, as a rule, they should go after graduation. In that case they can make the most of their stay abroad. This was the view that I put forward when I represented the Cambridge Indian Majlis before the above Indian Students' Committee. Much is made of public school training in Britain. I do not desire to express any opinion as to how it affects British people and British students. But so far as Indian students are concerned, I do not have a kind word for it. At Cambridge I came across some Indian products of English public schools and I did not think highly of them.[4] Those who had their parents living with them in England and had home influence to supplement their school-education fared better than those who were quite alone. Education in the lower stages must be

---

[4] Every rule has its exceptions, of course.

'national,' it must have its roots in the soil. We must draw our mental pabulum from the culture of our own country. How can that be possible if one is transplanted at too early an age? No, we should not, as a rule, countenance the idea of sending boys and girls to schools abroad quite alone at an immature age. Education becomes international at the higher stages. It is then that students can, with profit, go abroad, and it is then that the East and the West can commingle to the benefit of both.

In India members of the Civil Service used to be known formerly as 'subjunta', or one who knows everything. There was some justification for that because they used to be put up to all kinds of jobs. The education that they received did give them a certain amount of elasticity and a smattering of a large number of subjects which was helpful to them in actual administration. I realised this when I sat for the Civil Service Examination, with nine subjects on my shoulders. Not all of them have been useful to me in later life, but I must say that the study of Political Science, Economics, English History, and Modern European History proved to be beneficial. This was specially the case with Modern European History. Before I studied this subject, I did not have a clear idea of the politics of Continental Europe. We Indians are taught to regard Europe as a magnified edition of Great Britain. Consequently we have a tendency to look at the Continent through the eyes of England. This is, of course, a gross mistake, but not having been to the Continent, I did not realise it till I studied Modern European History and some of its original sources like Bismarck's Autobiography, Metternich's Memoirs, Cavour's Letters, etc. These original sources, more than anything else, I studied at Cambridge, helped to rouse my political sense and to foster my understanding of the inner currents of international politics.

Early in July, 1920, the Civil Service open competitive examination began in London. It dragged on for a month and the agony was a prolonged one. I had worked hard, on the whole, but my preparation was far below my expectation. So I could not feel hopeful. So many brilliant students had come down in spite of years of preparation that it would require some conceit to feel anything but diffident. My diffidence was heightened when I foolishly threw away about 150 sure marks in my Sanskrit paper. It was the translation paper, English to Sanskrit, and I had done it well. I prepared a rough copy of the translation first with the intention of making a fair copy in the answer-book. But so oblivious was I of the time that when the bell went, I had transcribed only a portion of the text I had prepared in rough. But there was no help—the answer-book had to be surrendered and I could only bite my fingers.

I informed my people that I had not done well and could not hope to find a place among the selected candidates. I now planned to continue my work for the Tripos. Imagine my surprise, therefore, when I got a telegram one night when I was in London from a friend of mine which ran thus— 'CONGRATULATIONS SEE MORNING POST'. I wondered what it meant. Next morning when I got a copy of the Morning Post, I found that I had come out fourth. I was glad. A cable went off to India at once.

I had now another problem to face. What should I do with the job? Was I going to give the go-by to all my dreams and aspirations, and settle down to a comfortable life? There was nothing new in that. So many had done it before—so many had talked big when they were young and had acted differently when grown up. I knew of a young man from Calcutta who had Ramakrishna and Vivekananda at the tip of his tongue in his college days, but later on married into a rich family and was now safely landed in the Indian Civil Service. Then there was the case of a friend from Bombay who had promised in the presence of the late Lokamanya Tilak that, if he happened to pass the I.C.S. Examination, he would resign and devote himself to national work.[5] But I had resolved early in life not to

[5] When Lokamanya B.G. Tilak visited Cambridge in 1919 he appealed to the Indian students not to go in for Government service but to devote themselves to national service. He regretted that so many bright and promising students were hankering after Government jobs. This friend in a fit of inspiration stood up and

follow the beaten track and, further, I had certain ideals which I wanted to live up to. It was therefore quite impossible for me to go into the Service unless I could make a clean sweep of my past life.

There were two important considerations which I had to weigh before I could think of resigning. Firstly, what would my people think? Secondly, if I resigned now in a fit of excitement, would I have any occasion in future to regret my action? Was I absolutely sure that I was doing the right thing?

It took me seven long months to make up my mind. In the meantime, I started a correspondence with my second brother, Sarat. Fortunately the letters I wrote have been preserved by him. The ones I received have all been lost in the storm and stress of a hectic political life. My letters are interesting inasmuch as they show the working of my mind in 1920.

The I.C.S. Examination result was declared about the middle of September, 1920. A few days later when I was taking a holiday at Leigh-on-Sea in Essex I wrote to him on the 22nd September as follows:

'I was so glad to receive the telegram conveying congratulations. I don't know whether I have gained anything really substantial by passing the I.C.S. Examination—but it is a great pleasure to think that the news has pleased so many and especially that it has delighted father and mother in these dark days.

---

announced that, though he was trying to qualify for the Indian Civil Service, if he manages to pass the examination, he would resign and then serve the national cause. He did not pass the first time but the next year he was successful and he is now in the service.

When Lokamanya Tilak was to visit Cambridge, the India Office and the Foreign Office became nervous. Lord Curzon, who was then the Foreign Secretary, wrote to the Vice-Chancellor requesting him to stop his visit if possible. The Vice-Chancellor sent for the Indian students in that connection, but they declared that since Lokamanya Tilak had already been invited, it was quite impossible to cancel his visit. Thereafter, there was no interference on the part of the University, Lord Curzon's letter notwithstanding.

The burden of Lokamanya Tilak's speech at Cambridge was that he demanded 'Home Rule within fifteen years'. Some English undergrads who had heard that Lokamanya Tilak was a firebrand came to the lecture expecting some hot stuff. After the lecture they remarked: 'If these are your extremists, we don't want to hear your moderates.'

'I am here as a paying guest of Mr B.'s family. Mr B. represents English character at its very best. He is cultured and liberal in his views and cosmopolitan in his sentiments.... Mr B. counts among his friends Russians, Poles, Lithuanians, Irishmen, and members of other nationalities. He takes a great interest in Russian, Irish and Indian literature, and admires the writings of Ramesh Dutt and Tagore.... I have been getting heaps of congratulations on my standing fourth in the competitive examination. But I cannot say that I am delighted at the prospect of entering the ranks of the I.C.S. If I have to join this service I shall do so with as much reluctance as I started my study for the I.C.S. Examination with. A nice fat income with a good pension in after-life—I shall surely get. Perhaps I may become a commissioner if I stoop to make myself servile enough. Given talents, with a servile spirit one may even aspire to be the Chief Secretary to a provincial Government. But after all is Service to be the be-all and end-all of my life? The Civil Service can bring one all kinds of worldly comfort, but are not these acquisitions made at the expense of one's soul? I think it is hypocrisy to maintain that the highest ideals of one's life are compatible with subordination to the conditions of service which an I.C.S. man has got to accept.

'You will readily understand my mental condition as I stand on the threshold of what the man-in-the-street would call a promising career. There is much to be said in favour of such a service. It solves once for all what is the paramount problem for each of us—the problem of bread and butter. One has not got to face life with risk or any uncertainty as to success or failure. But for a man of my temperament who has been feeding on ideas which might be called eccentric—the line of least resistance is not the best line to follow. Life loses half its interest if there is no struggle—if there are no risks to be taken. The uncertainties of life are not appalling to one who has not, at heart, worldly ambitions. Moreover, it is not possible to serve one's country in the best and fullest manner if one is chained to the Civil Service. In short, national and spiritual aspirations are not compatible with obedience to Civil Service conditions.

'I realise that it is needless to talk in this fashion as my will is not my own. Though I am sure that the C. Service has no glamour for you, father is sure to be hostile to the idea of my not joining. He would like to see me settle down in life as soon as possible.... Hence I find that owing to sentimental and economic reasons, my will can hardly be called my own. But I may say without hesitation that if I were given the option—I would be the last man to join the Indian Civil Service.

'You may rightly say that, instead of avoiding the service, one should enter its ranks and fight its evils. But even if I do so, my position any day may become so intolerable as to compel me to resign. If such a crisis takes place 5 or 10 years hence, I shall not be in a favourable position to chalk out a new line for myself—whereas today there is yet time for me to qualify for another career.

'If one is cynical enough one may say that all this "spirit" will evaporate as soon as I am safe in the arms of the service. But I am determined not to submit to that sickening influence. I am not going to marry—hence considerations of worldly prudence will not deter me from taking a particular line of action if I believe that to be intrinsically right.

'Constituted as I am, I have sincere doubts as to whether I should be a fit man for the Civil Service and I rather think that what little capacity I possess can be better utilised in other directions for my own welfare as well as for the welfare of my country.

'I should like to know your opinion about this. I have not written to father on this point—I really don't know why. I wish I could get his opinion too.'

The above letter shows that the conflict had begun but was still far from being resolved. On the 26th January, 1921, I reverted to the subject and wrote:

'....You may say that instead of shunning this wicked system we should enter it and fight with it till the last. But such a fight one has got to carry on single-handed in spite of censure from above, transfer to unhealthy places, and stoppage of promotion. The amount of good that one can do while in the service is infinitesimal when compared with what one can do when outside it. Mr R. C. Dutt no doubt did a lot of work in spite of his service but I am sure he could have done much more work if he had not been a member of the bureaucracy. Besides the question here involved is one of principle. On principle I cannot accept the idea of being a part of the machinery which has outlived the days of its usefulness, and stands at present for all that is connected with conservatism, selfish power, heartlessness, and red-tapism.

'I am now at the cross-ways and no compromise is possible. I must either chuck this rotten service and dedicate myself whole-heartedly to the country's cause—or I must bid adieu to all my ideals and aspirations and enter the service.... I am sure many of our relatives will howl when they hear of such a rash and dangerous proposal.... But I do not care for their opinions, their cheers or their taunts. But I have faith in your idealism and that is why I am appealing to you. About this time 5 years ago I had your moral support in an endeavour which was fraught with disastrous consequences to myself. For a year my future was dark and blank, but I bore the consequences bravely, I never complained to myself, and today I am proud that I had the strength to make that sacrifice. The memory of that event strengthens my belief that if any demands for sacrifice are made upon me in the future I shall respond with equal fortitude, courage and calmness. And in this new endeavour can I not expect the same moral support which you so willingly and so nobly lent me, five years ago?...

'I am writing to father separately this time and am appealing to him to give his consent. I hope that if you agree with my point of view you will try to persuade father to that effect. I am sure your opinion in this matter will carry great weight.'

This letter of the 26th January, 1921, shows that I had moved towards a decision but was still awaiting approval from home.

The next letter in which there was reference to the same topic was dated the 16th February, 1921. I wrote therein:

'.... You have received my "explosive" letter by this time. Further thought confirms me in my support of the plans I have sketched for myself in that letter.... If C. R. Das at his age can give up everything and face the uncertainties of life—I am sure a young man like myself, who has no worldly cares to trouble him, is much more capable of doing so. If I give up the service, I shall not be in want of work to keep my hands full. Teaching, social service, co-operative credit work, journalism, village organization work, these are so many things to keep thousands of energetic young men busy. Personally, I should like to take up teaching and journalism at present. The National College and the new paper *Swaraj* will afford plenty of scope for my activity.... A life of sacrifice to start with, plain living and high thinking, whole-hearted devotion to the country's cause—all these are highly enchanting to my imagination and inclination. Further, the very principle of serving under an alien bureaucracy is intensely repugnant to me. The path of Arabindo Ghosh is to me more noble, more inspiring, more lofty, more unselfish, though more thorny than the path of Ramesh Dutt.

'I have written to father and to mother to permit me to take the vow of poverty and service. They may be frightened at the thought that that path might lead to suffering in the future. Personally I am not afraid of suffering—in fact, I would rather welcome it than shrink from it.'

The letter of the 23rd February, 1921, is also interesting. Therein I say:

'Ever since the result of the I.C.S. was declared, I have been asking myself whether I shall be more useful to my country if I am in the service than if I am not. I am fully convinced now that I shall be able to serve my country better if I am one of the people than if I am a member of the bureaucracy. I do not deny that one can do some amount of good when he is in the service but it can't be compared with the amount of good that one can do when his hands are not tied by bureaucratic chains. Besides, as I have already mentioned in one of my letters, the question involved is mainly one of principle. The principle of serving an alien bureaucracy is one to which I cannot reconcile myself. Besides the first step towards equipping oneself for public service is to sacrifice all worldly interests—to burn one's boats as it were—and devote oneself whole-heartedly to the national cause.... The illustrious example of Arabindo Ghosh looms large before my vision. I feel that I am ready to make the sacrifice which that example demands of me. My circumstances are also favourable.'

It is clear from the above that I was still under the influence of Arabindo Ghosh. As a matter of fact it was widely believed about this time that he would soon return to active political life.

The next letter was written on the 6th April from Oxford where I was spending my holidays. By then I had received my father's letter disapproving of my plans, but I had definitely made up my mind to resign. The following extracts are interesting:

'Father thinks that the life of a self-respecting Indian Civil Servant will not be intolerable under the new regime and that home rule will come to us within ten years. But to me the question is not whether my life will be tolerable under the new regime. In fact, I believe that, even if I am in the service, I can do some useful work. The main question involved is one of principle. Should we under the present circumstances own allegiance to a foreign bureaucracy and sell ourselves for a mess of pottage? Those who are already in the service or who cannot help accepting service may do so. But should I, being favourably situated in many respects, own allegiance so readily? The day I sign the covenant I shall cease to be a free man.

'I believe we shall get Home Rule within ten years and certainly earlier if we are ready to pay the price. The price consists of sacrifice and suffering. Only on the soil of sacrifice and suffering can we raise our national edifice. If we all stick to our jobs and look after our own interests, I don't think we shall get Home Rule even in 50 years. Each family—if not each individual—should now bring forward its offering to the feet of the mother. Father wants to save me from this sacrifice. I am not so callous as not to appreciate the love and affection which impels him to save me from this sacrifice, in my own interest. He is naturally apprehensive that I am perhaps hasty in my judgement or overzealous in my youthful enthusiasm. But I am perfectly convinced that the sacrifice has got to be made—by somebody at least.

'If anybody else had come forward, I might have had cause to withdraw or wait. Unfortunately nobody is coming yet and the precious moments are flying away. In spite of all the agitation going on there, it still remains true that not a single Civil Servant has had the courage to throw away his job and join the people's movement. This challenge has been thrown at India and has not been answered yet. I may go further and say that in the whole history of British India, not one Indian has voluntarily given up the Civil Service with a patriotic motive. It is time that members of the highest service in India should set an example to members of the other services. If the members of the services withdraw their allegiance or even show a desire to do so—then only will the bureaucratic machine collapse.

'I therefore do not see how I can save myself from this sacrifice. I know what this sacrifice means. It means poverty, suffering, hard work, and possibly other hardships to which I need not expressly refer, but which you can very well understand. But the sacrifice has got to be made—consciously and deliberately.... Your proposal that I should resign after returning is eminently reasonable but there are one to two points to be urged against it. In the first place it will be a galling thing for me to sign the covenant which is an emblem of servitude. In the second place if I accept service for the present I shall not be able to return home before December or January, as the usual custom stands. If I resign now, I may return by July. In six months' time much water will have flowed through the Ganges. In the absence of adequate response at the right moment, the whole movement might tend to flag, and if response comes too late it may not have any effect. I believe it will take years to initiate another such movement and hence I think that the tide in the present movement must be availed of. If I have to resign, it does not make any difference to me or to any one of us whether I resign tomorrow or after a year, but delay in resigning may on the other hand have some untoward effect on the movement. I know full well that I can do but little to help the movement—but it will be a great thing if I have the satisfaction of having done my bit.... If for any reason I happen to change my decision regarding resignation, I shall send a cable to father as that will relieve his anxiety.'

In the letter written from Cambridge on the 20th April, I said that I would send in my resignation on the 22nd April.

In my letter dated the 23rd April from Cambridge I wrote as follows:

'I had a talk with the Censor of Fitzwilliam Hall, Mr Reddaway, about my resignation. Contrary to my expectations, he heartily approved of my ideas. He said he was surprised, almost shocked, to hear that I had changed my mind, since no Indian within his knowledge had ever done that before. I told him that I would make journalism my profession later on, and he said that he preferred a journalistic career to a monotonous one like the Civil Service.

'I was at Oxford for three weeks before I came up here and there the final stage of my deliberation took place. The only point which had been taxing me for the last few months was whether I should be justified morally in following a course which would cause intense sorrow and displeasure in many minds and especially in the minds of father and mother.... My position therefore is that, in entering a new career, I am acting against the express wishes of father and mother and against your advice though you have sent me your 'warmest felicitations in whatever course I choose.' My greatest objection to joining the service was based on the fact that I would have to sign the covenant and thereby own the allegiance of a foreign bureaucracy which I feel rightly or wrongly has no moral right to be there. Once I signed the covenant, it would not matter from the point of view of principle whether I served for three days or three years. I have come to believe that compromise is a bad thing—it degrades the man and injures his cause. . . . The reason why Surendra Nath Bannerji is going to end his life with a knighthood and a ministership is that he is a worshipper of the philosophy of expediency which Edmund Burke preached. We have not come to that stage where we can accept a philosophy of expediency. We have got to make a nation and a nation can be made only by the uncompromising idealism of Hampden and Cromwell. . . . I have come to believe that it is time for us to wash our hands clean of any connection with the British Government. Every Government servant whether he be a petty chaprasi or a provincial Governor only helps to contribute to the stability of the British Government in India. The best way to end a Government is to withdraw from it. I say this not because that was Tolstoy's doctrine nor because Gandhi preaches it—but because I have come to believe in it. . . . I sent in my resignation a few days ago. I have not yet been informed that it has been accepted.

'C. R. Das has written, in reply to a letter of mine, about the work that is already being done. He complains that there is a dearth of sincere workers at present. There will consequently be plenty of congenial work for me when I return home. . . . I have nothing more to say. The die is cast and I earnestly hope that nothing but good will come out of it.'

On the 18th May, I wrote from Cambridge as follows:

'Sir William Duke is trying to persuade me to withdraw my resignation. He wrote to *Bardada* about it. The Secretary of the Civil Service Board at Cambridge, Mr Roberts, also asked me to reconsider my decision and he said he was acting under instruction from the India Office. I have sent word to Sir William saying that I have acted after mature deliberation.'

This letter requires an annotation. Soon after I sent in my resignation, there was a flutter in the India Office dovecots. The late Sir William Duke, then Permanent Under-Secretary of State for India, who knew my father when he was Commissioner of Orissa, got into touch with my eldest brother, Sjt. Satish Chandra Bose, who was then qualifying himself for the Bar in London. Sir William advised me through my brother not to resign the service. I was also approached by lecturers in Cambridge and asked to reconsider my decision. Then there was a request from the Secretary of the Civil Service Board in Cambridge, the late Mr Roberts. All these moves taken from different directions intrigued me, but most interesting of all was the last move.

Some months earlier I had a passage-at-arms with Mr Roberts over some printed instructions issued to Civil Service Probationers by the India Office. These instructions were under the caption 'Care of Horses in India' and contained remarks to the effect that the Indian syce (groom) eats the same food as his horse—that Indian Bunnias (traders) are proverbially dishonest, etc. I naturally felt indignant when I received them and had a talk with other fellow-probationers who had also got them. We all agreed that the instructions were incorrect and offensive and that we should make a joint protest. When the time came for us to write, everybody tried to back out. Ultimately I grew desperate and decided to act on my own.

I went straight to Mr Roberts and drew his attention to the incorrect statements in the printed instructions. He flared up and said, 'Look here, Mr Bose, if you do not take up the official point of view, I am afraid you will have to clear out.' I was not to be browbeaten so easily and I had gone prepared for a scrap. So I calmly replied, 'Yes, but what do you mean by the official point of view?' Mr Roberts realised at once that browbeating would not do, so he changed his tone and voice and remarked gently, 'What I mean is that you should not look out for offences.'

I replied that I had not looked out for offences, but that the instructions were there in front of me. At the end he came round and said that he would draw the attention of the India Office to what I had told him. I thanked him and left.

A fortnight later Mr Roberts sent for me. This time he was very cordial. He read out a letter from the India Office in which they thanked me for drawing their attention to the printed instructions and assured me that when the instructions would be reprinted, the necessary corrections would be made.

After my resignation it was quite a different Mr Roberts that I met. He was so sweet. He argued long with me and tried to persuade me that under the new Constitution, I should try the service for a couple of years. It was possible under the new Constitution to serve the country while remaining in the service and if at the end of two years I found that I could not carry on, then I would be perfectly justified in resigning. I thanked him but told him that I had made up my mind because I felt that I could not serve two masters.

CHAPTER X

MY FAITH (Philosophical)

In 1917 I became very friendly with a Jesuit father. We used to have long talks on matters of common interest. In the Jesuit order founded by Ignatius Loyola I then found much that appealed to me, for instance, their triple vow of poverty, chastity, and obedience.[1] Unlike many Jesuits, this father was not dogmatic and he was well versed in Hindu philosophy. In our discussions he naturally took his stand on Christian theology as interpreted by his church, while I took my stand on the Vedanta as interpreted by Shankaracharya. I did not of course comprehend the Shankarite Doctrine of Maya[2] in all its abstruseness, but I grasped the essential principles of it—or at least I thought I did. One day the Jesuit father turned round to me and said—'I admit that Shankara's position is logically the soundest—but to those who cannot live up to it, we offer the next best.'

There was a time when I believed that Absolute Truth was within the reach of human mind and that the Doctrine of Maya represented the quintessence of knowledge. Today I would hesitate to subscribe to that position. I have ceased to be an absolutist (if I may use that word in my own sense) and am much more of a pragmatist. What I cannot live up to—what is not workable—I feel inclined to discard. Shankara's Doctrine of Maya intrigued me for a long time, but ultimately I found that I could not accept it because I could not live it. So I had to turn to a different philosophy. But that did not oblige me to go to Christian theology. There are several schools of Indian philosophy which regard the world, creation, as a reality and

---

[1] There is some analogy to the triple prayer of the Buddhist which has to be repeated daily—"I take refuge in Buddha: I take refuge in Dharma (Truth); I take refuge in the Sangha (Order)".

[2] In brief, this theory implies that the world as we perceive it through our senses is an illusion. It is a case of the rope being mistaken for a snake, the snake being the world of the senses.

My Faith (Philosophical)

In 1917 I became very friendly with a Jesuit father. We used to have long talks on matters of common interest. In the Jesuit order founded by Ignatius Loyala (then) I found much that appealed to me — for instance, their triple vow of poverty, chastity and obedience.[1] Unlike many other Jesuits, this father was not dogmatic and he was well-versed in Hindu Philosophy. In our discussions he naturally took his stand on Christian theology as interpreted by his Church, while I took my stand on the Vedanta as interpreted by Shankaracharya. I did not of course comprehend the Shankarite doctrine of Māyā[2] in all its abstruseness, but I grasped the essential principles of it — or at least I thought I did so. One day the Jesuit turned round to me and said — "I admit that Shankara's position is logically the soundest — but to those who cannot live up to it, we offer the next best."

There was a time when I believed that Absolute Truth was within the reach of the human mind and that the Doctrine of Māyā represented the attainable. thought that truth could be attained a quintessence of Knowledge. Today I would hesitate to subscribe to that position. I have ceased to be an absolutist (if I may use that word in my own sense) and am much more of a pragmatist. What I cannot live up to — what is not workable — I feel inclined to discard. Shankara's

1 There is some analogy to the triple prayer of the Buddhists which has to be repeated daily - ' I take refuge in Buddha ; I take refuge in Dharma (Truth); I take refuge in the Sangha (Ord

16, Herbert Street,
Cambridge.
22.4.'21.

The Right Hon. E. S. Montagu M. P.,
    Secretary of State for India.

Sir,

I desire to have my name removed from the list of probationers in the Indian Civil Service.

I may state in this connection that I was selected as a result of an open competitive examination held in August, 1920.

I have received an allowance of £100 (one hundred pounds only) up till now. I shall remit the amount to the India Office as soon as my resignation is accepted.

I have the honour to be,
    Sir,
Your most obedient servant,
    Subhas Chandra Bose.

Letter of resignation from the Indian Civil Service

not as an illusion. There is, for example, the theory of Qualified Monism according to which the ultimate reality is One and the world is a manifestation of it. Ramakrishna's view is similar, that both the One (God) and the Many (Creation) are true. Several theories have been advanced to explain the nature of creation. According to some the universe is the manifestation of Ananda or Divine Bliss. Others hold that it is the manifestation of Divine Play or 'Leela'. Several attempts have also been made to describe the One—the Absolute—God—in human language and imagery. To some, like the Vaishnavas, God is Love, to some like the Shaktas, He is Power; to others He is Knowledge; to still others He is Bliss. Then there is the traditional conception of the Absolute in Hindu philosophy as 'Sat-Chit-Ananda', which may be translated as 'Existence-Consciousness (or Knowledge)-Bliss'. The more consistent philosophers say that the Absolute is indescribable or inexpressible (anirvachaneeya). And it is reported of Buddha that whenever he was questioned about the Absolute he remained silent.

It is impossible to comprehend the Absolute through our human intellect with all its limitations. We cannot perceive reality as it is objectively—as it is in itself—we have to do so through our own spectacles, whether these spectacles be Bacon's 'Idola' or Kant's 'forms of the understanding' or something else. The Hindu philosopher will probably say that as long as the duality of Subject (Jnata) and Object (Jneya) remains, knowledge is bound to be imperfect. Perfect knowledge can be attained only when Subject and Object merge into oneness. This is not possible on the mental plane— the plane of ordinary consciousness. It is possible only in the supra-mental plane—in the region of super-consciousness. But the conception of the supra-mental, of the super-conscious, is peculiar to Hindu Philosophy and is repudiated by Western philosophers. According to the former, perfect knowledge is attainable only when we reach the level of the super-conscious through Yogic perception, i.e., intuition of some sort. Intuition as an instrument of knowledge has, of course, been admitted in Western philosophy since the time of Henri Bergson, though it may still be ridiculed in certain quarters. But Western philosophy has yet to admit the existence of the supra-mental and the possibility of our comprehending it through Yogic perception.

Assuming for a moment for argument's sake that we can comprehend the Absolute through Yogic perception, the difficulty about describing it will still remain. When we attempt to describe it, we fall back into the plane of normal consciousness and we are handicapped by all the limitations of the normal human mind. Our descriptions of the Absolute God are consequently anthropomorphic. And what is anthropomorphic cannot be regarded as Absolute Truth.

Now can we comprehend the absolute through Yogic perception? Is there a supra-mental plane which the individual can reach and where the Subject and the Object merge into oneness? My attitude to this question is one of benevolent agnosticism—if I may coin this expression. On the one hand, I am not prepared to take anything on trust. I must have first-hand experience, but this sort of experience in the matter of the Absolute, I am unable to get. On the other hand, I cannot just rule out as sheer moonshine what so many individuals claim to have experienced in the past. To repudiate all that would be to repudiate much, which I am not prepared to do. I have, therefore, to leave the question of the supra-mental open, until such time as I am able to experience it myself. Meanwhile I take up the position of a relativist. I mean thereby, that Truth as known to us is not absolute but relative. It is relative to our common mental constitution—to our distinctive characteristics as individuals—and to changes in the same individual during the process of time.

Once we admit that our notions of the Absolute are relative to our human mind we should be relieved of a great deal of philosophical controversy. It would follow that when such notions differ, they may all be equally true—the divergence being accounted for by the distinctive individuality of the subject. It would follow, further, that the notions of the same individual with regard to the Absolute may vary with time along with his mental development. But none of these notions need be regarded as false. As Vivekananda used to say, 'Man proceeds not from error to truth but from truth to higher truth'. There should accordingly be scope for the widest toleration.

The question now arises: Granting that reality as known to me is relative and not absolute, what is its nature? In the first place, it has an objective existence and is not an illusion. I come to this conclusion not from *a priori* considerations but mainly from the pragmatic point of view. The Doctrine of Maya does not work. My life is incompatible with it, though I tried long and hard to make my life fit in with it. I have, therefore, to discard it. On the other hand, if the world be real (not, of course, in an absolute but in a relative sense) then life becomes interesting and acquires meaning and purpose.

Secondly, this reality is not static, but dynamic—it is ever changing. Has this change any direction? Yes, it has; it is moving towards a better state of existence. Actual experience demonstrates that the changes imply progress—and not meaningless motion.

Further, this reality is, for me, Spirit working with a conscious purpose through time and space. This conception does not, of course, represent the Absolute Truth which is beyond description for all time and which for me is also beyond comprehension at the present moment. It is therefore a relative truth and is liable to change along with the changes in my mind.[3] Nevertheless, it is a conception which represents my utmost effort to comprehend reality and which offers a basis on which to build my life.

Why do I believe in Spirit? Because it is a pragmatic necessity. My nature demands it. I see purpose and design in nature; I discern an 'increasing purpose' in my own life. I feel that I am not a mere conglomeration of atoms. I perceive, too, that reality is not a fortuitous combination of molecules. Moreover, no other theory can explain

---

[3] There is nothing wrong in this—for as Emerson said, a foolish consistency is the hobgoblin of little minds. Moreover, what is progress if it does not involve change?

reality (as I understand it) so well. This theory is in short an intellectual and moral necessity, a necessity of my very life, so far as I am concerned.

The world is a manifestation of Spirit and just as Spirit is eternal so also is the world of creation. Creation does not and cannot end at any point of time. This view is similar to the Vaishnavic conception of Eternal Play (Nitya Leela). Creation is not the offspring of sin; nor is it the result of 'avidya' or 'ignorance' as the Shankarites would say. It reflects the eternal play of eternal forces—the Divine Play, if you will.

I may very well be asked why I am bothering about the ultimate nature of reality and similar problems and am not contenting myself with experience as I find it. The answer to that is simple. The moment we analyse experience, we have to posit the self—the mind which receives—and the non-self—the source of all impressions, which form the stuff of our experience. The non-self—reality apart from the self—is there and we cannot ignore its existence by shutting our eyes to it. This reality underlies all our experience and on our conception of it depends much that is of theoretical and practical value to us.

No, we cannot ignore reality. We must endeavour to know its nature—though, as I have already indicated, that knowledge can at best be relative and cannot be dignified with the name of Absolute Truth. This relative truth must form the basis of our life—even if what is relative is liable to change.

What then is the nature of this Spirit which is reality? One is reminded of the parable of Ramakrishna about a number of blind men trying to describe an elephant—each giving a description in accordance with the organ he touched and therefore violently disagreeing with the rest. My own view is that most of the conceptions of reality are true, though partially, and the main question is which conception represents the maximum truth. For me, the essential nature of reality is LOVE. LOVE is the essence of the Universe and is the essential principle in human life. I admit that this conception also is imperfect—for I do not know today what reality is in itself and I cannot lay claim to knowing the Absolute today—even if it be within the ultimate reach of human knowledge or experience. Nevertheless, with all its imperfection, for me this theory represents the maximum truth and is the nearest approach to Absolute Truth.

I may be asked how I come to the conclusion that the essential nature of reality is LOVE. I am afraid my epistemology is not quite orthodox. I have come to this conclusion partly from a rational study of life in all aspects—partly from intuition and partly from pragmatic considerations. I see all around me the play of love; I perceive within me the same instinct; I feel that I must love in order to fulfil myself and I need love as the basic principle on which to reconstruct life. A plurality of considerations drives me to one and the same conclusion.

I have remarked above that the essential principle in human life is love. This statement may be challenged when one can see so much in life that is opposed to love; but the paradox can be easily explained. The 'essential principle' is not fully manifest yet; it is unfolding itself in space and time. Love, like reality of which it is the essence, is dynamic.

What, now, is the nature of the process of unfolding? Firstly, is it a movement forward or not? Secondly, is there any law underlying this movement?

The unfolding process is progressive in character. This assertion is not quite dogmatic. Observation and study of nature point to the conclusion that everywhere there is progress. This progress may not be unilinear; there may be periodic setbacks—but on the whole, i.e., considered from a long period point of view, there is progress. Apart from this rational consideration there is the intuitive experience that we are moving ahead with the lapse of time. And last but not least, there is the necessity, both biological and moral, to have faith in progress.

As various attempts have been made to know reality and to describe it—so also have attempts been made to comprehend the law of progress. None of these efforts is futile; each gives us a glimpse of the truth. The Sankhya Philosophy of the Hindus was probably the oldest endeavour to describe the evolutionary process in nature. That solution will not satisfy the modern mind. In more recent times, we have various theories, or perhaps descriptions, of evolution. Some like Spencer would have us believe that evolution consists in a development from the simple to the complex. Others like von Hartmann would assert that the world is a manifestation of blind will—from which one could conclude that it is futile to look for an underlying idea. Bergson would maintain his own theory of creative evolution; evolution should imply a new creation or departure at every stage, which cannot be calculated in advance by the human intellect. Hegel, on the contrary, would dogmatise that the nature of the evolutionary process, whether in the thought world or in reality outside, is dialectic. We progress through conflicts and their solutions. Every thesis provokes an antithesis. This conflict is solved by a synthesis, which in its turn, provokes new antithesis—and so on.

All these theories have undoubtedly an element of truth. Each of the above thinkers has endeavoured to reveal the truth as he has perceived it. But undoubtedly Hegel's theory is the nearest approximation to truth. It explains the facts more satisfactorily than any other theory. At the same time, it cannot be regarded as the whole truth since all the facts as we know them, do not accord with it. Reality is, after all, too big for our frail understanding to fully comprehend. Nevertheless, we have to build our life on the theory which contains the maximum truth. We cannot sit still because we cannot, or do not, know the Absolute Truth.

Reality, therefore, is Spirit, the essence of which is Love, gradually unfolding itself in an eternal play of conflicting forces and their solutions.

Part II

LETTERS 1912–1921

LETTERS 1912-1921

These letters were written by Netaji Subhas Chandra Bose during his boyhood, adolescence and youth between 1912 and 1921. There are altogether 70 letters written by him to his mother Prabhabati Bose, brother Sarat Chandra Bose, boyhood friends Hemanta Kumar Sarkar and Charu Chandra Ganguly, Deshbandhu Chittaranjan Das and other friends. His historic letter to the Secretary of State for India tendering resignation from the Indian Civil Service is also included. Seven letters to Sarat Chandra Bose written in connection with his decision to resign from the Indian Civil Service have been published in full in this volume for the first time.

The letters to his mother and brother provide together with his autobiography, the source material with which to begin a study of Netaji's early mental and intellectual development. A long series of letters to Hemanta Kumar Sarkar, suitably edited, cover the period from his early college days to his resignation from the Indian Civil Service. It will be seen that these letters, rather than merely recording the many events and episodes, reveal the inner struggles of the writer. The two letters to Deshbandhu Das and the seven letters to Sarat Bose from England will, we hope, not fail to receive the special attention they deserve. They mark the first major decision in Subhas Chandra's life and what is historically most stimulating, they reveal for the first time the political visionary, planner and strategist that was about to enter the Indian political scene.

Except for the letters written to his brother in 1912–13 and again in 1920–21 all the rest had to be translated from the originals in Bengali. In rendering them into English—by no means an easy task—every effort has been made to preserve the spirit and tone of the originals, even if that has meant disregarding English idiom to a certain extent. In his letters to his friends and to Deshbandhu Das, Netaji used English expressions rather freely. These have been retained with necessary alteration in placement. For Bengali expressions and names which we have chosen to retain the non-Bengali reader will please refer to the section of References and Glossary.

The first nine letters were written by Netaji to his mother Prabhabati Bose. All of them were undated. But, checking up on events mentioned in the letters, it can be established that they were written in 1912–13.

The letters have been translated from the originals in Bengali. The traditional form of address used by the writer in the letters, if translated literally, would read: 'Submitted at the lotus-feet of my most revered mother'. For the convenience of the non-Bengali reader, this has been given in the translations simply as 'Revered Mother'.—*Ed*.

(1)

THE LORD BE WITH US

Cuttack,
Saturday

Revered Mother,

Today is the final day of the Puja; so you must now be in our country home—engrossed in the worship of the Goddess.

I expect the Puja this year will be performed with great pomp and ceremony. But, mother, is there any need of pomp and ceremony? It is enough if we invoke the One we seek to attain with all our heart and in all sincerity; what more is needed? When devotion and love take the place of sandal wood and flowers, our worship becomes the most sublime thing in the world. Pomp and devotion are incompatible. This year I have a pang in my heart. It is a great sorrow—not an ordinary one. This year I have been denied the fulfilment that comes through the *Darshan* of the Goddess *Durga*, the Queen of the three realms, our Savior from all misfortune and Protector from all evil, the Mother of the Universe,—attired in elaborate and magnificent robes and revealed in all Her resplendent glory with myriad lights shining around her; this time I have missed the happiness that comes from listening to the melodious chanting of the sacred hymns by our revered priest to the sound of the conch-shell and the gong; the satisfaction of sensing the sacred aroma of flowers, sandal-wood and incense and of sharing with others the holy food offered to the Goddess; on this occasion I have been deprived of the privilege of being blessed by the priest with the holy flowers and, above all, of the mental peace that comes from contact with the holy water of the *Puja;* I missed everything; all my five senses remain unsatisfied. If I could perceive the omnipresent and universal image of the Goddess, I would not be so mortified and I would not hanker after the wooden image; but how many are so blessed and fortunate as to have this perception! So, I remain unconsoled.

I shall be pining away at this place on the immersion day but at heart I shall be with you all. There will be no happiness for me on such a sacred day. There is no help for it now—tomorrow evening we shall send you our *pronams* from here. You and father will please accept the *pronams* and convey the same to all superiors.

We are all well. I hope all of you are in good health. My *pronams* to you and father.

Your devoted son
S<small>UBHAS</small>

P.S.—How is Sarada?

(2)

THE DIVINE MOTHER BE WITH US

Cuttack
Saturday

Revered Mother,

I was extremely happy to receive your letter this morning. The money order for Rs. 50/- came with it.

Please do not be in a hurry to reply to my letters—please do so at your leisure. If you have difficulty in reading through them, please get somebody else to read them out to you.

Pea seeds are being sown or will soon be sown in Jobra garden. Five or six days ago Raghua took the seeds from me. I did not visit the garden.

I was sorry to hear that Nagen *Thakur* was not able to perform the *Puja* this year. Has he recovered completely? Of all the Pujas that I have attended, those conducted by Nagen *Thakur* and our most revered *Gurudev* I have found to be the most effective in creating religious fervour. Nagen *Thakur's* chanting of the *Chandi* is most moving and even an unbeliever becomes a devotee.

I am delighted to learn that the house of our revered *Gurudev* in Kodalia has been completed. We shall take the first opportunity of visiting the house when we go to our village next. Please convey my respectful pronams to him when you see him. I am pained to hear of *Bardidi's* illness. How is she? We were anxious to learn that you had an attack of dengue fever. Please let us know how you are now and relieve our anxiety. The entire set of hymns of *Sankaracharya* are being sold from the office of *Basumati* at a very reasonable price. One book contains all his hymns and the price is only twelve annas or one rupee. Please do not miss this chance. Please ask *Kanchi Mama* to go and buy a copy. Please keep the book with you and bring it along when you come to Cuttack.

Mother, I have something to tell you. You are probably aware that I am particularly anxious to become a vegetarian. But lest people say something adverse or take it otherwise, I have not been able to fulfil my wish. A month ago I gave up all non-vegetarian food except fish. But today *Nadada* forced some meat on me. What could I do! I could not help eating it, but with great reluctance. I want to be vegetarian because our sages have said that non-violence is a great virtue. Not only the sages—but God Himself has said so. What right have we to destroy God's creations? Is it not a great sin to do so? Those who say that visual power diminishes if fish is not eaten, are wrong. Our sages were not so ignorant as to forbid eating of fish if that would cause blindness in people. What is your opinion in this regard?

I do not feel like doing anything without your consent. We are all well. My *pronams* to you all.

Your devoted son
SUBHAS

(3)

THE LORD BE WITH US

Cuttack
Saturday

Revered Mother,
Gopali told me that you have not gone to *Kashi* and that father has gone there alone. I learn from father's letter that it

was not possible for you to go because the *Raja* of Aal did not send money in time. Yesterday I sent you the prescription you mentioned but as I was in haste I could not write very much. I found two prescriptions of Nilratan Babu in your room. But I could not decide which one was wanted; so I sent both. Please ask *Chotdada* to pick the right one.

I finished my letter to *Didi* and mailed it yesterday. I am eager to know where and how Lily is.

Mejdada has written me a long letter at my request. I received it yesterday—my joy on receiving it knew no bounds. The trouble he has taken at my very humble request is embarrassing to me. I shall preserve the letter like a treasure till his return.

What more can I write? By God's grace, we are all well. Sarat Babu (*Jamaibabu's* brother) is here now. I suppose he will leave when he has been able to fix up his quarters.

Please let me know how our most revered *Gurudev* and the *Mother* are keeping? Please convey my respectful *pronams* to them. I remember them every day. How he used to gather flowers here and how we used to go to him to enjoy their fragrance—all this is still vivid in my memory. How he distributed the holy water and flowers after performing *Puja* one day still floats clearly before my mind's eye. I am writing like a mad man. You will probably have trouble reading my letter.

Our school will probably close on the 15th—I am not sure—the notice is not out yet. The rest of the news you will have from *Bardada*.

I am well. I expect you will find me stronger and heavier when you see me next. If that does not happen, it will not be my fault—I have to thank my stars for it. I doubt if others take as much care of their health as I do. But you seem to think that I am wilfully spoiling my health. I am feeling better now than a month ago.

The average daily expense is coming to Rs. 4/- to Rs. 5/- on some days and Rs. 3/- on others. The thirty rupees received from you have all been spent. Jagatbandhu gave me Rs. 37-8-0 annas from father's account. I am spending out of that for different items.

It is getting somewhat cool here very early in the morning—but winter is yet to come. Cauliflowers have not yet been planted. Two rupees worth of cauliflower seeds have been purchased—only tiny shoots have made their appearance.

Where are *Bowdidi, Mamima* and *Mejabowdidi* now and how are they? Convey my *pronams* to them. How is Asoke? Does he have all his teeth by now? All is well here. I hope all is well at your end too. Please accept our *pronams.*

Your devoted son
SUBHAS

(4)

Cuttack
Thursday

Revered Mother,

Please forgive me for not having written to you for so long. Please write to us about the present state of *Nadada's* health and allay our anxiety. Will it not be possible for him to take his examination this time?

Divine Mother's mercy is ever present with us—if one looks for it one can perceive it every moment of our lives. But, then, we are ignorant, non-believers and confirmed atheists—that is why we fail to realise the profundity of His mercy. And, we pray to him when we are in trouble—maybe with some degree of sincerity; but, once we are out of trouble and things begin to look up we stop praying and forget Him. That is why *Kunti Devi* had said, 'O Lord! Please keep me in adversity, all the time, so that I may be praying to you always with all my heart; happiness may lead me to forget you; so let me not be happy.'

The essence of human life—a continuous cycle of birth and death—is dedication to Lord *Hari*. Life is meaningless without it. The difference between me and an animal is that the latter cannot feel the presence of God or pray to Him, while we can, if we try. So my coming into this world will be of no avail if I fail to sing His Glory. Knowledge is vast—much too vast—my limited intellect cannot grasp it all; therefore, I must have Devotion now, not Knowledge. I do not want to (reason) argue—because I am utterly ignorant. I must therefore have only Faith—unquestioning Faith—Faith in the existence of the Lord; I want nothing else. Faith will bring Devotion and Knowledge will come from Devotion. The great sages have said: Devotion leads on to Knowledge. The aims of education are to sharpen the intellect and develop the power of discrimination. Education can be taken to have served its purpose if these two aims are fulfilled. If an educated person has no character, shall I call him a *Pandit?* Never. And, if an uneducated person is conscientious in his ways, believes in and loves God, I am prepared to accept him as a *Maha-Pandit.* Learning a few platitudes does not make a man learned; true knowledge comes from realisation of God. The rest is not Knowledge. I do not wish to lionize the learned or the Pandit. I worship the man whose heart is overflowing with the love of God. Even if he be of low caste, I am prepared to accept the dust of his feet as something sacred. And, one who shows all the signs of ecstasy at the mere mention of *'Durga'* or *'Hari'*—namely, perspiration, weeping, etc. is undoubtedly God Himself. The world is hallowed by their presence—we are just insignificant beings.

For nothing we hanker after riches, but we never care to think who is truly wealthy. In this world, one who is endowed with love of and devotion to God and such priceless attributes, is the wealthy person. Compared to him even the big kings are like beggars. That we are alive even after losing this priceless treasure is a wonder!

We become restless at the approach of 'examinations' but never stop to think that every moment of our lives we are being tested. We are on trial before God, before our *Dharma.* Educational tests are quite unimportant— and they are of temporary value. But the other tests are for eternity. We have to suffer their results in this life and those that follow.

He who goes through this life placing himself unreservedly at the hands of God is the blessed one—his life attains fulfilment and his coming into this world has meaning. But, alas, we refuse to accept this great truth. We are so blind, so unbelieving and so ignorant that we fail to realise this truth. We are not men, we are *rakshasas* of this sinful age.

Nevertheless, we have hope—God is merciful, He is always merciful. Even in the midst of the darkest sin, we can recognise His mercy. His compassion is immeasurable.

When *Vaishnava* religion was facing extinction, the greatest of the *Vaishnavas, Adwaitacharya,* mortified by the humiliation of his religion, prayed thus: 'O Lord, save us, religion is in peril in this sinful age; please come and save us.' Thereupon Lord *Narayana* appeared on this earth in the form of *Shri Chaitanya.* Such experience—that of emergence from time to time of the light of truth, knowledge, love and piety in the midst of darkness and sin—gives us hope that we are not beyond redemption yet; else why should He return to this earth in human form again and again. How much longer will you be staying in Calcutta? Please let us know how you all are and allay our anxiety. We are all well. Father is well.

Your devoted son
SUBHAS

(5)

THE DIVINE MOTHER BE WITH US

Cuttack
Sunday

Revered Mother,

I have not written to you for quite some time; I have some leisure today and so I wish to give myself and my pen the great privilege of writing these few lines to you.

Ideas come surging from within me from time to time

as when flowers come to bloom in a garden and I offer them at your feet as outpourings of my heart. But, I have become somewhat impatient as I have had no means of knowing whether they give you the sensation of some satisfaction as fragrant flowers do or whether they repel you because of their pungency.

I do not know in whom to confide the thoughts that come rushing inside me as untimely clouds in the horizon; and so I send them far away to you. I shall be delighted to know how you take them. But whether they please you or not, I dare to send them to you as the only offering that I can make from my heart.

Mother, what in your opinion is the purpose of our education? You are spending so much on us—you are sending us to school by car in the morning and fetching us again in the afternoon, giving us sumptuous food four or five times a day, dressing and clothing us, employing servants,—I wonder what are all this trouble, struggle and effort for? What after all is the purpose? I am unable to understand. After finishing our education we shall enter the life of activity, then go on toiling the rest of our lives like beasts of burden and thereafter depart from this world. Mother, what sort of career for us will please you most? In what sort of activity would you like us most to be engaged in when we grow up? I wonder what your desire is. I do not know if you will be the happiest if we grow up to be judges, magistrates, barristers or high-placed officials, or if we come to be admired for wealth and fortune by the men of the world, or if we come to possess abundant wealth, cars, horses, etc. and can command long retinues of servants, mansions, landed estates, etc. or if we earn the respect of the learned and the virtuous for having grown up to be "real men" even though we may be poor. I am most anxious to know what you would most like your son to be. Merciful God has given us this life, a sound body, intelligence and strength, which are all so precious, but why? He has given us so much of course for His worship and His work—but, Mother, do we do His work? We hardly pray to Him with all our heart once a day. Mother, it is most painful and disheartening to think that we hardly ever call out to Him—who is doing so much for us, who is always our friend, in prosperity or adversity, at home or in the wilderness, who lives always in our heart and is so close to us and who belongs to us. We weep over unimportant worldly things but have not a tear to spare for Him. Mother, are we not more ungrateful and heartless than even animals? Shame on this Godless education! One who does not sing His Glory has been born in vain! One can quench one's physical thirst by drinking water out of a pond or river, but is it so easy to satisfy one's spiritual thirst? No, it is never possible to quench spiritual thirst completely. That is why our sages have said:

"O Ignorant Man! Take refuge in Him! Resign yourself completely to Him."

In the current age, God has created something new, something that was not in existence in previous ages. This new creation is the *Babu*. We belong to this community of *Babus*. God has given us a pair of legs, but we are unable to walk 40/50 miles because we are *Babus*. We possess a pair of precious hands but we are averse to manual labour, we do not make proper use of our hands, because we are *Babus*. God has given us good physique but we look upon physical labour as behoving only inferior classes because we are of the class of *Babus*. For all sorts of work we cry out for servants—we have difficulty in working our limbs—because, after all, we are *Babus*. Though born in a tropical country we cannot bear the heat because we are *Babus*. We are so scared of the cold that we cover ourselves up with the heaviest possible clothing because we are *Babus*. We parade ourselves as *Babus* everywhere as we are after all *Babus*—but in fact we are animals in the garb of humans, devoid of all human attributes. We are even lower than animals because we have intelligence and conscience which animals have not. Being reared ever since birth in comfort and luxury, we have no capacity whatever to face difficulties—and that is why we cannot master our senses. We remain slaves of our senses throughout our lives and life becomes a burden to us. I often wonder when will the Bengalis rise to the full stature of manhood—when will they overcome their weakness for money and start thinking of the higher things of life—when will they learn to stand on their own legs in all matters—when will they start striving simultaneously for physical, mental and spiritual upliftment—when will they become self-reliant like other nations and proclaim their manhood? It pains me deeply to find that nowadays many Bengalis, under the influence of Western education, turn into atheists and spurn their own religion. It distresses me to see the present-day Bengalis drifting into a life of foppery and luxury and losing their character. What a pity that Bengalis nowadays have learnt to look down upon their own national costume! It hurts me deeply to find that among the Bengalis today there are very few strong, healthy and vigorous persons. And to crown it all, it is so tragic to see that very few among the Bengali gentlemen today pray to God as a daily duty. What can be more painful, Mother, than to find that Bengalis today have become ease-loving, narrow-minded, characterless, and given to jealousy and dabbling in other people's affairs! We are now being educated; if the aim is mere jobs and money, how can we be worthy of the education and of our manhood? Mother, will Bengalis ever come into their own? What is your view? Mother, we as a nation are heading towards perdition. Who will be our saviour? The saviour can only be Bengal's mothers; if Bengal's mothers bring their sons up in an entirely new way can Bengalis once again regain their manhood.

We are doing well. I have written to *Chotdada.* Father will be leaving for Gopanipalan on Monday. Please accept my *pronams.* I have raved a lot in this letter. If you have trouble reading it, please tear it up and forgive me.

Your devoted son
SUBHAS

(6)

THE DIVINE MOTHER BE WITH US

Cuttack
Sunday

Revered Mother,

India is God's beloved land. He has been born in this great land in every age in the form of the Saviour for the enlightenment of the people, to rid this earth of sin and to establish righteousness and truth in every Indian heart. He has come into being in many countries in human form but not so many times in any other country—that is why I say, India, our motherland, is God's beloved land. Look, Mother, in India you may have anything you want—the hottest Summer, the severest Winter, the heaviest rains and again, the most heart-warming Autumn and Spring—everything you want. In the Deccan, I see the *Godavari*, with her pure and sacred waters reaching up to its banks, wending its way eternally to sea, a holy river indeed! To see her or think of her at once brings to one's mind the story of *Panchabati* of the *Ramayana*—and I can see with my mind's eye the three of them, *Rama, Lakshmana* and *Sita*, spending their time in great happiness and in heavenly bliss on the banks of the *Godavari*, forsaking their kingdom and wealth; no worldly grief or anxiety affect the contented look on their faces; the three of them are spending their time in great joy in the worship of Nature and the Almighty. And, at the other end, we are all the time being consumed in the fire of worldly sorrows! Where is that happiness! Where is that peace! We are hankering after peace! There can be peace only though the contemplation and worship of God. If there is any way of having peace on this earth, every home must resound with the song of God. Again, when I look in the northerly direction, a more sublime scene comes before my mind's eye. I see the holy Ganges proceeding along her course—reviving in me another scene of the *Ramayana*. I see *Valmiki's* sacred abode of meditation in the wilderness—resounding all the while with the voice of the great sage, chanting *mantras* from the Holy *Vedas*—I can see the aged sage sitting on a deer-skin with his two disciples at his feet, *Kusha* and *Laba,* who are receiving instruction from him. Even the crooked serpent has lost its venom and is silently listening to the *mantras* with its head raised in attention; herds of cattle that come to the Ganges to quench their thirst are also stopping to listen to the blessed sound of the *mantras;* nearby a deer is lying on the ground and gazing intently at the face of the great sage. Every little thing in the *Ramayana* is so noble—the description of even a single blade of grass is so nobly done; but, alas, having forsaken religion, we are now unable to appreciate this nobility. I am reminded of another scene. The Ganges is on its course, carrying away all the filth of this world; the *Yogis* have collected on its bank—some have half-closed eyes engrossed in their morning prayers, some have built images and are worshipping them with sweet-smelling flowers collected from the forest and with burning sandalwood and incense, *mantras* chanted by some of them are being echoed and re-echoed through the atmosphere— some are purifying themselves with the holy water of the Ganges—some again are humming to themselves as they collect flowers for the *Puja.* Everything is so noble—and so pleasing to the eye as well as to the mind. But, alas! Where are those high-souled seers today? Do we hear their prayers any more? There is no more of their *yoga,* their prayers, their worship, etc.! It is a heart-rending situation. We have lost our religion, and everything else—even our national life. We are now a weak, servile, irreligious and cursed nation! O Lord! The same India has fallen on such evil days! Will you not come and resurrect us? This is Your land—but, look, O Lord, in what state she is now! Where is the eternal religion that your chosen men established here? The religion and the nation that our forebears the Aryans built up and established are now in ruins. O Merciful God, take pity on us and save us!

Mother, when I sit down to write a letter I lose all sense of proportion. I hardly know what I am going to write and what I am able to write. Whatever occurs to me in the first instance I put down—I do not care to think what I write and why. I write as I wish and as my mind dictates. You will forgive me if I have written anything improper.

When I think of the passing away of our most revered *Gurudev,* I hardly know if I should feel sorry or be happy. We do not know where man goes after leaving this world or what happens to him. But, ultimately our soul merges with the Eternal—and then is the happiest time for us—without any pain and sorrow—there are not any more the pangs of rebirth—we enjoy eternal bliss. When I think that he has left for a region where eternal peace prevails, that he is enjoying heavenly bliss in the company of Immortals, I do not find any reason to be sorry. Sorrow should not get the better of us when he has reached the abode of eternal happiness and the thought of his happiness should make us happy also. Whatever Merciful God does is for the good of the world. We were unable to realise this in the beginning because we were immature. When realisation comes we can appreciate with all our being that actually whatever our good Lord does is for the good. When God has taken him away from us for the fulfilment of His own purpose, we should not needlessly give into sorrow; after all, what belongs to Him He can take away at His Will—what right have we to interfere?

And, if, by the Will of God, he chooses to take on human form again to lead his misguided fellow-men along the path of righteousness and to inspire them with the tenets of the eternal religion, we have nothing to be sorry about. Because, the world will be benefited immeasurably thereby. We cannot as well go against something that is for the good of the world. Every human being stands to benefit from this. We are Indians—so India's good is our good. We should feel infinitely happy if he is reborn and seeks to bring our Indian brethren back to the path of religion. The Lord has Himself said in the *Gita.*

As are childhood, youth and old age, in this body to the embodied soul, so also is the attaining of another body. Calm souls are not deluded thereat.

We are all well. We are in His keeping and it is His Will. We are merely His playthings—how much power do we possess—all depends on His Mercy. We are gardeners—He is the owner of the garden. We work in the garden but we have no right to the fruits. We work in the garden and what fruits are grown we offer at His feet. We have the right to work, it is our duty to work—but the product belongs to Him, not to us. So, God has said in the Gita: "You have a right to action, but not to the fruits thereof".

Where is Lily now and how is she? I am not writing to her as I do not know where she is. Where and how are *Mamima* and my sisters-in-law? How are the brothers? How are all the rest? How is father and how are you? Please accept my *pronams*. What news have you of *Mejdada?* I have not received any letter from him for the last two or three mail days. How is *Natun Mamababu?*

I have heard that *Choto Mamima* is seriously ill. How is she? How is Sarada?

Your devoted son
SUBHAS

(7)

Ranchi
Sunday

Revered Mother,

I have not had any news of Calcutta for quite some time. I hope all of you are in good health. I presume you have not written for want of time.

How did *Mejdada* fare in his examination? Did you read the whole of my letter? I would be indeed sorry if you did not.

Mother, I wonder if Mother India in this age has one single selfless son—is our motherland really so unfortunate? Alas! What happened to our hoary past? Where are those Aryan heroes who would freely sacrifice their precious lives in the service of Mother India?

You are a mother, but do you belong only to us? No, you are the mother of all Indians—if every Indian is a son to you, do not the sorrows of your sons make you cry out in agony? Can a mother be heartless? No, that can never be—because a mother can never be heartless. Then, how is it that in the face of such a miserable state of her children, mother remains unmoved! Mother, you have travelled in all parts of India—does not your heart bleed at the sight of the present deplorable state of Indians? We are ignorant—and so we may be selfish but a mother can never be selfish because a mother lives for her children. If that be so, how is it that mother is unmoved when her children are suffering! Then, is the mother also selfish? No, no, that can never be—a mother can never be selfish.

Mother, it is not only the country that is in a pitiable condition! Look at the state of our religion! How holy and eternal the Hindu religion was and how degraded our religion is now! Think of the Aryans who hallowed this earth by their presence and look at us their fallen descendants! Is that holy eternal faith going to be extinct? Look, how atheism, lack of faith and bigotry have become rampant—leading to so much sin and so much misery for the people. Look, how the descendants of the deeply religious Aryan race have now become irreligious and atheistic! Worship, prayer and contemplation were then man's only duty; how many today invoke His name once in their lifetime? Mother, does not the sight of all this and the thought of all this move you too deeply and to tears? Do you not really feel this way? That can never be. A mother can never be heartless!

Mother, please take a good look at the miserable condition of your children. Sin, all manner of suffering, hunger, lack of love, jealousy, selfishness and above all, lack of religion, have made their existence a veritable Hell. And, look at the state of the holy eternal religion! And look, it is on the way to oblivion! Lack of faith, atheism and superstition have brought our religion down and vulgarized it. What is more, nowadays so many sins are being committed in the name of religion—so much sacrilege in the holy places! Look at the terrible state in which the *Pandas* of Puri find themselves! What a shame indeed! Look at the holy *Brahmin* of our olden days and the hypocritical *Brahmin* of the present time. Now, wherever religion is practised there is so much bigotry and sin.

Alas! What have we come to! What has our religion come to! Mother, when you think of such things, do you not become restless? Does not your heart cry out in pain?

Will the condition of our country continue to go from bad to worse—will not any son of Mother India in distress, in total disregard of his selfish interests, dedicate his whole life to the cause of the Mother?

Mother, how much longer shall we sleep? How much longer shall we go on playing with non-essentials? Shall we continue to turn a deaf ear to the wailings of our nation? Our ancient religion is suffering the pangs of near death—does that not stir our hearts?

How long can one sit with folded arms and watch this state of our country and religion? One cannot wait any more—one cannot sleep any more,—we must now shake off our stupor and lethargy and plunge into action. But, alas! How many selfless sons of the Mother are prepared, in this selfish age, to completely give up their personal interests and take the plunge for the Mother? Mother, is this son of yours yet ready?

We have attained human life after as many as eighty-four cycles of existence,—we have intelligence, conscience, soul, etc. But, in spite of having all these, if we remain satisfied like animals with mere eating and sleeping, if we remain slaves of the senses, if we remain occupied only with ourselves and like animals lead amoral lives,—then, what is the meaning of our being born humans? A life in the service of others is the only one worth living. Mother, do you know why I am writing all this to you? To whom else can I talk? Who will listen to me? Who else will take all this seriously? Those, whose lives are motivated only by selfish considerations, cannot afford to think on such lines—will not think on such lines—lest their self-interest should be impaired. But, a mother's life is not motivated by selfish considerations. Her life is dedicated to her children—to the country. If you read the history of India, you will see that so many mothers have lived for the sake of Mother India and have, when the need arose, sacrificed their lives for her. Think of Ahalya Bai, Meera Bai, Durga Bati—there are so many—I cannot remember all their names. We are reared on mother's milk—therefore, nothing can be more educative and elevating than what instruction and guidance we get from the mother.

If the mother tells her child 'Be satisfied with yourself,'—what can one say? The child must then be the unfortunate one. And you must take it that in this sinful age, good men will never appear. You have to presume that nothing is left of India's heritage! And there is no hope for the future! Nothing is left then but remorse! If that be so, if no hope is left of a recovery—if all that one can do is to sit and watch this degradation and misery,—then, what is all this trouble about? If I cannot achieve anything more in this life, why live?

I pray I may continue all my life in the service of others. I hope all are well there. All is well here. Please accept my *pronams*. Please do reply to this letter.

Yours ever affectionately
SUBHAS

(8)

THE DIVINE MOTHER BE WITH US

Ranchi
Sunday

Revered Mother,

I received your letter quite some time ago and I had also written a reply. But on looking through my letter I found that while in an emotional mood I had written many silly things. So I did not feel like sending it and I tore it up. It is my nature that I cannot restrain myself while writing letters—my heart gets the better of me. I dislike writing and reading letters on the worldly things of life—this explains my attitude—I want letters full of ideas.

I do not write when I do not feel like it. When I feel so inclined, I write letter after letter.

I do not always consider it necessary to write about physical well-being. If one has faith in God, worry, anxiety and fear keep away. What, after all, can one do even when misfortune befalls us? We have no such power that we can heal anybody as we may wish to. Why then must we worry? She—in whose keeping we all are—will protect us. When the Mother of the three realms is there to save us, what is there to fear or worry about? Lack of faith is at the root of all unhappiness and misfortune. But man fails to realise this. He thinks he can cure anyone if he so wishes. What ignorance! Uncle went down to Calcutta eight or nine days ago and he is keeping well. He is very fond of coconut water. And, in his present state of health it is very good for him. If you could get some coconuts down to Calcutta and sent them to him, you would be doing him a lot of good. He asked me to mention this to you.

All is well here. I am happy to know that you are all keeping well. When will *Mejdada* return?

Our examination results will probably be out by the middle of May. I do not know what the truth is, but I have heard that many have even come to know their marks.

Are you expecting *Sejdidi* and her family?

I am all the time tormented by the thought that I have already wasted so much of this precious but brief life. At times, it becomes intolerable.

Having been born as a man, if I fail to achieve the purpose of human existence, if I fail to fulfil its destiny,—what is the meaning of it all? As all rivers ultimately find their way to the sea, so do all human lives reach their finality in God. If one cannot realise God, his life is in vain—all ritual, worship and contemplation are in vain—they are nothing but hypocrisy. I no longer feel like wasting time in empty talk. I would rather shut myself up in a room and devote myself day and night to contemplation, thinking and study. Every day brings us nearer to Death—when is the time for us to strive for Him and achieve Him and earn eternal peace and rest? Till we have realized Him—the fountainhead of all happiness—there can be no happiness. How men can at all be content with wealth and property is something that often baffles me. Without Him—the repository of all happiness—there can be no bliss. One must reach Him—the source of all joy—only then can one achieve contentment.

Without realization and divine revelation, life is in vain. Worship, meditation, prayer, contemplation, etc. that man engages in, have only one aim—realization of the Divine. If this purpose is not fulfilled, all this is in vain. One who has tasted this heavenly bliss once, will never turn to the sinful material world.

He has sought to lead us into temptation with the material things of the world and reduced us to mere victims of *Maya*. The mother, as it were, is busy with her household and the child with his playthings—unless the child cries out to her with all his heart leaving all his toys behind, the mother does not come to him. Assuming that the child is at play, the mother feels no necessity to come to him. But when the child's wailing reaches her, she rushes to his side. The Mother of the Universe is playing the game with us. One cannot reach God unless his dedication is hundred per cent. If God could be realized with only fractional attention, why do such people who are steeped in worldly pleasures fail to achieve Him? Without Him, all is empty, absolutely empty,—life is a farce and an intolerable burden.

What do you say?

If I cannot reach Him, where shall my life belong—with what shall I occupy myself—with whom shall I communicate—where shall I seek happiness?

He epitomizes all beings—He has to be achieved and realised.

He can be attained only through *Sadhana*, deep meditation and intense prayer; only thus can He be realised quite speedily—even within the space of two or three years. One must persevere—success or failure is His Will. I must go on working—the ultimate result is in His hands—whether I succeed or I do not is His concern—we must continue and go on trying. One who has realised Him once has no need to strive or pray any more. I hope all of you are well. Please accept my *pronams.*

Your devoted son
SUBHAS

(9)

Ranchi
Monday (1913)

Revered Mother,

I was delighted to receive your letter yesterday. We had to extend our stay here so long on account of aunt's illness. She is better now—and the weather has also cleared. We shall be leaving here tomorrow and arrive in Calcutta early in the morning day after tomorrow.

We are all keeping well.

I had expected long before the examination and was almost certain that I would get a scholarship of Rs. 20/-. This was because I had wished it with all my heart—I had wished it not for my own sake because, after all, what need have I of money? I abhor money, as money is at the root of all evil. My wish was not in my personal interest—I had resolved not to spend a penny out of my scholarship on myself but to spend the whole of it for the good of others. And I hope I shall stick to my resolution. But I fail to see show I could secure such a high position. I had studied very little indeed prior to the examination,—and for quite some time I was paying inadequate attention to studies. I know it for certain that I do not deserve this position—I had expected to come seventh. If I can secure such a position without studying enough, what will become of those to whom nothing is higher than studies and who would even stake their lives on the pursuit of studies! But then,—whether I come first or I come last,—I have come to realise that pursuit of studies is not the highest goal of the student; students feel that by securing a stamp from the University they achieve their mission—but if one fails to acquire real knowledge in spite of obtaining this stamp from the University,—I say I hate this sort of education. Is it not more desirable to remain uneducated? To build his character is the student's primary duty—University education helps in building character—and we can tell one's character from what work he does. Work reveals character. I detest bookish knowledge with all my heart. I want character—wisdom—work. Character is all-inclusive, it includes devotion to God, love of country—the yearning to reach Him. Bookish knowledge is a worthless commodity of very little significance—but, alas! So many people brag so much about it.

There are certain advantages of studying in Calcutta and there are others of studying at Cuttack. I have not been able to make up my mind as to where to study—I shall decide on my return to Calcutta. But I think I should not be at the Presidency College because there are no facilities there for studying the subjects I want to take up. With my *pronams,*

Your devoted son
SUBHAS

The following four letters were written by Netaji to his elder brother Sarat Chandra Bose. Netaji was at the time 15 years old and he wrote them in English. The first letter was written when his brother was preparing to sail for England to qualify for the Bar and the other three when he was studying there. Netaji also wrote a number of very important letters to his brother in 1920–21 in connection with his resignation from the Indian Civil Service.—*Ed.*

(10)

Cuttack
The 22nd Aug, 1912.

My dear brother,

It is not without some reluctance that I am writing this letter as you are now very busy and anxious about your departure. But thinking that this will be the very last letter that you will receive from me while you are in India,

I venture to take my pen in hand.

In writing this, I have but one object—to make one request—that you will delight and instruct me by the descriptions of the various things you see on your journey to England and you will let me have a share of mind regarding how you feel among strange and foreign associations.

When your ship leaves the port of Bombay and moves farther and farther away from the shore—when you lose the last glimpse of the green vegetation and see the last blue line of your native land fade away like a cloud in the horizon and turn round to see the surging waves and the roaring billows with the ship cutting her way through them—the azure sky above, the monotonous deep below—will these elements of nature bring into your mind any strange feeling? Will they remind you of these lines of Irving—'It seemed as if I had closed one volume of the world and its contents and had time for meditation till I opened another' or will they make you repeat some lines of the same author—'It makes us conscious of being cast loose from the secure anchorage of settled life and sent adrift upon a doubtful world.' Surely anybody would choose the former rather than the latter.

You will have to pass some days, I think, before you come in sight of land again and that will be near Aden. How will you feel when land greets your eyes again after a short adieu?

In the sea, you can have a full and clear view of the sunset. It is indeed a glorious spectacle and those who have never been to sea envy the sight very much—it is so very beautiful! Will you not delight me with a brief description of a sunset at sea? What a beauty! That dazzling flood of ebbing light lighting up the entire expanse of the sea and playing up and down with the undulating waves! The Western horizon all rose-red in the rays of the setting sun! And the next moment you see the shades of evening stealing across the sky and in less than half an hour—the whole atmosphere enveloped in darkness—pierced here and there by the faint streaks of some pallid heavenly bodies! It is so very beautiful and so enchanting to the eyes and the soul!

Then after a monotonous sea-voyage lasting for a fortnight you are launched into the noise and tumult of another world—among an alien race and among fair skins and blue eyes. Will not these strange surroundings compare palpably with your former surroundings? Of course this will soon wear away in a day or two.

I hardly know what I have written. I have scrawled at random like a madman. But I hope I shall not be disappointed in my expectations. If it be not improper for the younger to say so, I ardently hope and wish, God-speed and comfort will attend your journey. We are well.

With love and due regards,

I am

Your very affectionately,
SUBHAS

(11)

Cuttack
17.9.12

My dear brother,

I hope you have received my letter addressed to London by this time. I wrote a letter to you while you were in Calcutta but I could not get any assurance as to whether the letter reached you. I went through your letter to mother from Aden and from that I learnt to my great delight that it did reach you. When I wrote it, I never for a moment thought that it would give you any satisfaction but I was so glad to learn that it gave you pleasure to read it. This is due to the fact that what I wrote came from my heart. The heart always appeals to the heart and so it was the case. The thoughts that come direct from the heart are far more effective than those that do not come from the heart even if the former be clothed in a simple and graceful style while the latter are gaudily attired in an ornate style.

I do not know why I wrote it—I cannot recall anything. I was suddenly overpowered with emotion and instantly took my pen in hand. I do not know what or why I wrote—I simply gave utterance to the thoughts that were then uppermost in my breast. Perhaps it was the dead stillness of the night, for it was then close upon midnight, that contributed to the rearing up of such weird feelings. I believe everybody experienced such feelings and especially those who attended the parting ceremony, and more violently too—for it was such a critical moment and it would have been too much for me. But, no, I must not talk of the past and give your feelings an unpleasant shaking.

You will there perhaps hear and read a good deal about the Bengali poet and venerable sage, Rabindranath Tagore. We feel so proud to read of him and the high honour shown to him by an alien people that for the time we become optimistic about the future of Bengal and of India. I am almost stung with self-reproach when I think how indifferent Bengal has been in showering laurels upon him and has suffered his genius, super-human though it is, to lie in the shade of neglect, whereas a foreign people, speaking an alien tongue and cherishing ideas and sentiments, diametrically opposed to ours in some cases, have lifted him up from this shade to sunshine and have extolled him as the greatest poet the world has produced. What a strange people we are! We have so little of reverence in us. So the poet has sung:

'Let knowledge grow from more to more
But more of reverence in us dwell'.

I hope a time will come when I shall be able to appreciate the poems of Rabi Tagore.

Have you met any of your old friends and Mr. Biren Bose among the number?

Englishmen speak very highly of the natural scenery of their motherland. Is it really so? I think you are in a position to draw a comparison between the sceneries of India and England.

We are pretty well here. Hope this will find you in the best of health.

With due regards and *pronams,*

I remain

Yours v. affly.

SUBHAS

(12)

Cuttack,

11.10.12

8 P.M.

My dear brother,

Your voluminous letter was to hand only this evening. I do not know how I am to express my sincere gratitude for the extreme trouble you have taken for the gratification of a childish request of mine. Language fails; for it half expresses and half conceals thoughts. I wish man could make it more perfect, it falls so short of expression. I cannot express to you how heartily I enjoyed your descriptions—vivid and appealing as they are. The scenes you have described seem to dance before my inward vision and seem to be living and real—and not only that—they call up other scenes that my eyes once took in and which were lying dormant for want of recollection and inspiration. The beautiful scenes of fair Darjeeling are now coming back to me—one by one—like the films of a bioscope—the sea, the blue, blue sea at Puri is dashing with fury against the sandy shores—the blue waters, flecked here and there with touches of white, stretching out to meet the blue sky in the horizon are now before me—the bare, rocky and barren hills of Naraj rising up to a noble height on the banks of the lordly and majestic Mahanady—the historic caves of Udaigiri and Khandagiri at Bhuvaneswar— these are all that I have seen—are now playing their part in the stage of my mind. Here I have before me a picture of 'Happy Snowdon'—it is such a beautiful thing. The playful and transient colours of the sky are casting their reflection on the snowy peaks—the icy lakes below are all catching a reflection of the glorious colours—the snow-covered rocks are tinged with bright red—the whole scene seems to be a picture of *Hemkut Parbat* of Hindu mythology or of Olympus, the abode of the gods of Greece.

I do not know what I am writing all this nonsense for and detaining you for nothing but something within urges me to go on. I do not know—this may be tiresome to you.

About a fortnight ago you sent mother a packet of the choicest picture post-cards. You have made a nice selection, a combination of such beautiful post-cards is one of rare choice. When asked by mother to choose the best, I replied that all of them were above comparison and superb. The pictures are so fine and, of course, exaggerate the beauty so much that it seems to make a Heaven of Hell. Though they are not faithful they are charming. We enjoyed the pictures heartily and I have kept some with me.

The descriptions you have given are so vivid that had I known something of drawing I would have attempted to represent them—only to make the impressions more deep and to satisfy my mind. But ignorant as I am of that art I must rest content with merely picturing them in my mind.

I can well imagine the state of your mind when you were between Bombay and Suez, tired of the monotony of the blue sea and the azure sky and longing to catch a glimpse of living nature. I do not like to stay in Calcutta for more than a month at a stretch, for I long to feast my eyes on the fresh beauty and the smiling appearances of nature. Without nature to soothe one's soul and to inspire him in his moments of weakness, man, I think, cannot lead a happy life. Without nature as one's companion and instructor life is no better than banishment in a desert—life loses all its freshness and activity and the sunny side of life grows gloomy.

I cannot do more than thank you over and over again for the trouble you have taken for me and for your exquisitely beautiful descriptions.

I hope you have by this time received the letters I wrote to you at London.

16.10.12

Today is the mail-day and I must post my letter. Last Monday I received a letter from you. I am glad to learn therein that you are putting up quite close to Captain and Mrs. Webb and that you meet them often.

When does the sun rise and set in London now? Is the parliament in session now? Have you experienced London's fog as yet—now that winter has come?

Glad to learn that you have met your old friend 'Sudhir Roy'.

Did you halt at Paris on your way to London from Marseilles?

I have already asked you to spare yourself the trouble of writing to me separately whenever you are busy. May I repeat it—you have so many letters to write and so limited a time at your disposal.

I am sending your 'long letter' to *Mejojamai Babu* and shall ask him to send it to *Sejajamai Babu* after perusal. But I shall have it back again.

School is closed and we are enjoying a pretty long vacation till Nov. 11th. Nadu, *Rangamamababu* and myself shall be here during the vacation. The rest are in Calcutta now. *Nadada* has come down here. Father and mother are doing well there.

I think this will find mother's letter as its companion in the G.P.O. in Calcutta. Please accept our *Bijaya pronams* though it is late. With due regards, I am

Yours v. affly.
SUBHAS

(13)

Cuttack
8.1.13.

My dear brother,

Another year has rolled by and we find ourselves responsible to God for the progress or otherwise that we have made during the last twelve months.

When I survey my last year's work, I cannot help

reflecting on the goal of life. Tennyson, I think, is a staunch optimist and strongly believes that the world is progressing day by day. Is it really so? Are we really nearing our longed for goal? Is our dear country, India, on the high-road to progress? I can't think so. May be, good may come out of evil—may be India is wading through sin and corruption towards peace and progress. But as far as the eye of prudence, prophecy or foresightedness can behold, all is darkness—dense darkness with here and there a faint ray of hope to cheer up the earnest worker or the high-souled patriot. Sometimes the rays seem to brighten up—sometimes the gloom seems to darken. The future history of India is like the condition of the gloomy sky, during a storm. England and of course the whole of Europe may be progressing. The star of religion is rising in the sky of Europe but it is steadily declining in the sky of India. What was India and what is she now? What a terrible change! Where are those saints, those sages, those philosophers—our forefathers who had explored the farthest limits of the realm of knowledge? Where is their fiery personality? Where is their strict Brahmacharya? Where is their realization of God? Where is their unification with the supreme soul, of which we now simply talk of. All is gone! Hushed is their vedic strain! No more are the songs of the Sama Veda to be heard resounding on the banks of the sacred Ganges! But there is hope yet—I think there is hope yet—the angel of hope has appeared in our midst to put fire in our souls and to shake off our dull sloth. It is the saintly Vivekananda. There stands he, with his angelic appearance, his large and piercing eyes and his sacred dress to preach to the whole world, the sacred truths lying embedded in Hinduism! The evening star is up—the moon of course must come. A brighter future is India's destiny. God is ever good. Through sin, irreligiousness, corruption and every other vice He is leading us towards our only goal. He is the magnet round which all things revolve and to which all creation inevitably moves. We must move—the road may be dangerous and stony—the journey may be a laboured one, but we must march. We must ultimately lose ourselves in Him. The day may be far off—but it must come. That is the only hope I now cherish—otherwise everything is disappointing and disheartening to me.

Don't we feel that He is pulling us towards Him with magnetic force?—I think we do. Has He not spread nature's charms around us only to remind us of His existence? Has he not bidden the stars to speak for Him and the infinite sky to teach man that He is infinite? Has He not instilled love in our hearts, to remind us of the love He bears towards us? Alas! He is so good—and we, so naughty.

Dear brother, I don't know why I feel inclined to scribble in this fashion. I have marked that at certain intervals, I feel tempted to disburden my heart. Perhaps, this is one of those strange moments.

I was very glad to receive your letter by the last mail. I was feeling all these days that distance had distanced you from me but this sacred messenger more than made up for this feeling of absence.

We like to keep a memorial of our late Asst. Headmaster (Now Headmaster, Sambalpur Zillah School) Babu Suresh Ch. Gupta in our school. We would like very much to have a life-size bust direct from England. If it costs a pound, it is certainly very cheap. How much do you think will be the freight? Will Rs. 35 or 40 be sufficient for getting it from England direct?

We are having our Test Exam. now and we are faring quite well. We are doing pretty well here. Hope you are in the best of health.

With *pronams* to you,

I am,
Ever affly. yours,
SUBHAS

The following thirty-one letters were written by Netaji to Hemanta Kumar Sarkar, a friend of younger days, during 1914–1919. They have been translated from the Bengali. English expressions used in the original letters have been retained. The first letter deals with the circumstances of his return home after his wanderings in search of a *Guru* to which Netaji has referred in his autobiography.—*Ed.*

(14)

Thursday
Afternoon
19-6-14

I got off the street car, braced myself up and entered home. I met Satyen *Mama* and another acquaintance in the front room. They were rather surprised. I met *Pishamahasaya* and *Dada* inside the house. Mother was informed. Half way up I met her. I made *pronams* to her—she could not help weeping on seeing me. Later, she only said, 'it seems you have come into this world to kill me. I would not have waited so long before drowning myself in the Ganges; only for the sake of my daughters have I not done so.' I smiled within myself. Then I met father. After I had made my *pronams,* he embraced me and led me to his room. On the way he broke down and in the room he wept for quite some time holding on to me. When he was weeping with myself in his arms, I could not help feeling that although I had tried to forget everything else for that youthful face, innocent as the full moon,—I had not been able to do so with all my being. Then he lay down and I massaged his feet—it appeared as if he was feeling some heavenly pleasure. Thereafter both of them went on enquiring at length where I had been. I told them everything frankly—I mentioned about the money. They had come to know about Haripada; it was not necessary to tell them about you and so I did not say anything. *Mama* asked me and so I told him. But that matters little. They only asked me why I had not written at all.

Telegrams were sent to and enquiries made at various places. Mother was active. Father was passive, his attitude being that things would take care of themselves. The matter was not reported to the police—a relative who happened to be a police officer having advised against it. Mother was almost mad at the thought that I had left home for good. So, another *Mama* (America-returned) went out in search of me; he wrote a letter after making exhaustive enquiries at Baidyanath and Deoghar which reached here today;

I know its purport. He went to Balananda. Another Brahmachari told him, 'If he has gone out unprepared, he will get a hard knock and return; if it is the contrary, it is useless to try to get him back.'

Enquiries were made at Belur, a wire was sent to the Ramakrishna Mission at Hardwar—the reply was negative. An astrologer of Howrah was approached. He said that I would return in nineteen or twenty days, that I was well and not alone but had two companions and further that I was somewhere in the North-West the name of the place starting with 'B'. I think I was then at Benares. He added that I would not become a Sannyasi owing to some contrary influence but would return to the world. He may go to Hell! He knows nothing at all. Of all people, Ranen *Mama's* attitude is most favourable. Satyen advised me to be most obedient—as if that is his life's ideal. The rest did not say very much.

There is a gentleman I have known for some time. He is quite reasonable. He said that I should boldly discuss matters, talk the matter over and then be a Sannyasi. Who after all, he asked, could stand in my way?

I had long talks with father again in the afternoon. They related to various views of life, meeting Sannyasis and about my wanderings. I told him I did not like anybody. I also told him immediately what my ideal was. What he wanted to drive at during the discussion was: (1) whether it was possible to practise *Dharma* while leading a worldly life, (2) that renunciation needs preparation, (3) whether it was right to shirk one's duty. I said in reply—(1) Everybody cannot have the same medicine because everybody has not got the same disease and the same capacity—(2) Whether or not renunciation is possible depends on how much cleansing one needs—all may not require much in the way of polishing up—(3) Duty is relative—higher call may completely supersede lower calls when Knowledge comes, action becomes redundant.

He asked me if indivisibility of the Divine Spirit, that is to say that 'the Spirit alone is true, the world is all false', was not a mere theory. I said that so long as it was a mere platitude it was a theory, but it becomes true when it is realised and that such realisation was possible. Those who said so realised its truth and have also said that we could realise it. He asked, 'Who were able to do it and what is the proof?' I answered that the *Rishis* achieved it and then quoted the *Sloka* beginning with 'Vedahamiti.' He then said that once upon a time Maharshi Devendra Nath, Keshab Chandra and Paramhansa were in Calcutta—and people were able to achieve what they were capable of. I said that Vivekananda's ideal was my ideal.

He said at the end, 'When your higher call comes, we shall see.' I have so far not opposed father actively—passively I have won the victory. Now he is unable to force anything upon me. And, when I go away next time, he will probably give up the idea and the effort to get me back.

However, I now see that I have done well in coming back.

Mother is a fanatic and says that next time I go, she will also leave with me and not return home again. I think I will not be able to understand her. I find father very reasonable.

I am quite well. Please let me know how you are.

Yours—

All have a very good impression of Beni Babu and they respect him. Beni Babu did not say much. He mentioned the Sannyasi but did not mix you up at all in my austere activities. The man in him revealed himself again in this matter.

(15)

21-6-14.

I have become so callous. I really do not know why I have turned so stone-hearted. I do not feel at all for my parents—they wept and I could not help smiling. It is true there is no love in my heart—if there was any, I would give it to you unreservedly. I had a talk with father today. He gave me three pieces of advice and said that when I regained my sanity, he would discuss other things with me. He is trying to make me adopt the worldly way of life.

I did not say anything today—I maintained passive silence implying non-submission. Later on I might, if I feel so inclined, talk to him more frankly. It is not possible to reason with mother—she is displeased with me—she thinks I do not care for her in the least...

People generally take maternal love to be the deepest and the most selfless and say that a mother's love is immeasurable. But, my dear friend, I do not rate maternal love so highly. Beni Babu has probably not experienced any other love in his life and that explains his view. Is a mother's love really completely selfless? I do not know; nevertheless, so long as a mother cannot accept any other boy from the street equally as her own son, can her love be called selfless? Her attachment is born of having reared her child herself...

But compared to the love I have tasted in this life, the ocean of love I find myself in, mother's love is like a puddle. In this self-centred world, man's only refuge is mother's love and that is why they raise it so high. For one you have brought up yourself you may well develop affection—is there much credit in that? But, somebody who can give a man from the street the highest place in his heart—how big is his heart—how sublime is his love! People will refuse to understand this.

Do I have it all wrong?

(16)

38/2 Elgin Road
Calcutta
18/7/14.
Saturday 11 a.m.

I just received your letter. I probably forgot to mention in my letter yesterday that parents and others were reaching Calcutta on Monday. You better come again—because later when the house fills up, I do not quite know if it will be convenient or not for us to meet. Please come on Sunday any time you like. He is always present. Even if He is not physically close to me, I can always feel His invisible presence and His good wishes are all the time leading me along the right path.

One may also serve through the Soul and through love that is not outwardly evident. What pleasure it gives me to think that you are doing your work! Incidentally, did you miss your supper day before yesterday? You must not be too hard on yourself; your penance will not be in the usual form—it is all His will, His love and His work—what more can I write—you can well understand what I mean. I am quite well. Yesterday morning the minimum temperature was 97° and in the evening the maximum was 100.2°; today the minimum was 97.4°. I am well and you need not worry. We shall talk when we meet. On Sunday you may stay from morning till afternoon or evening—who dares interfere? It will be better if you come alone.

(17)

Calcutta
Friday Evening
3/10/14

The greatest gift is to give one's heart away. When this is done, there is nothing else left to give away. Is not the one who receives this gift also the most fortunate? Is there anybody more fortunate or happier than he? But who is more—than one who cannot reciprocate this gift? What is the result? The result is peace for both.

* * *

A vision rises before my eyes. It is the Kali temple at Dakshineshwar. In front of me I see Kali the Mother, sabre in hand, a picture of happiness—poised on the seat of *Shiva*, with lotuses all around her. Facing her is a boy—more childlike than his age—sobbing and appealing to somebody in his yet indistinct words: 'O Mother, accept my offering, what is good as well as what is bad, what is sinful as well as what is virtuous'. The fierce and fiery Mother is not satisfied so easily—She wants to devour everything, so She must have the good as well as the bad, the virtues as well as the vices. The boy must give up everything. He cannot have peace otherwise and the Mother will not let him go.

* * *

It is most painful. Mother must have everything. She is not satisfied at all. So he is weeping and repeating, 'Take all, Mother, take all'. Gradually, the flow of tears stopped,—his cheeks and breast dried up—peace came back to his heart. His heart was now empty—no trace of the great pain was left—and everything became peaceful. His heart was all sweetness now and he rose. He had nothing to call his own any more—he had given everything away. The boy is Ramakrishna.

(18)

27-3-15

I shall be going with father towards the end of April. The house of the Maharaja of Burdwan has been fixed up for us. I shall feel most uncomfortable in the midst of luxury and domestic limitations but I shall stick it out. While there I shall occupy myself with extensive study. My studies will be in four parts:
  (1) Study of man and his history
  (2) General study of the Sciences—first principles
  (3) The problem of Truth—the goal of human progress, that is, philosophy
  (4) The greatness of the world.
Besides these, I propose to go through all my college books once. I feel very enthusiastic about studies now. I find things are now completely reversed. The examinations are over and my interest in studies grow! I now feel like devouring all the books.
  I wish to take Honours in Philosophy in my B.A. and come out first. I am unable to decide now if I should take up Sanskrit or Economics thereafter—you cannot live in this modern world without some knowledge of Economics. Sanskrit one can study by himself. Now the question is

whether the economics that is taught in the college is of much use in the practical field. However, I shall make my mind up soon. If you are well, I shall go to Germany. In order to decide upon our duties in the future and how we shall proceed step by step, it is necessary that we meet once.

If considerations of health warrant it, I shall not study in Calcutta. The advantage of studying in Calcutta is that there are good professors here. The advantage of studying in Cuttack is that the climate there is better; there are better opportunities of work there because of the considerable influence we command among the public; this will be so at least as long as father is alive. If necessary, I can study in Cuttack or Hazaribagh. I have written to Hazaribagh for the prospectus. After my return from Kurseong I shall, if need be, discontinue my studies in Calcutta. If it comes to that, you will have to repay my loans to you,—initially you may give me small sums, because there will not be any more tuition work. And I have to give some to Dutta Gupta also.

(19)

Cuttack
Saturday
3-4-15

You have probably received my last two letters. Important events took place yesterday and the day before. It is not possible to write everything openly just at present. Besides, Girish and Sureshda have particularly requested me to tell you about it some time later. I shall be in Calcutta within a month—I shall see you then and let you know the whole thing. There has been a most wonderful reconciliation— Girishda was some sort of a mediator. Sureshda said that he thought the relationship to be undesirable but not unhealthy. He said further that he was never in the least doubtful as regards purity, but he was quite pained to receive complaints from all the rest about our exclusiveness.

He told me also how a sense of remorse grew in him day by day on account of our behaviour. I said whatever I had to say. I am most impressed by Girishda's faith and his character. He added that if the East Bengali had nursed any suspicions in his mind, he would call him a liar to his face. However, all's well that ends well and let us close that chapter. We committed one mistake (and we have to be very careful about this in future) and that is, we failed to realise that each word or action on our part carried so much weight. What a profound effect they had on our brothers.

Sureshda told me that we must mix with the public on equal terms, so that nobody gets to know how much a particular person loves another.

(20)

18-7-15

Well, is it possible for man to realise Absolute Truth? Everybody takes one relative truth to be the absolute in his life and then uses that as the yardstick to judge good and evil, happiness and sorrow of this life. Nobody has really the right to interfere in anybody else's individual philosophy of life or to speak against it, but the fact remains that the basis of that philosophy has got to be sincere and true, as Spencer's theory is—'he is free to think and act so long as he does not infringe the equal freedom of any other individual'.

* * *

Intellectual preparation is necessary in the first instance. Then, thinking and work will go on simultaneously. Ultimately one has to lose himself completely in work. Initially, one must have some make-shift activities so as not to lose the capacity to work.

Look, there are two sides to a life—intellect and character. It is not enough to offer only character to your country—you must be able to produce an intellectual ideal.

* * *

It will not do to know something of everything but to organise them into a systematic whole—and to know everything of something. Simple assimilation will not do—but creative genius is necessary.

I shall give you an inkling of my intellectual career. Only a vague outline of it has formed in my mind. The idea is indeed grand—I do not know if I can translate it into reality in my own life. Even if that does not happen,—if the idea is really good, somebody else may be able to fulfil it.

* * *

(21)

27-7-15

I have not got anything special to do at present,—except working for the Famine Relief Fund. For the time being, all else remains suspended.

(22)

29-7-15

I am not doing anything special at the moment. Poor fund—debating—magazine have not started as yet. Since a week ago I have stopped coaching. It affects your own studies. But I shall remain an auxiliary—I shall teach if I am in want and it is necessary. They have made me the Secretary of the College Famine Fund. I must work for it to a certain extent. There is no one else available.

I should like to go out to do relief work—one can thus gain practical experience. And, experience of famine is something that you cannot have all the time. My emotions want me to go—in fact I am eager to go—but reasoning is bidding me not to—

(1) I may lose my health, because I cannot help exerting myself to the utmost.

(2) Work of the College Relief Committee will suffer.

(3) If I go I should go on behalf of the College organisation—as I am in it.

I have told them I shall give them an answer after due deliberation. Most probably my answer will be in the negative. Will you please let me have your opinion?

Nevertheless, I greatly desire to see the world as it actually is. I must however suppress the desire.

(23)

38/2, Elgin Road, Calcutta
31-8-15

In my article I have expressed my attitude in an indirect manner—I have described it as supreme and sublime indifference. I am realising more and more as time passes that I have a definite mission to fulfil in life and for which I have been born, and I am not to drift in the current of popular opinion. It is the law of this world and people will criticise but my sublime self-consciousness will enable me not to be influenced by them. If the treatment I receive in this world brings about a change in my attitude, that is, makes me unhappy and despondent, I have to assume that it is all due to my own weakness. But, as one who is aiming to reach out to the skies is oblivious of hills or wells on the way, so also is one whose mind is directed towards his mission to the exclusion of everything else, completely unconcerned by other things. I must move about with the proud self-consciousness of one imbued with an idea.

Well, I now understand that to be a man in the real sense there are three prerequisites:

(1) Embodiment of the past
(2) Product of the present
(3) Prophet of the future

(1) I must assimilate the past history, in fact all the past civilisations of the world.

(2) I must study myself—study the world around me—

both India and abroad and for this foreign travels are necessary.

(3) I must be the prophet of the future. I must discover the laws of progress—the tendency of both the civilisations and therefrom settle the future goal and progress of mankind. The philosophy of life will alone help me in this.

(4) This ideal must be realised through a nation—begin with India.

Is not this a grand idea?

* * *

The more we lift our eyes heavenwards the more we shall forget all that was bitter in the past. The future will dawn upon us in all its glory.

Why have you not written about your health? Please reply soon and let me know how you are.

I have plenty to talk to you about. When shall we meet?

(24)

16-9-15

Your letter is to hand.

Many people ask: when philosophy cannot lead you to any conclusion and is ever-growing—one man lays down certain theories, another comes, goes beyond his predecessor and puts forward bigger ideas; when such is the way of philosophy, why go in for philosophy and the philosophic way of life? When Hegel's philosophy was first preached in this world, all people thought as if his was the last word—as if that was the final conclusion. But the world is unfortunate. The march of philosophy has now left Hegel behind. Nevertheless, if you have to live, you must face such questions. Just as fragrance is the inevitable accompaniment of a blooming flower (there is nothing to question about it) so also are such searching questions inevitable in life.

What is the good of studying philosophy? It is this—that you come to know your own questions, your own doubts. . . . You come to know how so many others have thought about them. You may then organise and properly direct your line of thinking.

Nobody who is not eccentric can attain greatness. But, all eccentric people do not become great men. All mad men do not become great men of genius. Why? Only madness does not suffice. Something more is necessary. You cannot arrive at solutions to your questions if eccentricity robs you of self-control. One must remain calm even in the midst of emotion. Then and only then can you build your life on a constructive basis. One must control his emotions and think deeply. Without emotion, thinking is impossible. But with nothing but emotion, thinking cannot be fruitful. Many are quite emotional but do not want to think—many others do not know how to think.

* * *

....Once you have come to know the technique of thinking, there is nothing to fear—to reach a conclusion will still be difficult but not impossible. That is why I believe that my yearning, questions, doubts will not end in nothing but will bring me something positive. You may now have the same expectation.

If there is an ideal, it can be realised—this is my faith. For example, if perfection be the ideal man can become perfect, otherwise there is no such ideal as perfection.

Any way, whatever the ideal may be—it can be realised—this is the basis of my life-philosophy.

One must not be impatient. How can we find an answer to a question in a day, in search of which so many people have laid down their lives!...

* * *

But, then, unless I can find a fundamental principle on which to build my life, with what do I go forward?

Do you know what Kant's philosophy is like? It assumes something to be true, analyses it and criticises it ruthlessly and then gives it up. And having given it up, it arrives at a higher truth. Then, once again, the latter is analysed and criticised in the same manner—and ultimately you arrive at the highest truth.

Life is like that. By all means build up a philosophy in order to harmonise all your present activities in life. Then proceed in accordance with that philosophy. On the other hand, in the inner recesses of your mind, destroy and reconstruct it every moment of your life. Life progresses through continuous construction and destruction. Construct something, then destroy it, build something else and destroy it again and so on.

Something cannot come out of nothing. Man proceeds from Truth to higher Truth. We must pass through inconsistencies. They fulfil life.

If emotions get the better of you, you lose reason, critical power, analytic and synthetic power. Because, only in cool moments can one make proper use of these qualities.

20-9-15

The state of my health is such that I cannot imagine being able to achieve anything special in life. Vivekananda was perfectly right when he said: 'Iron nerves and a well intelligent brain and the whole world is at your feet'.

If the change helps me to recoup my health completely, I shall begin to believe again that life is worth living.

(25)

26-9-15

I have just read Lodge. I do not quite understand why you have asked for my views regarding the Jesuit movement.

That community in question has both good and bad sides. What is good will continue to be good for the present age. What is bad is not intrinsically bad—it was all right for the bygone ages—but is not suited to the needs of the present age.

What is the reason? The concept of human 'freedom' has changed. In ancient times, by 'freedom' people of India meant spiritual freedom—renunciation—freedom from lust, greed, etc. But this freedom also included freedom from political and social bondage. The *Sannyasi* could, if he so wished, cut across social and political barriers with impunity—he could even change rules of government.

The western world, however, is now engaged in finding solution to political and social problems. There has been a rise of individualism among them. They are seriously considering what should be the relationship of the individual to society and the ruling class.

This conflict has made an adjustment of mutual rights necessary. Now we can see that in society and in relation to the State, every individual has certain rights; he is free so long as he does not misuse them or violate them. Everybody is conscious that he is a human being and has certain rights and a voice.

We have been born in this democratic age in a democratic atmosphere. So, if you reject this, you cannot get anywhere in the current age.

But then, individualism may bring harm to the organisation. What is the way out? The answer again is adjustment. There is a way—there is nothing to fear. Germany is trying to solve this problem to a certain extent. In peace time all are enjoying their freedom (the State has no control over the universities there)—but when the call comes all voluntarily renounce their freedom and present themselves most obediently and ready with their arms. Such is the law for all co-operative endeavour; ordinarily for transaction of business, everybody has a voice. . . .

Autocracy results in the dearth of competent men, and the cause suffers as a result. Naturally and constitutionally, one who is the superior in knowledge, wisdom, experience, etc. shall have a bigger voice in the Council and the rest will pay more attention to him. But they will follow him and accept his advice for its intrinsic worth and not because it is coming from him.

If this is the yardstick of judging an organisation, it is not difficult to criticise the Jesuit community. Now let us have a look at the similarities:

1. Protestantism—Western civilisation and Western influence.
2. Counter reformation—Indian renaissance in national and spiritual life.

3. Loyola—began as a man of action, ended life as a religious man.
4. Paris—!
5. Church—religious and country.
6. Chastity—poverty and obedience (absolute).
7. General—the absolute Commander.
8. Relief from ordinary duties of life.

* * *

The history of every community or fraternity is about the same.

Their motto is on the whole not bad. Chastity and poverty are obligatory. Then, I have already mentioned obedience. One must fashion himself and function in accordance with the demands of the age. If this is taken into account, there is much in common between the present and the past ages. It is only natural that this has attracted your attention.

Tuesday

Your letter reached me yesterday. I am tolerably well. It is not certain yet where I shall go; most probably it will be Kurseong. Because father is also thinking of going there. Father's health has improved but it will take him some time to recover. It would be good if he could give up work, but then the difficulty is how to keep the family running.

So long.

(26)

26-9-15.

Despondency does sometimes cast its shadow on my mind but hope returns as naturally as lightening in the sky. Who can suppress it? That light once again renders life desirable and I find anew that life is worth living.

(27)

3-10-15
Saturday

On the one hand one is reminded of the message of Brahmananda and on the other, of the Western ideal—Life is activity. On one side there is the silent and peaceful life of an introspective... the Yogi who has realised the futility of the world; on the other I see the great laboratories of the West, their scientific way of life, their wonderful inventions, discoveries and knowledge. Then I feel like going over to their continent and spend ten or twelve years there in a single-minded pursuit of knowledge; after all, only one who has earned something is in a position to give. I have the desire also to take a plunge for once into their life of activity and then see if, instead of being merely carried along by the current, I can direct it myself....

(28)

19-10-15

Mr. Sentimentalist,

Your letter reached my hands yesterday. I now weigh one maund and twenty-one and a half seers. I am rather surprised at this, because at Cuttack my weight was one maund and sixteen and a half seers. Any way, I am here for a month. I expect to gain another five seers.

Since coming here I have been well from all points of view. That is why I like the hills so much. Occasionally rains bother you a little—otherwise there is no trouble at all. Bright sunshine and dry fog make ideal weather here. So far I have not been able to study at all. Let me see if I can do better hereafter.

* * *

The mountains are most wonderful; I think these slopes are the most fitting abode of the heroic Aryans. One should not live in the degenerate plains. Of course, it is no use just saying this because it cannot be helped. But, it is much better to have a house in the hills than to build one on two *cottahs* of land in Calcutta at a cost of fifty thousand rupees. There is no better way of reviving our Aryan blood than to consume meat and scale mountains.

That pure Aryan blood no longer flows in our veins. Slavery of ages—so much of adulteration. . . .

As I wander about the hills, I think of this very often. The sense of power must permeate our entire being. We again have to leap across mountains—it was only when the Aryans did such things that they were able to produce the *Vedas.*

The Hindu race no longer has that pristine freshness—that youthful vigour and those unmatched human qualities. If we want to get them back we must begin from the land of our birth—the sacred Himalayas. If India has something priceless, something noble—something to be proud of—it is the memory of all that is linked up with the Himalayas. That is why when you are face to face with the Himalayas, such memories come back to your mind. . . .

Yours
Rationalist

(29)

Hawk's Nest, Kurseong
21-10-15
Thursday

Your letter reached me yesterday.

* * *

You went to the hills with a sick mind; that is why you were not able to enjoy the trip. You must go once again when your mind is at peace.

In the hills physical vigour increases very considerably and one can have perfect peace of mind. In the peaceful solitude of the hills, life can be dreamt away—the misty veil hanging about the hills is but the dreamy veil of fair poetry. Was it Pope or somebody else who said:

'Thus let me live unseen, unknown, etc. etc. . . .

Thus unlamented let me die, steal from the world and not a stone tell where I lie.'

You can appreciate the spirit behind these words when you come to the hills; but one must admit that only one facet of human life is brought out into the open—while another side, that is, ceaseless and frantic activity and movement, which you see in Calcutta, lies dormant. In Calcutta, my mind is always occupied with some work or other. The mind is, as it were, forced to work; the seriousness of life—complexity and variety of life become apparent to you, problems of life weigh heavily on your mind. But, here, you can afford to be a lotus-eater for a while—why should life all labour be?

* * *

Yours
Rationalist

(30)

26-10-15

* * *

Most of my thinking is related to my own self.

I am amazed to see how so many conflicting desires and motives influence man in his life. So many desires come from where one does not know and then, after some time, they go away. Why and where do such desires come from—I cannot tell. The first chapter of human life is completely irrational. We take pride in saying that man is very rational—but man is more irrational than rational. Man acts by instinct and sentiment like animals rather than by reason. I cannot find the cause and meaning of so many of our actions. How strange!

Today I found the solution of a long-standing question in my mind. As I sat inside the temple reflecting the answer came.

* * *

Yours
Western Philosopher

(31)

29-10-15

I have come to know through conversation, the history of the Jesuits in its broad outline. It is not easy to write all that in a letter; so, I shall tell you when we meet. They bitterly complain that they have been given a very inferior position in modern history, because most of the historians are Protestants and even the Royalty is the same. Further, they have not got a place in the history of Philosophy. In Schwegler's *History of Philosophy*, which we read, medieval philosophy has for the most part been omitted.

I had a mind to learn something of medieval or scholastic philosophy, in other words, theology. But, when I learnt that they have to study theology for four years before taking the D. D. degree, I did not make the attempt. Besides, it will not work now because of lack of time.

Jesuits say that whatever philosophy there was in the Middle Ages was nothing but theology and the Jesuits were in the forefront of all literary and educational activity. Education all over Europe was in their charge.

Their doctrine and forms are extremely dogmatic—I shall tell you about them later. But, from a certain point of view, their organisation is most attractive. They do not worship the Founder—and bigotry has not made inroads into their organisation. Their dogmatism does not vary quantitatively—it is all defined. One who will not accept the defined doctrines has no place among them.

Yours
Rationalist

(32)

Vishram Kutir
Kurseong
7-11-15

My dear Poet,

I was sorry to receive your letter as you have showed me up as a mischievous person. You know very well that

I have always been a 'good boy'—am I capable of any naughtiness? So, what is the meaning of this accusation of yours? Can one who has always been a 'good boy' be up to any mischief at any time? So, I cannot be a 'naughty boy' and any mischief on my part is impossible.

I am not at all a thinker, nor a poet; how, then, can I appreciate the essence of poetry or the sentiments of lyrics? Having failed to appreciate the thoughts behind your perfect, deeply introspective and great poems, I have merely criticised their outward form. Those who are devoid of the finer sensibilities and are not connoisseurs only see the ant-hill around *Valmiki,* the boisterous blank verse of Madhusudan, the Calcutta language of Rabindranath and skeletal images of Abanindranath. So, is there any wonder that a reader of this category should seek lapses in rhyme in your thoughtful poetry....

If I have committed an offence, the fault lies in my lack of discriminative power and in my want of appreciative faculty. And I offer my apologies for such poverty of my mind.

Professor Prafulla Chandra has left. I have had some talks with him—of this later.

* * *

In the matter of writing articles of your own way of life, you cannot afford to go by other people's opinions. What you have got to say, you will say—regardless of others.

As to my article, it will appear meaningless if one does not know why and in what spirit I wrote it. It is not surprising that some people will find it so. But what does it matter?

In such a society or organisation, a particular person may attain a very high position; but I can now well understand that in a different set-up, his place may be at the *very bottom;* one's judgment of things depends on his own ideas and his estimate of man.

* * *

So, how can appreciation or non-appreciation of other people affect you? Yes, you are right in saying that you must be guided by the light within you.

Yours
Foolish and Poor
Correspondent

(33)

Vishram Kutir
Kurseong
17th November (1915)

It is only natural for you to be impressed with the teachings of Lord Buddha—but I shall be happy only if you will follow them to the letter. Will you do so?

* * *

I have very largely solved my life's problem. All of a sudden I found the answer today. I have solved it intellectually—I have decided upon the main principles although some minor details remain to be worked out. I now want the iron will to carry out the plan into systematic details. I lack system—I cannot function systematically. I must rectify this by effort and practice.

* * *

We are most probably going to Darjeeling tomorrow morning. From there we want to go up to Senchal hill. On a clear day you can see Mt. Everest from Senchal hill. We shall return in two or three days.

(34)

Craig Mount
Darjeeling
Saturday
20-11-15

* * *

We came here day before yesterday. In a sense this place is better than Kurseong. You get better things to eat and a lovelier view of Nature. In addition, there are a number of places worth visiting. We have been to Observatory Hill, Botanical Gardens, Museum, Race Course,

Military Barracks and Mount Senchal. Kanchenjungha is of course visible from Mount Senchal—we also saw Everest. Senchal is at a height of about 8400 feet—we went there this morning. One has to go about six miles uphill. Fortunately the sky was clear and we had a good view of Everest.

However, this town is—'Calcutta transferred to the hills' and that is its drawback. Now it is not crowded—people have left for the plains—I am therefore enjoying it here.

We get a clear view of the snows from our verandah. There are mountains and mountains all around and—the sky-scraping, shining white peaks of Kanchenjungha covered with perpetual snow. How fascinating is this place! When you see it you can hardly control your emotions. From one end of horizon to the other there are ranges of snow-capped mountains—like waves lashing against the sky. Far, far away, nestled in mountain slopes there are monasteries of Buddhist *Lamas*. If one wants to lead an extremely individualistic life, there is nothing more satisfying than the life of a wandering pilgrim. I feel like crossing the mountains to Sikkim and Nepal. There is a road to Tibet also. This is used for trade and commerce.

But, in the current age the life of a wandering pilgrim in not for the youth of Bengal. He has very onerous duties to shoulder.

One gentleman asked me in Kurseong how I was enjoying my stay there. As a matter of courtesy, I replied, 'Very well'. But I felt in my own mind that the days of enjoyment had passed. I remember our great delight when we came to Darjeeling for the first time during the Puja holidays eight years ago. We had of course come here for enjoyment then. But what a change has come upon me now! I had said then as an expression of boyish emotion, 'The happiest day in my life will be when I shall become independent and a still happier one when I shall go to Darjeeling'.

But, today, my life is not for my own enjoyment. My life is of course not devoid of happiness but is not for enjoyment—my life is a mission—a duty. The gentleman in question probably came to Kurseong to enjoy himself but I have come for physical and moral improvement. I loathe to leave these mountains. Bengal of course has other attractions, but, apart from that, this rustic hilly country is incomparable. Verily, the Himalayas are the abode of the Gods—a paradise. Our illiterate Brahmin cook, pointing towards the Kanchenjungha said, 'That way is paradise'. All others laughed at him. But I realised that his words were metaphorically true.

Well, if I try to tell you everything, I will never finish.

I am putting up here with a rich relation. They are taking very good care of me—more than one could expect. I have come here with a maternal uncle. People here knew about my waywardness and now having seen me have come to know more of it.

Now,—I have written a lot about myself. We shall go down to Kurseong tomorrow and leave for Calcutta the day after. The day after we shall reach Sealdah at 11 a.m. I shall try to go to College the same day.

When I meet you, I shall have to undertake a sort of judicial enquiry about yourself. I shall have to investigate why you neglect your health.

I do hear from you but you write hardly anything about yourself. This you also have to explain.

(35)

Wednesday Evening
8-12-15

There was a meeting today at the University Institute to accord a reception to Jagadish Chandra. I went there in high hopes of listening to a few words from Jagadish Chandra's own lips,—just to see him and to hear him speak. I do not know why since childhood I have always had the deepest respect for two persons—Jagadish Chandra and Vivekananda. I had been attracted to them by the pictures I saw of them and ever since I came to know something of them from other people. The ostensible purpose of the meeting was of course 'to honour him by a reception'. But none other than a patriot at heart will understand how Bengalis and above all, Bengali students, have insulted and humiliated him. The entertainment consisting of songs, local instrumental music, poetry reading, etc. were quite good, but, then, there was also English drama; the actors were students—and you can well imagine what the themes were like, and, at the end,—God save the King! When I found that acting was on the programme, I once thought of leaving. But in fond expectation of hearing him speak, I tried to have a nap for the duration of the drama. Amongst a gathering of boisterous young men, I sat with my eyes closed like a stern puritan. The meeting drew to a close but my wish was not fulfilled. I returned broken-hearted and thought to myself that until we learnt to honour our great men properly, there could be no deliverance for us Bengalis, or for that matter, of India! Honouring the great with a theatrical performance! What a shame! Poor India! O Bengalis, to what depths have you descended?

This incident has pained me deeply. I am reminded again and again of what the most revered *Dharmapala* said at a meeting: So long as men run after sensual pleasures, India will not rise. I do not remember his exact words. But that was the burden of his speech. I saw that with the Bengalis, the desire for sensual pleasure had gone deep down into the marrow of their bones. And, this was the principal reason of their weakness in spite of their intelligence.

What is the way out? I feel that to counteract this, we need a band of outstanding young men of stern puritanic principles. Our countrymen must have their eyes opened. Indeed, Ramakrishna got at the root of our national character.

I do not know in what light Jagadish Chandra took this reception. Jagadish Chandra the patriot will no doubt accept whatever his country has to offer him—be it fragrant flowers or be it dumb ash. But there can be little doubt that this reception pained him.

I am writing an article for our Debating Club in the column 'Next Monday's Reading'—the subject being 'The civilization of India in the Vedic and Pouranic Age'. It will help matters if you will send me in the meantime one or two books or let me have your hints regarding some titles, etc. or your own notes.

(36)

Sunday
19-12-15

* * *

Nowadays I have become too rational and intellectual. All sentiments have almost died out and a stoic sternness is getting hold of me. As days pass, the nature of life's ideal becomes clearer to me,—but I have not the necessary strength to fulfil it.

* * *

In order to be able to mix with everybody in this world, one must come out of his shell. Have I succeeded in doing so?

(37)

Friday
27-12-15

* * *

We are back once again in December and January is not far behind. About this time two years ago we were in Santipur. The most pleasant memories of that band of *sannyasis* of Santipur are coming back to me.

India has lost almost everything—she has even lost her soul, but still, we must not worry, we must not lose hope; as the poet has said, 'You must regain your manhood'. Yes, we must be men again. The beautiful land of India is now haunted by creatures who are but the embodiments of ghosts of the dead past. All over the place, there is lack of hope—and death, luxury, disease, limitless sorrow—'Dark clouds of misfortune have overcast the entire horizon of India.' But, regardless of all this hopelessness, stillness, poverty and squalor and starvation, and drowning the wailings of half-starved beings on the one hand and pompous noise made by those wallowing in riches and luxury, we must once again sing the national song of India. And, that is—Arise, Awake!

(38)

Wednesday Evening
2-2-16

* * *

Please take care of your health. You should take proper exercise, morning walks, have milk and eggs and not over-tire yourself. Your whole life is in front of you; there is no necessity of foolishly over-working yourself now on the plea of making proper use of time.

Sureshda left yesterday. He was sorry not to have been able to meet you. He had to leave yesterday on some pressing work. The hostel has been changed—a shift from 2/11 to 45/1 Amherst Street. The other house was very damp and had to be given up. All living in that Calcutta mess excepting one or two are about to develop pharyngites. Sureshda suspects that you are showing signs of pharyngites (I am not sure of the spelling). Does your throat still bleed? It is my request that you get yourself treated both for this and for dysentery. You may get yourself examined by Jnanda or somebody else and then take medicines as required. Please do not neglect this.

Arabinda has been spreading news of your ill health all over the place. Many have asked me about you. If you wish to teach Arabinda a lesson and avoid discomfiture for yourself, you better get yourself cured. In that case when people come to see you, they will find you in better health.

I heard from Bidhu that Sureshda has pharyngites. Any way, it has been proved that even a strong physique may break down as a result of over-work under unhealthy conditions.

You have the bad habit of trying to suppress physical

illness by will power. This is how you fell so seriously ill on the last occasion. You may be taken ill this time also if you are not careful. So, it is my earnest request to you to take care of your health while there is still time. So long.

The next two letters deal with the Oaten affair in the Presidency College, Calcutta, to which Netaji has referred in his autobiography.—*Ed.*

(39)

38/2, Elgin Road
Calcutta
29-2-16

Hemanta Kumar,

I did not write to you for a day or two as there was nothing special to write about. You cannot afford to be restless or impatient on my account. We have to wait patiently for a while.

In view of my representation to the Syndicate, they will not issue any orders on my case now—they will probably wait till the Committee's report has been published. Today I applied to the Committee requesting them to record my evidence and reconsider my case. The Committee is now recording the evidences of professors. I think it will take another three or four days hearing the professors and thereafter the boys will be called. We shall then appear and give evidence. The terms of reference of the Committee are quite wide. They will enquire into the following:

(1) Relation between European and Indian Professors in Presidency College.

(2) Relation between European Professors and Indian students.

(3) Relation between Indian Professors and Indian students.

(4) Cause of indiscipline leading on to the strike.

(5)   Do   leading on to assault.

The Government will probably try to carry out certain

reforms and run the Presidency College according to necessary new regulations on the basis of the recommendations of the Committee. This is with a view to avoiding any kind of trouble in future. So, you can well understand that the matter is quite serious. Ashu Babu is there, so we hope the rights of students will not suffer. If the Committee find us innocent or give us the benefit of doubt, we shall apply to the Syndicate to reinstate us as students of Presidency College. If they do not reinstate us, we shall ask to transfer. If we are given transfer certificates, there will be no difficulty in getting admission to other colleges. In case we fail to obtain this, I shall be practically rusticated. However, they usually do not rusticate in such cases for more than a year. For offences of a very grave nature, they may order rustication for life—which of course means that studies end for good.

But then, I have much in my favour. I am well-known as a 'good student'. I am known at least by name in high circles, the vast majority of the public feel that I am innocent. Ashu Babu knows of me personally and the evidence of the orderly against me is much too weak. So, there is every possibility of my being found innocent and let off. At least, I should get a transfer.

If ultimately everything fails, we might file a law suit.

(40)

38/2, Elgin Road
Calcutta
6-3-16
Monday

Hemanta,

I am feeling worried not having heard from you. Have you not received my letter? Our letters are being intercepted. I think I wrote my last letter on the day after I appeared before the Committee. You may have heard that the hostel has been closed and the college will probably not reopen before the holidays are over. It appears that the attitude of the Committee towards us is favourable and we hope that even if we are not declared to be innocent, we shall be given the benefit of doubt. Anyway, for the present we have to wait and see. It may be desirable for you to destroy my letters.

Please let me have all news. I had a discussion with Beni Babu one of these days. He criticised the boys severely and sympathised with Mr. James.

How is your health? Please write how you are. I hope you are taking proper care of yourself and I shall not have to remind you again of this. Please reply early.

Yours
SUBAS CHANDRA

(41)

Tuesday
4-7-16

When I left you I could see that your mental state was far from good. Even so, I had to come away. I did not write to you for the last few days. But, was that any reason why you should not have written? I had a mind to see you the next morning but could not do so for some special reason. Anyway, please let me know in detail how you are. I should like to know what sort of comments people are making regarding your health.

It appears I shall have to discontinue my studies. I am facing a serious problem. So long I have been seeking help and advice from this person and that. I now see that the solution rests very largely with myself. Besides, my mental state at present is not good—I do not know if I shall survive this. Nevertheless, one of the experiences of my life has been that a sense of hope always keeps me going and never allows me to turn away from life. Who knows if this is mere illusion! Will you turn away from me at this crisis in my life?

I could never imagine that the problem I am facing today would turn out to be so enormously difficult.

What more can I write? Please write to me at length. How is everything over there?

(42)

Friday
(1917)

My dear Hemanta,

I just received your letter. I met Atul Babu—he failed to find suitable quarters for me. There is some hope that the University may open a new mess. I do not see any other way than to wait for that. The places that Atul Babu found out about are not convenient at all. On the first floor of the mess on Sambhu Chatterjee Street, there is a room available—but it is poorly lighted and ill-ventilated. It cannot therefore be taken.

I have secured admission to the third year class in the Scottish Church College.

I did not quite appreciate the purport of your letter. I was not born in a poor family. This is indeed true—but am I responsible for that? What penance do I have to do on that account? I do not see any other way than to take full advantage of the domestic and social situations in which we have been born. Of course, the case is different with those who are full-fledged *Sannyasis*. And I am not one.

And then, I do not find any change in me. To external appearance there may have been some change as a result of necessity, but inside me there has been none. Well, the impetuosity of youth is calming down. With advancing age and cumulative experience, one's mind gets steadier. That is most probably what has been happening to me. Ideas which seek to fight their way out against all opposition when one is young, tend to sober down with advancing age.

Of course there is another consideration. If one comes to believe that there has been a change in the mental make-up of the other person, he can never again be convinced by explanation and persuasion that that is not so. In such situations, if one tries too hard to explain himself, others tend to get more convinced of exactly the opposite. Let us leave it at that!

If anybody believes that there has been a change in my mental make-up or that I am not what I was, this is a matter of great sorrow and misfortune for me. I never expected that you would do so.

In the kind of age and world we are living, we cannot afford to give full and uninhibited play to all our sentiments. We have to keep them inside us. The whole of nature is forcing us into this.

This root of the matter is that the disease is yours, nobody else's. And it is a kind of mental aberration—of which I have been warning you for quite some time and which I have tried to cure as much as I could. So long as you are not cured of this, the whole world—why me alone—will appear to you to be abnormal.

Have you received any answer from the Presidency College?

Yours

SUBHAS

In the following two letters Netaji relates his experiences with the Calcutta University Unit of the India Defence Force in 1917–18. The relevant writing in his autobiography will be found in Chapter VIII.—*Ed.*

(43)

Y.M.C.A.
Calcutta University Infantry
Shooting Camp
Belghurria, E. B. Rly.
5-4-18

I have received your letter. I did not go to the University Institute on that day as I was supposed to go to Camp. The doctor having advised against it, I could not go to camp either. We came here day before yesterday and shall be here for two to three weeks. Rifle practice started today. I find it quite interesting. I do not expect we shall get leave before the 24th April. So, it will not be possible for me to be present at the annual meeting of the Night School at Krishnagar on the day mentioned by you.

I am keeping reasonably well. The rest is O.K. How is your health?

SUBHAS

(44)

Calcutta
Tuesday
30-4-18

Hemanta,

Your letter was to hand duly. All of us returned home on Friday last. I am keeping well. I do not expect there will be much work for me during the vacation—as there will be very few people left in Calcutta during the holidays. I cannot say, however, what will happen after the Pujas. I suppose we shall know the trend from the proceedings of the big assembly in Delhi. Capt. Gray will take charge of General I.D.F. from the 1st May next. After their training has been completed, he will go out on recruiting work. Of course, it will take another month and a half to complete their training.

Our experience has been quite pleasant on the whole, and there is no doubt that all of us have benefited to some extent from what we have learnt. But then, the effect of three months' training cannot be very lasting and how much one gains from any experience is determined by the type of trainee in question.

There is not much of romance in our experience. That is why while we were in Calcutta things sometimes appeared rather monotonous. But in Belghurria, when one day our camp was washed away by rain and storm and the next day there was continuous firing from dawn till 4.30 in the afternoon, we felt as if we were in field service. Moreover, building latrines, collecting drinking water from far-off villages, doing patrol duty at night and above all, taking part in night operation brought a lot of satisfaction. And, then, in the shooting competition at Belghurria, the British instructors were beaten by the boys. The last few days at the camp were quite decent and we came to love the life there. All of us felt a pang in our hearts, more or less, when we had to leave.

Yesterday, I met Nilmoni and Mondal. I may see them again today. I heard that you were too busy with your studies to meet any people. What happened to your trip to Bolpur? Will you spend the holidays at Goari or go somewhere? I wish to have news of your health.

I shall probably stay on in Calcutta. From time to time however I am feeling like going to Puri. I have a mind to visit your place also.

I am keeping reasonably well. I have not resumed my studies yet. I shall write an article on camp life for the College Magazine. I shall show it to you when it is complete. Please let me have an early reply.

SUBHAS

P.S.— You have enquired about my promotion. I did not get any promotion—I remained a private till the last. One reason for this was that under Capt. Gray's orders, the N.C.O.s were deprived of their stripes and instead of nominations, a fresh election was held by vote. I was absent (sick) at the particular time. And all the posts were filled up.

The following letter was written to Bholanath Roy, fellow-student and friend.

(45)

38/2 *Elgin Road,*
12-4-19

My dear Bholanath Babu,

I ought to have informed you earlier as to how I have fared in the examination. However better late than never.

I have done well in the first four papers but have not been able to do satisfactorily in the last two (viz: History of Philosophy and essay). The questions were not quite suitable.

It is needless for me to tell you that your hints were of great value to me within the examination hall. I got your essay (Religion and Morality) in time. Rajen Babu was kind enough to send it to me by post. I am going to return it to him again as I have done with it.

Hope you are doing well. We are mostly well here.

Yours affly,
SUBHAS

P. S.—Relation between ethics and theology was one of the questions in the ethics paper.

SUBHAS CHANDRA BOSE

Bholanath Roy Esq. M.A.
18, Ram Mukherjee Lane,
Sibpur.

The following letter was written to Hemanta Kumar Sarkar.

(46)

38/2, *Elgin Road,*
Calcutta
26-8-19

I am facing a most serious problem. Yesterday the family made an offer to send me to England. I have to sail for England immediately. There is no chance of getting into any good University in England just at present. It is their wish that I should study for a few months and appear at the Civil Service examination. It is my considered view that there is no hope of my passing the Civil Service examination. The rest are of the view that in case I fail the examination I might get into London or Cambridge University in October next. My primary desire is to obtain a university degree in England; otherwise I cannot make headway in the educational line. If I now refuse to study for the Civil Service, the offer to send me to England will be put into cold storage for the time being (and for all time). Whether it will ever materialise in future I do not know. Under the circumstances, should I miss this opportunity? On the other hand, a great danger will arise if I manage to pass the Civil Service examination. That will mean giving up my goal in life.

Father had been to Calcutta. He made the offer yesterday and I had to give my consent in course of the day. Father left for Cuttack yesterday. And I have agreed to sail for England. But, I am at a loss to understand what my duty is and a discussion with you is most necessary. It would be very good indeed if you could make a trip to Calcutta soon. I heard you were due here on the 4th. But that will delay matters unduly.

The following letter was written to Bholanath Roy.

(47)

38/2 *Elgin Road*
1-9-19

My dear Bholanath Babu,

Your letter was to hand on the 20th August and I had given Schwegler's book to a friend of mine for making it over to you. In the meantime events so turned out that I had to take the book back. You will doubtless be surprised to learn that I am sailing for England on the 11th September from the Kidderpore Dock. I intend to make an attempt for the I.C.S. and failing that, to go up to Cambridge. Of course I shall not be going to Cambridge before October 1920—but shall reside at present in London. As I mean to take up Philosophy both in the I.C.S. and at Cambridge, I think it advisable to take my Philosophy books with me and if possible to make some study on board. Shall I not be so fortunate as to see you before I leave? I had been to college today but could not find you.

With love,

Yours affly,
SUBHAS

Bholanath Roy
18, Ram Mukherjee Lane
Sibpur

The following letter was written to Hemanta Kumar Sarkar.

(48)

38/2, Elgin Road, Calcutta
3-9-19

The last few days I have been through a mental turmoil. I had consented to go abroad after a long struggle—yet I was not able to convince myself that my decision had been right. Anyway, I felt much relieved on receiving your letter.

I was frightfully busy yesterday and so could not write to you. I shall be sailing on the morning of the 11th September from Calcutta—provided of course I can by then complete all necessary arrangements.

Whether or not letters of introduction will be necessary I shall decide after a personal discussion with you. I must also consult with you about my studies. Well, once you are here, all that will be taken care of. You need not rush down because I shall be constantly on the move for the next two or three days. I hope, after that, I shall have some leisure. Your impending examination makes things rather difficult.

The following letter was written to Jogendra Narayan Mitra.

(49)

City of Calcutta
at Indian Ocean
20th Sept. 1919

My dear Sir,

It certainly appeared ungrateful and unbecoming on my part to neglect to see you once before leaving Calcutta, after all that you had done for me. But I hope you will pardon me considering the fact that I was naturally very busy just before my departure. I might have written to you before coming, but up till the last I hoped to go and see you at your residence and when I failed, there was no time for writing to you. You must have been very anxious to know what became of the certificate and passport that I was so urgently in need of and to say the least it was extremely unkind on my part to leave you in that state of anxiety when even a few lines might have been welcome to you. Though it is so late in the day still you will be glad to learn that I got the age certificate from the Commissioner in time and the P.A., Mr. F. M. Mukherjee, was very kind to me and did his utmost to hasten the granting of the Certificate. If you have occasion to meet him in the future kindly convey to him my warmest gratitude. I also got the Passport in good time and for this I am grateful to Mr. J. N. Bose the Assistant Commissioner and some other gentlemen. I cannot say how greatly they helped me in that critical moment. I have stood the sea well and have not been sick since I left. We are about twelve Bengali students on board and we have all managed to make friends. But for their company I might have felt lonely and uncomfortable.

We reach Colombo during the course of the day and on the whole it will take us about 30 days to reach London. When I reach London I hope to write to you again.

I am doing quite well on board. Hope this will find you all in the best of health. Before closing allow me once more to tender my warmest gratitude and my best respects to you.

Yours affly,
SUBHAS CHANDRA BOSE

I am anxious to know whether this letter reaches you. If you find time kindly drop me a line at your convenience. My address for the present will be

C/o. Thomas Cook & Son
Ludgate Circus
London.

SUBHAS

Jogendra Narayan Mitra Esq.
Deputy Magistrate & Dy.
Collector, Alipore
4, Kartic Bose's Lane
Off Grey Street
Calcutta.

The following two letters are to Hemanta Kumar Sarkar.

(50)

8, Glenmore Road
Belsize Park
London N.W. 3
Undated (1919)

Hemanta,
   I am writing a long detailed letter to you—but it is yet unfinished. I am writing this just to inform you of my safe arrival and my address. I am very busy at the moment because I have not been able to fix things up about my studies. I shall write to you at length by the mail. My eldest brother is also staying in this house. I arrived in London on the 20th October. Please tell Pramatha that Jugalda is still in Marseilles. He will be going to India with his regiment in November or December. They will be demobilised there probably in April 1920. I got this information from Dhiren's father Mr. M. M. Dhar. I shall be writing myself to Jugalda for news and then let you know.
   Mr. Bharat Ch. Dhar's son is also living in this house. He has come to London to study for the B.Com. I find it very cold here now. I shall stop here today. In haste,

Yours
SUBHAS

(51)

Fitz William Hall
Cambridge
12-11-19

* * * *

   Those from whom I did not expect any letters have written to me while none came from you. Never mind, I hope you will be writing in future.
   I told you in my last letter that I had secured admission to Cambridge University and that I had arrived here. I succeeded in getting a seat thanks to a friend's help and

partly also to my service with the I.D.F. Despite scarcity of accommodation, I have been lucky enough to find living quarters also.

I am planning to take the Civil Service examination next year and, whether I pass or fail, to appear at the Moral Science Tripos examination in May 1921.

I must take a degree here because that will stand me in very good stead in future.

Indians have an association here called the 'Indian Majlis'. Meetings are held weekly and from time to time guest speakers come from outside. Mrs. Sarojini Naidu once spoke on 'Kingdom of Youth'. Mr. Andrews has spoken on 'Indentured Labour System' and on the present grievances of Indians living in the Fiji Islands. Before I arrived the great Tilak paid a visit here. India House tried to prevent his coming but without success. Indians here are of extremist temperament and there were protests at his mild speech.

It has been snowing here for the last two days. Whether one wills it or not, the climate of this country makes people energetic. The activity you see here is most heartening. Every man is conscious of the value of time and there is a method in all that goes on. Nothing makes me happier than to be served by the whites and to watch them clean my shoes. Students here have a status—and the way the professors treat them is different. One can see here how man should treat his fellow man. They have many faults—but in many matters you have to respect them for their virtues. How are you? How did you fare in the examination? I am anxious to know what you plan to do next. Please write to me in detail. Suniti Babu is doing research work in London. I am well. Jugalda is in France.

The following letter is written to Jogendra Narayan Mitra.

(52)

Fitz William Hall
Cambridge
19-11-19

My dear Sir,

On my way to London I dropped a letter to you at one of the ports. I hope the letter reached you duly.

It looks monstrous on my part not to see you and bid you good-bye before leaving Calcutta after all that you had done for me. I must apologise to you once more and I hope you will excuse me in consideration of the fact that I was so very busy at that time. I was hoping till the last day to be able to find time to go and see you but I failed.

The voyage was a pleasant one though rather long and tedious. I reached London on the 20th October and was there for a few days with my brother. I was advised by many people in London to prefer Cambridge to London and so I came over here. I intend to sit for the I.C.S. examination in August 1920 and to take the Moral Science Tripos in 1921.

I am quite well and comfortable here. Hope this will find you all in the best of health.

With my best regards
I am
Yours affly
SUBHAS CH. BOSE

The following six letters were written to Hemanta Kumar Sarkar.

(53)

Fitz William Hall
Cambridge 7.1.20.

Hemanta,

Your letter (of the 27th November) reached me a few days ago. Why have you not written to me for so long?

* * *

You have received by now the news of my coming over to Cambridge from my letter. I found this place suitable for studies and so I decided to come here. To have found a seat was a matter of good luck,—it was partly due to my University result—and above all, thanks to a friend's help.

* * *

What will Prafulla do now? Please send me a copy of the article in *Bharatvarsha* after it has been published.

Is Prafullada still working in Presidency College or has he been transferred elsewhere? Please write to me fully about your talks with Sureshda. He says he wants to start a school, but can he get himself relieved of his employment? Jugal wrote to me about a month ago that he would be relieved soon. But I do not see any sign of that happening soon.

Sureshda has in a sense given me up. If I do not enter the Service, there is a possibility of reunion with him. Whether I join the Service or not, I do not understand how that can terminate the relationship between man and man. Is this sort of shopkeeper's mentality the proper mental attitude? Anyway, I do not wish to quarrel with anybody—I shall continue to do my duty—and in doing so, it will be very good if I come close to other people; if I do not, there is nothing to lose.

I saw Suniti Babu in London.

How is Beni Babu? Please write to me in detail about things back home and let me know also some of your thoughts.

In your letter I discovered a sorrowful note of some deep-seated pain. Why this pain?

I am quite well. If you meet Pramatha, Hemendu or Charu, please ask them to write to me. When you see Priyaranjan, please tell him that I have received his letter. I shall reply to him by the next mail.

Yours
SUBHAS

(54)

Cambridge
Monday
19th January (1920)

Hemanta,

I was happy to receive your letter. I have the feeling that you have taken too much work at the same time. One has to spend a lot of energy in teaching at the University—then there is the shop and on the top of that so much more! When you understand that your health is deteriorating day by day, there can be no justification for such behaviour. It is a fault with the way of life in our country that those who do not work just do nothing at all and those who do, try to do too much and by trying to achieve everything in a day lose their health and all the rest of it. If your original plan was to try for the P.R.S. and do some teaching at the same time, it would have been better for you not to have gone for the shop. If one is desirous of achieving something of permanent nature, he has to remain occupied with it for many years,—that is not possible in a year or two. So, if you wish to do something permanent for your country, you should function in such a manner that you may retain your capacity to work for many years. True enough, nobody can tell when the call to depart comes—but even so, there is nothing to be gained by stabbing yourself or by spooling your health by over-work. I am writing in very strong terms. But I feel sure you will not misunderstand me. It is a pity, you take too much on yourself and sometimes even though your health fails, you complete your assignment by will power. This is not at all a desirable situation.

Wednesday, 21st January

I am happy to have details of your examination results. I am all the more happy to learn that you have been given various duties at the University. I feel confident that you will give a good account of yourself in all this work—but my only anxiety is about your health.

The 'natives' of this country have certain qualities which have made them so great. First, they can work strictly to time with clock-work precision; secondly, they have a robust optimism—we think more of the sorrows of life, they think more of the happy and bright things of life. Then, they have a strong commonsense—they appreciate their national interest very well. Now to sum up, there is something wrong with the air we breathe—we must bring about a change in that.

The principal cause of your neglect of yourself and your health is that—Oriental indifference.

'What is the good of taking care of the body, when it lasts only a few days and will return to the dust in a few days!'—such indifference is most undesirable for a Hero of Labour. You need a little air from the West if that will bring you that robust optimism.

I have written a letter to Beni Babu. I have not written to Mr. Dutta Gupta yet.

* * *

I have nothing more to say. If you lose your health at this young age as a result of your own neglect—the fault is entirely yours. Man has no hand in many matters—but, apart from that, to neglect one's health is an offence—an offence not only to one's self but also to others and above all to one's country. If the youth of our country lose their physical capacity at an early age, then it must be said that there is something wrong or small in their ideal. Your body is not your own—you are merely the trustee. That is why I am so brutal in what I am saying. I believe you will not neglect that trust.

I have not been able to write a detailed letter,—probably it will not materialise. I made a mistake in thinking that after reaching England I would take my time to write a detailed letter. It is very difficult at the present time to have the leisure.

I do not yet understand if I have swerved from my ideal. I do not want to deceive myself and persuade myself to believe that studying for the Civil Service is a good thing.

I have always hated it—and probably I still do—in the circumstances I do not quite understand if working for the Civil Service is a sign of my weakness or a good augury for the future. My only prayer is that my wellwishers may not form any hasty opinion about me.

The meaning of many events cannot be properly assessed till the very end. Is the same not possible in my case as well?

Yours
SUBHAS

(55)

Cambridge
4th February, 1920

Hemanta,

I am happy to receive your letter. Almost all the newspapers and the important monthly journals of our country come here. But, there is no time to read them—I get to know news from home from my friends.

I am pleased to know about Prafulla. Is it a fact that Surhit has received the nomination?

*   *   *

My detailed letter to you is still in my mind—parts of it have been written down. I wanted to write it more or less in the form of a travel diary. For the present it will not materialise for want of time.

How much work will you take upon yourself simultaneously? The shop, teaching, studies, Night School,—and what more. What will be the result? You will spoil your health and become useless within a short period of time. There is something so wrong with our climate that we cannot strike a balance between moderation and enthusiasm. Where there is enthusiasm there is no moderation and where there is moderation there is no enthusiasm and no vitality. However much you may consider yourself to be practical,—you have not learnt to be practical in such matters.

How are you now? I am quite well. I have not written to Dutta Gupta yet—I shall probably do so by the next mail.

Yours
SUBHAS

(56)

Fitz William Hall
Cambridge
2nd March 1920

Hemanta,

For some time now I have not heard from you, neither have I written to you. When the time at your disposal is limited, you can only write to such people for whom just a few lines suffice.

The other day there was the Annual Dinner at the Indian Majlis. Mr. Horniman attended as our guest. Some local foreign friends also came. On Sunday last Mrs. Ray gave a lecture at a meeting of the Majlis on the 'Rights of the Indian Mother'. Really, when will Indian women once again assume their role as educators of society? So long as India's women will not wake up, India will never wake up. When I heard Mrs. Sarojini Naidu speak here the other day, I could hardly contain the happiness that was surging within my breast. On that day I could see that even today a woman of India had such erudition, inspiration, qualities and character that she could face the Western world and express herself. Later I came to know Dr. Mrigen Mitra's wife in London. I found Dr. Mitra a moderate in politics and Mrs. Mitra an extremist and my happiness knew no bounds. And then I came to know Mrs. Dhar—Girishda's mother—she is also an extremist. After seeing all this I have come to believe that the country which has women of such high ideals, cannot but make progress. I believe a deep sense of patriotism develops in Indian women who come to this country, because a mother's heart is very sensitive and deep.

Let us leave it there—I am just rambling. Do you meet

Girishda? Where is he and how is he doing? Please ask him to
write to me when you see him. What is all the other news of
the shop? I have heard Jagadish Babu has become an F.R.S.
Labour leaders had told him—'The country which can tolerate
Amritsar massacres deserves it'. Horniman is a true friend of
India. He is very keen to return to his land of adoption. He is
not getting his passport.

* * *

I do not know which way I am drifting. Neither do I know
at which port my voyage will end. However, I have faith that
if you all do not deny me your love and blessings, I shall not
go astray.

My handwriting is probably getting worse everyday. So
much for today. Please give me all your news.

(57)

Cambridge
10th March (1920)

Hemanta,

I have received your long letter. I shall not be able to
answer it before reading it over and over again. I am therefore
not replying to it by this mail—I am confining myself to
business matters only.

1. Re: Expenses

If you leave out the initial expenses on account of clothing
and personal effects, I think one can get along with £250/-.
I suppose you will not be admitted as an ordinary student—so
lecture fees can be left out. It is quite difficult for an ordinary
student to carry on—but I believe it should not be at all hard
for a research student. Here there are three terms in a year.

After thinking it over seriously, I feel it is very difficult
to say if £250/- will do. It is impossible to manage boarding
and lodging etc. here for less than fifteen or sixteen pounds
for four weeks (you may take it as a month). In some
colleges the expenses are much higher. Then, you have to

provide for University fees and books. You will have one advantage in that your lecture fees will be less than those for an ordinary student. All University charges here are billed at the end of the term. There are three terms in a year, the terminal bill is quite a fat one and in some colleges bills are very heavy. During term it is not possible for you to manage with £21/-. But one hopeful feature is that terms take only six months. During the remaining six months there are no expenses other than board and lodging. So, for that period, the expenses should not exceed fifteen pounds per month. Therefore at the end of the year one may manage with £250/- but one cannot be dead sure about it. Personally I feel you should provide yourself with some extra funds—it may come handy in case of need. Probably Hem Babu (Dutta Gupta) will be willing to give you a loan. This money will be on fixed deposit in your name. If it is not needed, he will get the money back with interest. And in case it is spent, you will return it later on out of your earnings.

What you will get out of your scholarship for initial outfit will probably not be enough for all the expenses.

2. Re: Studies

In the matter of studies, there are three avenues open to you in England—London D.Litt or Oxford degree or Cambridge. I do not know much about Oxford—I shall make enquiries and let you know. In Cambridge, now there is only the B.A. Degree; you may obtain this degree either by sitting for the examination as an ordinary student or by submitting a thesis as a research student.

You will of course be a research student. A new proposal has been mooted to start Ph.D. in Cambridge from this year. I guess all arrangements in this regard will be completed before the October term. Dr. Taraporewalla should be able to tell you which place—London, Oxford or Cambridge will be suitable for your work. London is most convenient from the point of view of expenses. But, at the London University they often do not exempt you from the M.A. examination and taking the M.A. examination means a lot of trouble. Suniti Babu was exempted but they did not want to exempt Sushil Dey. The atmosphere of London is not good at all for studies.

I am of opinion that—it is best to work for Ph.D. at Oxford or Cambridge and I hope arrangements for Ph.D. will be completed before October.

When you are a Govt. scholar, you should apply to all the three places through Prof. Cozajee. Nowadays it is difficult to gain admission to Oxford or Cambridge but I believe there will be no difficulty at all for a research student. Suniti Babu will be able to tell you what were the advantages as well as disadvantages of being in London.

As Michaelmas term starts in the beginning of October, there is not much gain in coming here very early. After June comes the long vacation here. So, once it is not possible for you to come for the April term, it is better for you to come for the October term. So much for today.

Yours
SUBHAS

(58)

Cambridge
23-3-20

I am happy to learn that you are coming here on a State Scholarship. Whatever it is, you should come to a quick decision as to where you wish to get admitted and put in your application here. Then there is the question of money. In addition to your scholarship you have to arrange for £50/- per year. May be you will not need it—but most probably you will. Then there is the question of outfits. I heard that Government scholarship does not provide anything for outfits. I think the entire range of outfits will cost nearly one thousand rupees—of course that includes everything.

I duly received the M.A. list you sent.

There are many truths in your long letter. But you are not right about two things. I am not offended even now if I am called a *Sannyasi*. I may not now deserve to be called a *Sannyasi*—but I still feel proud of myself as before if I am called one.

Secondly, I have not told anyone that I shall not return to Bengal after passing the I.C.S.

I approve of almost everything in your letter. If I have to give a reply, it will become very long. Now that you are coming, we shall talk things over and settle accounts face to face. Let us postpone it for the present.

I am fairly well. How are you?

The following letter was written by Netaji to Mr. Charu Chandra Ganguly, a fellow student and friend.—*Ed.*

(59)

Cambridge
23rd March (1920)

Charu,

I was happy to receive your letter and to know your examination result. Now you will be facing the trials of life—I hope you will be equally successful in all the tests to come.

So far I have not had the time to mix with a large number of people—I expect I shall have sufficient leisure after the 'August' examination.

Nilmoni, Satyen Dhar and others are well. Prankrishna Parija is doing good research work here—his subject is Botany.

Is there no hope of your coming abroad?

We get all news about India here—and there is also a lot of discussion on India. Even one who has never thought of his own country cannot help doing so after coming here.

I have a complaint to make. You have not replied to all my letters. And, should you not write to me even if you do not hear from me?

You have to do me a service—I want the pamphlets which Dr. P. K. Roy has written on Dr. Ward's psychology. Besides, I want your M.A. Psychology notes. I have no time now to read books—so I have.to depend on notes. After coming here and observing people here and their methods of work, I have been feeling that in our country two things are especially needed—(1) Spread of education among the common people—(2) Labour Movement.

Swami Vivekananda used to say that India's progress will be achieved only by the peasant, the washerman, the cobbler and the sweeper. These words are very true. The Western World has demonstrated what the 'power of the people' can accomplish. The brightest example of this is,—the first socialist republic in the world, that is, Russia. If India will ever rise again—that will come through that power of the people.

In all the countries of the modern world which have made progress, the same 'power of the people' has come into its own.

Swami Vivekananda has said in his *Bartaman Bharat* that the dominance of the three castes, *Brahmana, Kshatriya* and *Vaishya* is a thing of the past. Among the Western peoples, the *Vaishya* caste is made up of—Capitalists and Industrialists,— their days are numbered. The *Sudras* or the untouchable caste of India constitute the Labour Party. So long these people have only suffered. Their strength and their sacrifice will bring about India's progress. That is why we now need mass education and labour organisation.

I better stop here today; there is hardly any time. Please send the books by all means. I am fairly well. I hope this will find you all in good health.

Yours
SUBHAS

The following letter is written to Sarat Chandra Bose.

(60)

Leigh-on-Sea
22.9.20

My dear brother,

I was so glad to receive the telegram conveying congratulations. I don't know whether I have gained anything really substantial by passing the I.C.S. Examination—

but it is a great pleasure to think that the news has pleased so many and especially that it has delighted father and mother in these dark days.

I am here as a paying guest of Mr. Bates's family. Mr. Bates represents English character at its very best. He is cultured and liberal in his views and cosmopolitan in his sentiments. He is altogether unlike the ordinary run of Englishmen—who are proud, haughty and conceited and to whom everything that is non-English is bad. Mr. Bates counts among his friends Russians, Poles, Lithuanians, Irishmen and members of other nationalities. He takes a great interest in Russian, Irish and Indian literature and admires the writings of Romesh Dutt and Tagore.

I am thinking of presenting him with something which can stand as a representative of Indian art and culture. It strikes me that it will be a good thing to present him with a miniature model of the Taj Mahal. The Taj Mahal is undoubtedly one of the finest specimens of our art and I am sure that such a present will be cordially welcomed by him. But the difficulty in sending such a delicate commodity is to pack it properly so that it may be proof against all damage. Miniature models of the Taj can be bought in Calcutta but failing that, can you order for one in the Jaipur art school? I have no idea of its price but *Bardada* told me that it would not cost more than twenty or thirty rupees. If the price is not prohibitive, i.e., if it is on this side of forty rupees, can you order for one to be sent to Mr. Bates? The best thing would of course be to send it straight to Mr. Bates instead of sending it to me. But it won't be worthwhile sending it if the suppliers cannot guarantee that the thing will not be damaged on the way.

I have sent father a copy of the mark sheet which has been sent to us. I have asked him to send it on to you after he has done with it.

I am returning to Lond: on the 24th. I shall be back to Camb: about the 7th of Oct: My present plan is to prepare for the Moral Science Tripos in May (or June) next. I shall have to prepare for the I.C.S. final examination in Hindusthani, Riding, etc. also. This will be held in

September next year.

I have been getting heaps of congratulations on my standing fourth in the competitive examination. But I cannot say that I am delighted at the prospect of entering the ranks of the I.C.S. If I have to join this service I shall do so with as much reluctance as I started my study for the C.S. Examination with. A nice fat income with a good pension in afterlife—I shall surely get. Perhaps I may become a Commissioner if I stoop to make myself servile enough. Given talents with a servile spirit, one may even aspire to be the Chief Secretary to a provincial Govt. But after all is service to be the be-all and end-all of my life? The Civil Service can bring one all kinds of worldly comfort but are not these acquisitions made at the expense of one's soul? I think it is hypocrisy to maintain that the highest ideals of one's life are compatible with subordination to the conditions of service which an I.C.S. man has got to accept.

You will readily understand my mental condition as I stand on the threshold of what the man-in-the-street would call a promising career. There is much to be said in favour of joining such a service. It solves once for all what is the paramount problem for each of us—the problem of bread and butter. One has not got to face life with any risks or any uncertainty as to success or failure. But for a man of my temperament who has been feeding on ideas which might be called eccentric—the line of least resistance is not the best line to follow. Life loses half its interest if there is no struggle—if there are no risks to be taken. The uncertainties of life are not appalling to one who has not, at heart, worldly ambitions. Moreover it is not possible to serve one's country in the best and fullest manner if one is chained on to the Civil Service. In short, national and spiritual aspirations are not compatible with obedience to Civil Service conditions.

I realise that it is needless to talk in this fashion as my will is not my own. Though I am sure that the C. Service has no glamour for you, father is sure to be hostile to the idea of my not joining the C. Service. He would like to see me settled down in life as soon as possible. Moreover if

I have to qualify for another career it will add considerably to the financial burden which is already on your shoulders and I am not so heartless as not to feel what that burden means for you. Hence I find that owing to sentimental and economic reasons, my will can hardly be called my own. But I may say without hesitation that if I were given the option—I would be the last man to join the Indian Civil Service.

You may rightly say that instead of avoiding the service one should enter its ranks and fight its evils. But even if I do so, my position any day may become so intolerable as to compel me to resign. If such a crisis takes place 5 or 10 years hence, I shall not be in a favourable position to chalk out a new line for myself—whereas today there is yet time for me to qualify for another career.

If one is cynical enough one may say that all this "spirit" will evaporate as soon as I am safe in the arms of the service. But I am determined not to submit to that sickening influence. I am not going to marry—hence considerations of worldly prudence will not deter me from taking a particular line of action if I believe that to be intrinsically right.

Constituted as I am, I have sincere doubts as to whether I should be a fit man for the Civil Service and I rather think that what little capacity I possess can be better utilised in other directions for my own welfare as well as for the welfare of my country.

I should like to know your opinion about this. I have not written to father on this point—I really don't know why. I wish I could get his opinion too.

If the ঘটকs [match-makers—Ed.] come to trouble you again, you can ask them straight away to take a right about turn and march off.

I am pretty well here. How are you all doing? Where are father and mother?

Yours v. affly
SUBHAS

The following two letters were written to Deshbandhu Chittaranjan Das and were sent by Netaji through a friend for being delivered to him personally. In his letter to Sarat Chandra Bose from Cambridge of the 28th April, 1921, Netaji mentioned the reply that he received from the Deshbandhu to one of his letters. The letters have been translated from the originals in Bengali. The form of address used in the Bengali originals, literally translated, would read: 'I beg to submit with salutations.' The appropriate English form 'Sir' has been given in the translations.—Ed.

(61)

The Union Society
Cambridge
16th February (1921)

Sir,

I am probably a stranger to you. But you will perhaps recognise me if I tell you who I am. I am writing this letter to you on one very important matter—but before I come to business I must first prove my sincerity. Therefore I shall first introduce myself.

My father Mr. Janakinath Bose is a practising advocate at Cuttack and was the Government Pleader there a few years ago. One of my elder brothers Mr. Sarat Chandra Bose is a barrister of Calcutta High Court. You may know my father and you surely know my elder brother.

Five years ago I was a student of Presidency College. During the trouble in 1916 I was expelled from the University. After losing two years I obtained permission to resume my college studies. Thereafter in 1919 I passed the B.A. examination and got a first class in Honours.

I arrived here in 1919 in the month of October. I passed the Civil Service examination in August 1920 and secured the fourth place. In June this year I shall take the examination in Moral Science Tripos. The same month I shall get the B.A. degree here.

Now I shall come to business. I have no desire at all to enter government service. I have written to my father and brother at home that I wish to give up the Service. I have not had their reply yet. In order to get their consent, I have to convince them of what tangible work I want to do after giving up the service. I know very well that if after quitting the service I plunge into national work with resolute determination, I shall have plenty to do, viz. teaching at the National College, writing and publishing books and newspapers, organisation of village societies, spreading education among the common people, etc. But, if I can now show to my family what tangible work I wish to undertake—it will probably be easier for me to obtain their permission to leave the service. If I can give up the service with their agreement there will be no need to do anything against their will.

You know best about the situation in the country. I heard you had established National Colleges in Calcutta and Dacca and that you wanted to bring out a newspaper 'Swaraj' in English and Bengali. I have heard also that in various places in Bengal village societies, etc. have been established.

I should like to know what work you may be able to allot to me in this great programme of national service. Of education and intelligence I have but little—but I believe I have the enthusiasm of youth. I am a bachelor. As regards my education, I have read something of philosophy because that was my Honours subject in Calcutta and I am doing the same subject in my Tripos here. Thanks to the Civil Service examination I have had an all-round education up to a certain standard—such as, Economics, Political Science, English and European History, English Law, Sanskrit, Geography, etc.

I believe that if I can join this work, I shall be able to bring one or two Bengali friends from here into it. But until I personally enter the field, I cannot drag anybody else into it.

I cannot visualize from here which are the suitable fields of work in our country at present. But I have the feeling that on my return to my country, I should be able to take up two kinds of work, teaching in college and writing for newspapers. I desire to give up the service with clear-cut plans. If I can do that, I shall not have to spend time in thinking and I shall be able to enter the field of work immediately after throwing up the service.

You are today the high priest of the festival of national service in Bengal—that is why I am writing this letter to you. Echoes of the great movement that you have launched in India have reached here through letters and newspapers. The call of the motherland has thus been heard here also. A Madrassi student from Oxford is suspending his studies for the time being and returning home to start work there. Not much work has so far been done at Cambridge although a lot of discussion is continuing on 'non-co-operation'. I believe if one person can show the way there will be people here to follow in his footsteps.

You are the apostle of our national service programme in Bengal—I have therefore come to you today—with whatever little education, intelligence, strength and enthusiasm that I may possess. I have nothing much to dedicate at the altar of our motherland—all that I have is my conscience and my weak physical frame.

My purpose in writing to you is only to ask you what work you may be able to give me in this gigantic programme of national service. If I know that, I shall be able to write to my father and brother at home accordingly and I shall be able to prepare my mind in that light.

I am now in a sense a government servant. Because I am now an I.C.S. Probationer. I did not dare to write to you direct lest my letter is censored. I am sending this letter through a trusted friend of mine Mr. Pramatha Nath Sarkar—he will deliver this letter personally to you. Whenever I shall write to you, I shall be doing so in this way. You may of course write to me because there is no danger of letters being censored here.

I have not told anybody of my intentions here—I have written only to my father and brother at home. I am now a government servant—so, I hope, you will not mention this matter to anyone till I have resigned from the service. I have nothing more to say. I am now ready—you have only to command me to go into action.

My personal feeling is that if you start with the English edition of Swaraj, I may be working as one of the sub-editorial staff. Besides, I may be teaching the junior classes of National College.

I have quite a few ideas in my mind regarding the Congress. I think there must be a permanent meeting place for the Congress. We must have a house for this purpose. There will be a group of research students there who will be carrying on research on various national problems. As far as I am aware, our Congress has no definite policy relating to Indian currency and exchange. And then, it has probably not been decided what sort of attitude the Congress should adopt towards the Native States. It is perhaps not known what the stand of the Congress is in regard to franchise (for men and women). And further, the Congress has not probably made up its mind as to what we should do about the Depressed Classes. Because of lack of effort in this regard (that is, about the Depressed Classes), all non-Brahmins of Madras have become pro-Government and anti-nationalist.

My personal view is that the Congress has to maintain a permanent staff. They will do research on individual problems. Each one will collect up-to-date facts and figures, and after all such facts and figures have been collected, the Congress Committee will formulate a policy vis-a-vis every individual problem. Today the Congress has no definite policy with regard to many national problems. That is why I think the Congress must have permanent quarters and a permanent staff of research students.

Besides, the Congress should open an Intelligence Department. It has to be so arranged that all up-to-date news and facts and figures about our country are available in the Intelligence Department. Booklets will be published in every provincial language by the Propaganda Department and will be distributed free among the general public. Apart from that, a book will be published by the Propaganda Department on each and every question in our national life. In such a book the policy of the Congress will be explained and the grounds on which such a policy has been formulated will also be given. I have written so much. These questions are not new to you. I could not help writing about them as to me they appear to be quite new. I feel that tremendous work lies ahead of us in connection with the Congress. If you so wish, I shall probably be able to make some contribution in this respect.

I shall be awaiting your views. I am anxious to know what are the different kinds of work you may be able to assign to me. If you desire to send somebody to England to learn journalism, I am prepared to take this work up. If I am given this work, expenses on account of passage and outfits will be saved. I shall of course resign from the service before I take up this work. You will no doubt pay for my board and lodging because after giving up the service there will be no justification for my accepting money from home.

My personal wish is to leave for home in the month of June if I quit the service. But I am prepared to forego that wish if necessary.

You will forgive the great length of this letter. I hope you will let me have your reply as early as possible. Please accept my *pronams*.

I am
Yours respectfully,
SUBHAS CHANDRA BOSE

My address:
Fitz William Hall,
Cambridge

(62)

The Union Society
Cambridge
2nd March, 1921

Sir,

I wrote you a letter a few days ago—I hope you received it in due time.

I expect you will be happy to learn that I have all but made up my mind to resign from the service. I have told you in my previous letter what different kinds of work I may be suitable for. I cannot visualize clearly from here what sort of work offers the best scope at the present time. You are now actively in the field—you will therefore know very well what kind of work presents the best possibilities and what sort of workers are needed at present.

It is my request that you may kindly not mention this matter to anybody till you receive news of my resignation from the service. If I give up the service, I should like to return home towards the end of June provided of course I can secure a passage in time. I am eager to know what sort of work awaits me at home—because I wish to prepare my mind accordingly. Besides, it is also possible to undertake studies here according to the nature of the work that I shall be taking up on my return home. I hope you will let me have a reply on this point as early as possible.

Certain ideas are coming to my mind—I am communicating them to you.

(1) I may take up teaching at the National College. I have read a little of Western philosophy.

(2) If you publish a daily newspaper in English, I may work as one of the sub-editorial staff.

(3) If you open a research department for the Congress, I may also work there. I have written about this at some length in my previous letter. I think we must have a band of research students. They will deal with individual problems in our national life and collect facts about them. Then the Congress will appoint a committee and that committee will consider all such facts and formulate the policy of the Congress on each question.

Our Congress has no distinctive policy regarding Currency and Exchange, neither has the Congress a clear-cut policy about Labour and factory legislation. Then, our Congress has no definite policy about Vagrancy and Poor Relief and, again, the Congress has probably no determined policy as to the type of the Constitution we are going to have after the attainment of Swaraj. In my view the Congress-League scheme is entirely out-of-date. We must now frame the Constitution of India on the basis of Swaraj.

You may well say that the Congress is now engaged in pulling down the existing order, so until this work of demolition has been completed it is not possible to start constructive activity; but I am of the view that right from now when the work of destruction is going on, we must begin to create. To be able to formulate a policy in respect of any problem of our national life will require thinking and research over a long period of time. So research should start right from now. If the Congress can draw up a complete programme, we shall not have to worry about our policy in respect of any question when we have achieved Swaraj.

And then, there has to be an Intelligence Department of the Congress, where all information about the country will be available. It will be necessary for this department to publish booklets. One book will deal with one particular problem—for instance, the rates of birth and death during the last decade and the mortality rates due to different diseases.

Further, India's position in the last decade as regards revenue and expenditure will be published in another book—what have been the sources of revenue and what have been the items of expenditure. Thus we shall have to spread information throughout the country on all aspects of our national life through small publications.

(4) There is plenty of scope for work directed to the spread of education among the common people. Simultaneously with such activity, it will be necessary to establish Co-operative Banks.

(5) Social Service.

It is my view that there is scope for work in the above directions. But it will be for you to consider in which department you would have me. Of course teaching and journalism are the sort of work that appeals to me. I may make a beginning with these for the present and then, as opportunities present themselves, take part in other activities also. To me, giving up the service means taking the vow of poverty; so I shall not refer at all to my emoluments; bare subsistence will be enough for me.

If I can take up the work with full determination, I believe I shall be able to bring one or two Bengali friends here into it.

In Bengal you are the high priest of the great movement of national service that is now being organised. I have come to the end of what I had to say—now it is for you to let me participate in your great work.

As soon as I quit the service, people here will be asking me what I shall do on my return home. So, for my own satisfaction and in the interest of self-justification to others, I am most anxious to know how you can utilise my services.

I hope you will please keep all these matters confidential for the present.

Please accept my *pronams*.

I am
Yours respectfully,
SUBHAS CHANDRA BOSE

The following four letters are written to Sarat Chandra Bose.

(63)

Cambridge
16-2-21
Wednesday

My dear brother,

I was expecting copies of some of the photographs taken at Shillong. I suppose they are on their way now.

Has Saroj Babu started an independent firm of his own? It appears so, from the letter he has written to me.

Your letter of the 20th Jan. reached me on Saturday last. I am glad to learn how the children are getting on. I am told Asoka has improved considerably of late. From what I know of the Bolpur School I think it is a jolly good idea to send Bimal there. I hope *Bardidi* will approve of this plan.

You have received my 'explosive' letter by this time. Further thought confirms me in my support of the plans

I have sketched for myself in that letter. The only difficulty is what I may call social opposition. No man of the world will approve of my rash enterprise. The ordinary man lacks the idealism which alone can conceive of a life different from the one we ordinarily live. I am sure you will support me. If C. R. Das at this age can give up everything and face the uncertainties of life—I am sure a young man like myself, who has no worldly cares to trouble him, is much more capable of doing so. If I give up the service, I shall not be in want of work to keep my hands full. Teaching, social service, co-operative credit work, journalism, village organisation work—there are so many things to keep thousands of energetic young men busy. Personally, I should like to take up teaching and journalism at present. The national college and the new paper "Swaraj" will afford plenty of scope for my activity.

As for my livelihood, I hope to earn enough to make both ends meet—either as a teacher in the National College or as a member of the Editorial Staff of any of the nationalist papers, or as both. My wants are few and I shall be satisfied with little.

When I persuaded myself, a few months ago, that I should accept the service at present, my idea was to save an amount roughly equivalent to the money spent over me and then to resign the service and join public life. That amount I wanted to set apart for the higher education of Gopali or Sati or for the upbringing of *Bardidi's* children. I felt (and I still feel) that I owed a duty to the members of our family—having myself enjoyed the benefit of an education abroad. But I have begun to doubt whether that is the best way I can fulfil the moral responsibility which hangs on my shoulders. I have further begun to think that the sum total of good I can do if I resign the service is more than what I can do if I stick to the service and simply save money. It is for you to decide whether I can better fulfil the moral responsibility which rests on me by resigning the service or remaining in it. Personally I have no doubt that I can do much more if I am not in the service. A life of sacrifice to start with, plain living and high thinking, wholehearted devotion to the country's cause—all these are highly enchanting to my imagination and inclination. Further, the very principle of serving under an alien bureaucracy is intensely repugnant to me. The path of Arabindo Ghosh is to me more noble, more inspiring, more lofty, more unselfish though more thorny than the path of Romesh Dutt.

I have written to father and to mother to permit me to take the vow of poverty and service. They may be frightened at the thought that that path might lead to suffering in the future. Personally I am not afraid of suffering—in fact, I would rather welcome it than shrink from it.

I am pretty well here. How are you all doing?

I shall keep all this a secret until a decision is arrived at.

Yours v. affly
SUBHAS

P.S.— If I resign, I intend to return home as soon as possible. The Tripos comes off early in June and the results will be declared within a fortnight. So I shall be in a position to return in June along with *Bardada*. I shall of course have to refund to the India Office the total sum I get as allowance by that time. I shall get the second instalment of the allowance (£50/-) by the end of March and the 3rd instalment by the end of June.

S. C. BOSE

(64)

Cambridge
23-2-21

My dear brother,

I did not hear from you by the last mail. You were too busy at the time—I presume.

I have already written to you more than once about my desire to resign the Civil Service and take up public service instead. I have submitted this desire of mine to a severe analysis and to a mature deliberation. I can assure you that I have not arrived at such a decision in a moment of mental excitement. The decision may be a regrettable one from a certain point of view but it is based on my whole outlook on life. Ever since the result of the I.C.S. was declared, I have been asking myself whether I shall be more useful to my country if I am in the service than if I am not. I am fully convinced now that I shall be able to serve my country better if I am one of the people than if I am a member of the bureaucracy. I do not deny that one can do some amount of good when he is in the service but it can't be compared with the amount of good that one can do when his hands are not tied by bureaucratic chains. Besides, as I have already mentioned in one of my letters, the question involved is mainly one of principle. The principle of serving an alien bureaucracy is one to which I cannot reconcile myself. Besides, the first step towards equipping oneself for public service is to sacrifice all worldly interests—to burn one's boats as it were—and devote oneself wholeheartedly to the national cause.

You will realize that the conditions under which an I.C.S. man has got to live and work are incompatible with my temperament, training and general outlook on life. Under these circumstances it would be a most illogical thing for me to accept conditions in the midst of which I am sure to feel miserable. On the other hand I know that a life of sacrifice, of suffering and even of poverty is heartily welcome to me if only it is in the interests of our national cause.

I have already said more than once that the uncertainties of life are powerless to intimidate me. I am fully aware that I am deliberately courting pecuniary loss and physical discomfort. But I am prepared for the untoward effects of my action—both immediate and remote.

The illustrious example of Aurobindo Ghose looms large before my vision. I feel that I am ready to make the sacrifice which that example demands of me. My circumstances are also favourable. Our family is fairly well-to-do (expect for *Bardidi* and her children) and I have no pressing worldly responsibilities. I believe I have an ascetic frame of mind which will enable me to bear with patience any misfortune which may visit me in future. Lastly, I am unmarried and hope to remain so. Who can ever expect such easy circumstances?

My plan is to return home in June after taking my degree—with *Bardada* if possible. I desire to take up teaching work in the National College on my arrival in Calcutta. In addition to this I intend to join the staff of one of the nationalist daily papers in Calcutta. I have other plans also in my mind viz. social service, mass education, co-operative credit society and the organisation of a research department for political and economic problems in connection with the National Congress. But these plans will be taken up later on when men and money are forthcoming. In any case I shall have plenty of work to do to keep my hands full when I arrive in India.

I am sure you will respond favourably to this proposal of mine. The only obstacle is that hardly any one else among our relatives will approve of my eccentric plans. There will be a terrible hue and cry everywhere but I do not think that that should scare us if we take our stand on truth.

You have done all that you could for me and all that I could expect from you—and without being solicited either. I feel that I have been placed under a kind of moral obligation—the meaning and depth of which I do not sufficiently comprehend. The result is that I feel that my proposal to resign is, to say the least, a cruel one. Such a proposal means that the sum of Rs. 10,000/- spent for my sake will yield no return whatsoever. But when I appeal to you to consent to my resignation I do so, not as a personal favour but for the sake of our unfortunate country which is in dire need of wholehearted devotees. You will have to look upon the money spent for my sake as a gift laid at the feet of the mother without any expectation of return in any shape or form.

This is my last letter to you on the subject of my

resignation. I am making a similar appeal to father and mother also. I am sure I shall get your consent. The next riding examination comes off on or about the 23rd April. I hope to get a reply to this before that date and in all probability I shall not have to appear at the next riding examination.

I realize that it will require more strength of mind on your part to consent to my proposal than has been required of me in formulating this proposal. But I am fully confident that you possess the requisite strength of mind. I am sure that if you are convinced of the soundness of my proposal you will not allow any other consideration to withhold your consent.

Aurobindo Ghose is to me my spiritual guru. To him and to his mission I have dedicated my life and soul. My decision is final and unchangeable, but my destiny is at present in your hands.

Can I not expect your blessings in return and will you not wish me Godspeed in my new and adventurous career?

Yours v. affly
SUBHAS

P.S.— Glad to receive your letter of the 2nd inst: and to learn that all of you are doing well.

We are pretty well here. How are you all doing?

SUBHAS

(65)

Oxford
6th April '21

My dear brother,

Your letter of the 12th March was to hand duly. I have been profoundly impressed by the sentiments expressed in that letter. I am gratified to find that you corroborate my point of view even though you do not accept my conclusions.

Since the 15th of August last, one thought has taken possession of me—viz. how to effect a reconciliation between my duty to father (and mother) and my duty to myself. I could see from the very outset that father would be against my proposal—in fact, my idea would seem to him preposterous. It was not without a shudder therefore—shudder at the thought of causing him pain—that I asked you to communicate my intention to father. In fact, I did not then have the heart to write to him direct. That was in September last and the result of that attempt you know very well.

Since then the struggle has been going on in my mind—a struggle intensely painful and bitter in view of the issues involved. I have failed to arrive at any reconciliation. We who have grown up under the influence of Swami Vivekananda on one side and Aurobindo Ghose on the other—have, fortunately or unfortunately, developed a mentality which does not accept a compromise between points of view so diametrically opposed. It is quite possible that I have been nurtured on a wrong philosophy. But it is the characteristic of youthful minds to have more faith in themselves than in others. It is perhaps an unfortunate fact but it is a fact all the same.

You know very well that in the past I had occasion to cause great pain not only to father and mother but to many others including yourself. I have never excused myself for that and I shall never do so. Nevertheless, conditioned as I was by temperament and circumstance, there was no escape for me out of an intellectual and moral revolt. My only desire then was to secure that amount of freedom which was necessary for developing a character after my own ideals and for shaping my destiny after my own inclination.

Since then, circumstances have considerably changed. Bereavement after bereavement has overtaken us. Father and mother are not in the same state of health in which they were some years ago. It will be cruel—exceedingly cruel—for me to cause them grievous pain in their present state of mind and health. I know I shall never be able to excuse myself in afterlife for being instrumental in bringing so much pain and worry. But what can I do? Should I abandon my own point of view?

I realise that all along I alone have been instrumental in introducing so much discord into our otherwise quiet family. The reason is that certain ideas have taken possession of me and these ideas have unfortunately been unacceptable to others.

Father thinks that the life of a self-respecting Indian Civil servant will not be intolerable under the new regime. And that home rule will come to us within ten years. But to me the question is not whether my life will be tolerable under the new regime. In fact I believe that even if I am in the service, I can do some useful work. The main question involved is one of principle. Should we under the present circumstances own allegiance to a foreign bureaucracy and sell ourselves for a mess of pottage? Those who are already in the service or who cannot help accepting service may do so. But should I, being favourably situated in many respects, own allegiance so readily? The day I sign the covenant I shall cease to be a free man.

I believe we shall get Home Rule within ten years and certainly earlier if we are ready to pay the price. The price consists of sacrifice and suffering. Only on the soil of sacrifice and suffering can we raise our national edifice. If we all stick to our jobs and look after our own interests, I don't think we shall get Home Rule even in 50 years. Each family—if not each individual—should now bring forward its offering to the feet of the mother. Father wants to save me from this sacrifice. I am not so callous as not to appreciate the love and affection which impels him to save me from this sacrifice, in my own interests. He is naturally apprehensive that I am perhaps hasty in my judgment or over-zealous in my youthful enthusiasm. But I am perfectly convinced that the sacrifice has got to be made—by somebody at least.

If anybody else had come forward, I might have had cause to withdraw or wait. Unfortunately nobody is coming yet and the precious moments are flying away. In spite of all the agitation going on there, it still remains true that not a single civil servant has had the courage to throw away his job and join the people's movement. This challenge has been thrown at India and has not been answered yet. I may go further and say that in the whole history of British India, not one Indian has voluntarily given up the civil service with a patriotic motive. It is time that members of the highest service in India should set an example to members of the other services. If the members of the services withdraw their allegiance or even show a desire to do so—then and then only will the bureaucratic machine collapse.

I therefore do not see how I can save myself from this sacrifice. I know what this sacrifice means. It means poverty, suffering, hard work and possibly other hardships to which I need not expressly refer but which you can very well understand. But the sacrifice has got to be made—consciously and deliberately.

Father says that most of the so-called leaders are not really unselfish. But is that any reason why he should prevent me from being unselfish? If anybody wants to be unselfish he will unavoidably cause suffering and worry in his own family. We cannot complain that other people are not self-sacrificing if we ourselves are not prepared to be so.

From the above considerations I conclude that on behalf of our family I must come forward with my little offering and since this sacrifice must be undergone we might as well do so with a light heart. Father is afraid that I am ruining my career and that I may bring untold suffering on myself in future. I do not see how I can persuade him that the day I resign will be one of the proudest and happiest moments of my life.

Your proposal that I should resign after returning is eminently reasonable but there are one or two points to be urged against it. In the first place it will be a galling thing for me to sign the covenant which is an emblem of servitude. In the second place if I accept service for the present I shall not be able to return home before December or January, as the usual custom stands. If I resign now, I may return by July. In six months' time much water will have flowed through the Ganges. In the absence of adequate response at the right moment, the whole movement might tend to flag and if response comes too late it may not have any effect. I believe it will take years to initiate another such movement and hence I think that the tide in the present movement must be availed of. If I have to resign, it does not make any difference to me or to anyone of us whether I resign tomorrow or after a year but delay in resigning may on the other hand have some untoward effect on the movement. I know full well that I can do but little to help the movement—but it will be a great thing if I have the satisfaction of having done my bit.

As to my programme when I return home—that will depend on the conditions then existing in Bengal and on the needs of that province. Apart from the work I do, I shall have to devote a lot of time to a study of the different problems of our national life. Only a profound study of these problems can equip a man intellectually for the task of intelligent service.

A couple of years' service—specially under Lord Sinha's regime—will not help me in my future work. A couple of years' work as district officer will no doubt afford valuable experience. But it will take about eight years to be a district officer and two to three years in order to be a sub-divisional officer. The first year is devoted more or less to official, or rather clerical, work.

The movement—as you say—is now in a nebulous and chaotic condition. But it is for us to shape it in the proper manner. It will serve no useful purpose if we adopt the Asquithian policy of wait and see. The movement will either succeed or fail. If it succeeds it will do so in spite our indifference which one may call criminal. If it fails, the responsibility will be ours for having kept aloof from the movement.

I have no exaggerated opinion about the progress of

events at home. If I were sure that the movement would progress favourably, I could easily have waited. The apprehension of failure or slackening impels me to throw myself into the movement before it is too late to mend matters.

I do not know who has spread the rumour in Calcutta that I have resigned already. Some people perhaps presume to know more about myself than I do.

The application for a military commission refers to myself though there has been some misunderstanding on this score. The Indian students at Cambridge have been agitating for admission into the Officers' Training Corps there. I was one of those who applied in Michaelmas Term 1920, for enlistment. But we only wanted training during our stay at Cambridge. I expressly mentioned in the application that I was a probationer in the I.C.S. It is clear that when I resign the I.C.S., I can have nothing to do with H.M.'s Army.

I may do some teaching work immediately [after] I return but as a permanent profession I shall choose journalism. That will help me to earn my living as well.

If for any reason I happen to change my decision regarding resignation, I shall send a cable to father as that will relieve his anxiety.

How are you all doing? We are all pretty well here.

Yours v. affly.,
SUBHAS

(66)

Cambridge
20-4-21

My dear brother,

I have not heard from you for the last two weeks. I am particularly anxious on *Mejdidi's* account.

I do not know how the rumour spread in Calcutta about 2 months ago that I had resigned. I had written only to one man in Calcutta about my desire and he has not given it out. I believe the expectations of certain people took shape in the form of a rumour which soon gained currency.

I am going to send in my resignation day-after-tomorrow. I have written this week to two persons in Calcutta about it and have requested them not to make a fuss over it. The fact that I am definitely going to resign has leaked out here only within the last few days. Unfortunately it seems to have created a sensation among the Indian Community. I am afraid, therefore, that some of the people here will send word to India and some people there will try to make a sensation over it. I am anxious to avoid creating a sensation for several reasons. In the first place, I dislike both sensation and popular applause. Secondly, if there is no sensation there is not likely to be any difficulty about my getting home as soon as possible. Thirdly, I would like to hide the fact of my resignation from father's knowledge, in view of Mejdidi's present state of health. I have not written to father anything about my resignation since I heard of Mejdidi's illness. But I am afraid it is impossible to keep it a secret. Still, I shall try my best.

I had a very stormy time at Oxford—stormy—from the mental point of view. I shall write to you in my next letter all the reasons which finally persuaded me to choose the path of resignation.

You need not bother about sending me any money at present—especially in view of the unfavourable rate of exchange. Some of my friends have offered to lend me sufficient money which will keep me going till I reach home. I have not hesitated in accepting the offer because I have been assured that they are lending out of their surplus stock which they have at present. I shall borrow in pounds and if the rate of exchange improves during the next few months, it will be convenient for me to repay the amount from India. They will not lose anything by lending me the money (except the bank rate of interest) whereas it may be of great help to me. I expect the rate of exchange to improve during the next few months.

I shall apply for a passage early next week. I intend to leave for home by the end of June. I shall try for a berth in the Messageries Maritimes and failing that, in the B.I.S.N. or City Line.

You have said too many kind words about me in your letters which I know how little I deserve. The magnanimous spirit revealed in your letters has touched me profoundly. I know that that spirit is worthy of you and all I shall say is—I am proud of you. In spite of the difference of opinion, I feel sure that no one could have expected a more cordial and sympathetic response from one's elder brother.

I know how many hearts I have grieved—how many superiors of mine I have disobeyed. But on the eve of this hazardous undertaking my only prayer is—may it be for the good of our dear country.

Yours v. affly.,
SUBHAS

Letter of resignation from the Indian Civil Service.

(67)

16, Herbert Street,
Cambridge
22-4-'21.

The Right Hon. E. S. Montagu M.P.
    Secretary of State for India.
Sir,

I desire to have my name removed from the list of probationers in the Indian Civil Service.

I may state in this connection that I was selected as a result of an open competitive examination held in August, 1920.

I have received an allowance of £100/- (one hundred pounds only) up till now. I shall remit the amount to the India Office as soon as my resignation is accepted.

I have the honour to be
Sir,
Your most obedient servant,
SUBHAS CHANDRA BOSE

This letter to Mr. Charu Chandra Ganguly was written by Netaji on the day he sent in his resignation from the Indian Civil Service.—*Ed.*

(68)

Fitz William Hall, Cambridge
22nd April, 1921

My dear Charu,

You are aware that once before I sailed forth on the sea of life at the call of duty. The ship has now reached a port offering great allurement—where power, property and wealth are at my command. But, the response from the innermost corner of my heart is—'You will not find happiness in this. The way to your happiness lies in your dancing around with the surging waves of the ocean.'

Today, in response to that call, I am sailing forth again with the helm in His hands. Only He knows where the ship will land.

I have not been able to decide yet what I shall do. Sometimes I feel like joining the Ramakrishna Mission. At other times I feel like going to Bolpur. And, then again, I have the desire to become a journalist. Let us see what happens.

Yours
SUBHAS

The following two letters are written to Sarat Chandra Bose.

(69)

The Union Society
Cambridge
23-4-'21

My dear brother,

I have not heard from you for the last two weeks. I learn from father's letter that you had been to Cuttack during Easter Week. I am anxious to know how Mejdidi is doing, but all of you are maintaining what appears to me a suspicious silence about her.

I had a talk with the Censor of Fitzwilliam Hall, Mr. Reddaway, about my resignation. Contrary to my expectations, he heartily approved of my idea. He said he was surprised, almost shocked, to hear that I had changed my mind, since no Indian within his knowledge had ever done that before. I told him that I would make journalism my profession later on and he said that he preferred a journalistic career to a monotonous one like the Civil Service.

I was at Oxford for three weeks before I came up here and there the final stage of my deliberation took place. The only point which had been taxing me for the last few months was whether I should be justified morally in following a course which would cause intense sorrow and displeasure in many minds and especially in the minds of father and mother.

I wrote to you in one of my previous letters that I felt that, having had the advantage of an education abroad, I should try my best to extend the same advantage to some other members of our family or at least to contribute to the material welfare of our family in some other way. Strictly personal questions did not in any way trouble me as I did not have any worldly ambition to start with and as I had further resolved to live a life of celibacy. But it occurred to me that before I turned my back on all family interests I should be convinced that I was really acting under the inspiration of some higher duty. The apt saying of Christ that he who hates his brother and says that he loves God is a hypocrite—reminded me that it is often possible to neglect mundane duties under a delusion of working for higher ends.

I have always felt that it is unfair from our point of view to place such a huge financial burden on your shoulders— though I could never effect any other practical solution of our financial problem. Consequently I felt that I should try to decentralize the burden and take some responsibility on my shoulders. This appeared to me all the more imperative since in order to help father to retire you would have to take over some further financial responsibility. I wrote to you what I felt on this matter and received your reply to it. The reply was magnanimous as it could be and you tried therein to absolve me of the moral obligation under which I felt I had been placed. Nevertheless I feel that I have not been absolved of the moral obligation and shall not be absolved—until and unless I prove to my own satisfaction that I have done sound and solid work in the career which I am now going to follow.

I need not make it a secret that I felt I was responsible more to father, mother and yourself for what I did, than to anyone else. You have tried to absolve me of the moral obligation though moral obligation which is deeper than legal obligation cannot be disowned at the will of either or both parties. The obligation I own to father and mother is not to displease them to the best of my ability. They are inspired by a desire to look after my own interests and they are naturally afraid that if I resign the Civil Service I shall be courting financial ruin and poverty for myself in the future. I have not been able to persuade them that the course I intend to follow will bring me the greatest amount of happiness—that real happiness cannot be measured in terms of pounds, shillings and pence and that if I stick to the service I shall always feel that I am a criminal who has not got the courage of his convictions. Their view follows naturally upon a materialistic interpretation of life but I quite realize that out of their affection for me they are anxious to see me getting on well in life instead of being plunged once more into a sea of uncertainties.

My position therefore is that in entering upon a new career I am acting against the express wishes of father and mother and against your advice though you have sent me your "warmest felicitations in whatever course I choose".

My greatest objection to joining the service was based on the fact that I would have to sign the Covenant and thereby own the allegiance of a foreign bureaucracy which I feel rightly or wrongly has no moral right to be there. Once I signed the Covenant, it would not matter from the point of view of principle whether I served for three days or three years or thirty years. I have come to believe that compromise is a bad thing—it degrades the man and injures his cause. When I was hauled up for assaulting Oaten, I denied any complicity in the affair. I was then labouring under a delusion that the end justifies the means. Later on when in joined the I.D.F., I took the oath of allegiance to the higher authorities—though in my heart of hearts there was no feeling of allegiance. I have learnt from all this that one compromise always leads to another. The reason why Surendra Nath Banerji is going to end his life with a Knighthood and a ministership is that he is a worshipper of the philosophy of expediency which Edmund Burke preached. We have not come to that stage where we can accept a philosophy of expediency. We have got to make a nation and a nation can be made only by the uncompromising idealism of Hampden and Cromwell.

I feel, very strongly, as a result of my past experience that compromise is a very unholy thing. If I had stood up before James in 1916 and admitted that I had assaulted Oaten, I would have been a better and truer man and would have served the students' cause better—though perhaps with unfavourable consequences to myself. Similarly, I would have been true to myself and to my principles if I had refused to join the I.D.F. under the existing conditions and had refrained from coming to England for the Civil Service. But the past is past and I cannot bring it back again. The future is still in my hands and it is for me to decide whether I should continue further—and perhaps irretrievably—in the path of compromise or whether I should stand up for a principle regardless of all consequences.

I do not believe that one cannot do any good to the country while in the service. Neither do I believe that one must live like a European in order to get on well in the service. I quite realize that the true man will always be able to shape his circumstances instead of being moulded by them. These considerations, therefore, were minor ones and to me the most vital consideration was that of principle.

I have come to believe that it is time for us to wash our

hands clean of any connection with the British Government. Every Government servant whether he be a petty chaprasi or a provincial Governor only helps to contribute to the stability of the British Government in India. The best way to end a government is to withdraw from it. I say this not because that was Tolstoy's doctrine nor because Gandhi preaches it—but because I have come to believe in it.

I have come to believe, further, that the national liberty which we want cannot be attained without paying for it dearly in the way of sacrifice and suffering. Those of us who have the heart to feel and the opportunity to suffer should come forward with their offering. I do not expect that those who have been long in the service and have financial responsibilities to shoulder can do this. Nevertheless each family in this wide land of ours must come forward with its own humble tribute and as long as we do not do our duty, we have no right to complain that the leaders are selfish.

I feel that we have not yet contributed our share and therefore I should make the sacrifice. Sacrifice and suffering are not in themselves very attractive things but I can't avoid them as I have been convinced that without them our national aspirations can never be fulfilled. It is purely an accident that I should be coming forward for the work and not somebody else. If we would approve of the sacrifice in the case of a third person there is no reason why we should not approve of it in our own case.

Besides, I find that fortunately I am fitted for this task by my temperament and previous training.

These considerations lead me to think that I am right in giving up the service—that father's desire that I should serve is unreasonable and is actuated only by natural affection for me and solicitude for my worldly prosperity.

My resignation will bring some amount of suffering—it may for instance hinder *Sejdada's* promotion later on. But I think we should accept some amount of suffering as inevitable.

I hope it will not appear from this long letter that I am

sermonising. Any such thing is farthest from my mind. My desire in writing the above has been to tell you what considerations have led me to decide upon a course of action which is opposed to the wishes of almost all of you. I have taken up an attitude of disobedience only after being convinced that sacrifice and suffering are inevitable for gaining one's ends and that under the circumstances I am best fitted to undergo the sacrifice.

It is not for me to judge whether this constitutes a moral justification for acting on my own initiative in the face of all advice to the contrary. I know I have hurt father beyond measure and I shall never excuse myself for having done so. Time alone will prove whether I am right or not. If you think that I have been guilty of rashness and indiscretion I pray that you will suspend your judgment and restrain your condemnation till my folly is thoroughly exposed by time. If you think I am not wrong in my choice I am sure your blessings and good wishes will always attend on me in my future career.

I received a letter from mother saying that in spite of what father and others think she prefers the ideal for which Mahatma Gandhi stands. I cannot tell you how happy I have been to receive such a letter. It will be worth a treasure to me as it has removed something like a burden from my mind.

I sent in my resignation a few days ago. I have not yet been informed that it has been accepted.

C. R. Das has written, in reply to a letter of mine, about the work that is already being done. He complains that there is a dearth of sincere workers at present. There will consequently be plenty of congenial work for me when I return home.

I intend to sail for home by the end of June. I shall apply for a berth as soon as my resignation is accepted. You need not bother about sending me any money now. I have been offered a loan which will keep me going till I reach Calcutta.

I am relieved to learn that *Mejdidi* has come round. I am therefore writing to father to say that I have resigned.

I hope and pray that he will be able to stand this piece of bad news.

I have nothing more to say. The die is cast and I earnestly hope that nothing but good will come out of it.

I have not heard from you for three weeks at least. Your silence surprises me. Are you doing quite well?

We are all pretty well here. How are you all doing? Does Ami still remember me? He will be a big boy by the time I return.

Yours v. affly.,
SUBHAS

(70)

The Union Society
Cambridge
18-5-21

My dear brother,

I am anxious to hear from you as I have not received any letter from you for a long time. The Indian mail has arrived but the first instalment of it did not contain any letter from home.

Sir William Duke is trying to persuade me to withdraw my resignation. He wrote to *Bardada* about it. The Secretary of the Civil Service Board at Cambridge, Mr. Roberts, also asked me to reconsider my decision and he said he was acting under instructions from the India Office. I have sent word to Sir William saying that I have acted after mature deliberation.

My examination (Tripos) comes off on the 1st June.

According to my present plan I shall sail from Marseilles towards the end of June or the beginning of July. I shall book my passage as soon as I receive intimation that my resignation has been accepted.

How are you all doing? I am pretty well here. *Bardada* will be going to Oxford shortly on a visit.

I intend to travel by one of the Nippon Yasen Kaisha boats and shall land at Colombo.

The Japanese Crown Prince is receiving a magnificent reception all over England. He came here yesterday to receive the Hon. L.L.D. He had a splendid ovation here as well.

Yours v. affly.,

SUBHAS

Part III

APPENDICES

APPENDIX 1

GENEALOGICAL TREE OF THE BOSES OF MAHINAGAR

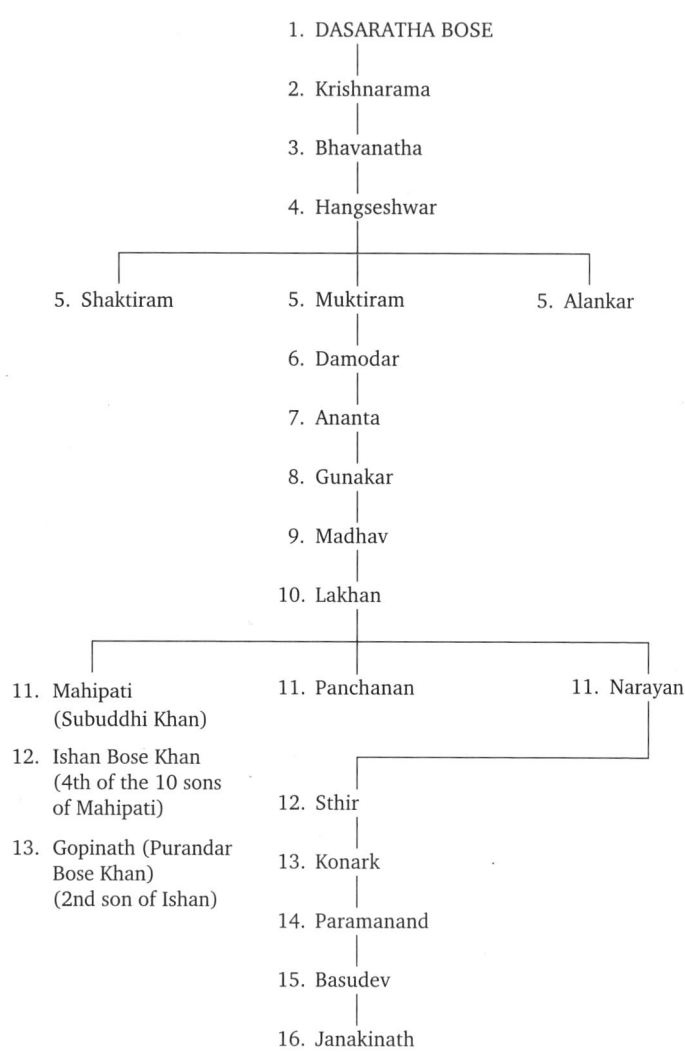

1. DASARATHA BOSE

2. Krishnarama

3. Bhavanatha

4. Hangseshwar

5. Shaktiram   5. Muktiram   5. Alankar

6. Damodar

7. Ananta

8. Gunakar

9. Madhav

10. Lakhan

11. Mahipati   11. Panchanan   11. Narayan
(Subuddhi Khan)

12. Ishan Bose Khan
(4th of the 10 sons
of Mahipati)   12. Sthir

13. Gopinath (Purandar
Bose Khan)
(2nd son of Ishan)   13. Konark

14. Paramanand

15. Basudev

16. Janakinath

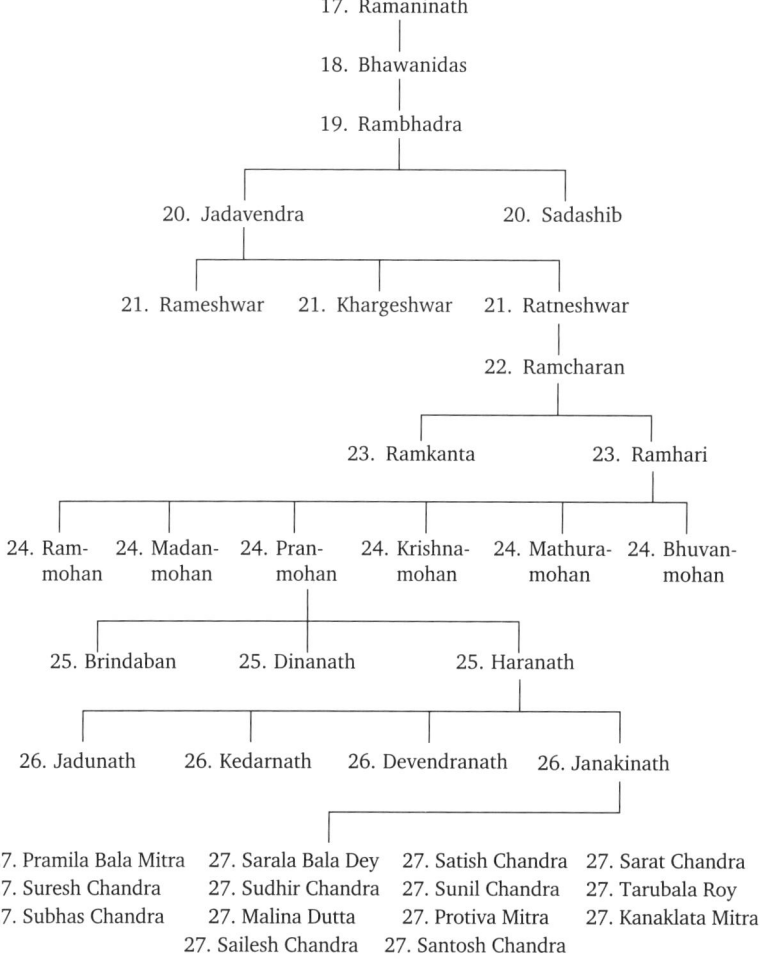

17. Ramaninath
18. Bhawanidas
19. Rambhadra

20. Jadavendra   20. Sadashib

21. Rameshwar   21. Khargeshwar   21. Ratneshwar

22. Ramcharan

23. Ramkanta   23. Ramhari

24. Ram-   24. Madan-   24. Pran-   24. Krishna-   24. Mathura-   24. Bhuvan-
mohan   mohan   mohan   mohan   mohan   mohan

25. Brindaban   25. Dinanath   25. Haranath

26. Jadunath   26. Kedarnath   26. Devendranath   26. Janakinath

27. Pramila Bala Mitra   27. Sarala Bala Dey   27. Satish Chandra   27. Sarat Chandra
27. Suresh Chandra   27. Sudhir Chandra   27. Sunil Chandra   27. Tarubala Roy
27. Subhas Chandra   27. Malina Dutta   27. Protiva Mitra   27. Kanaklata Mitra
27. Sailesh Chandra   27. Santosh Chandra

GENEALOGICAL TREE OF

KASI NATH DUTT

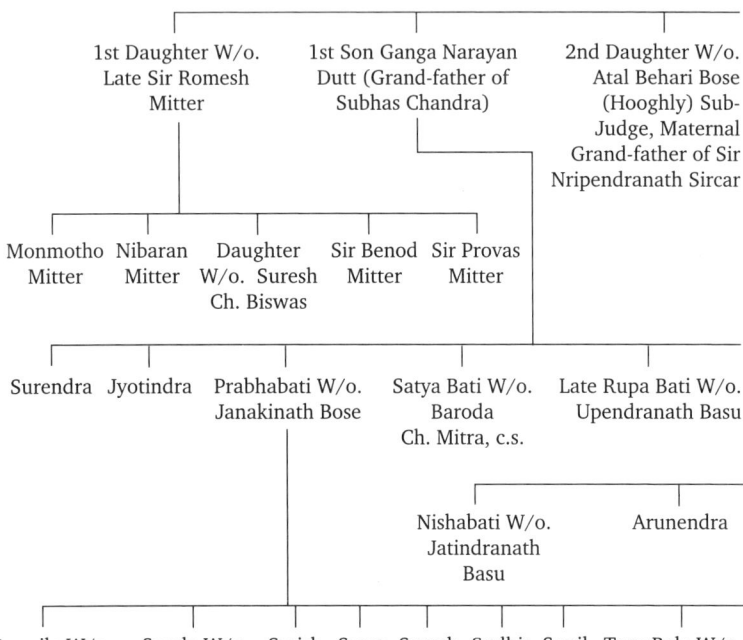

DIX 2

THE DUTTS OF HATKHOLA

of Baranagore

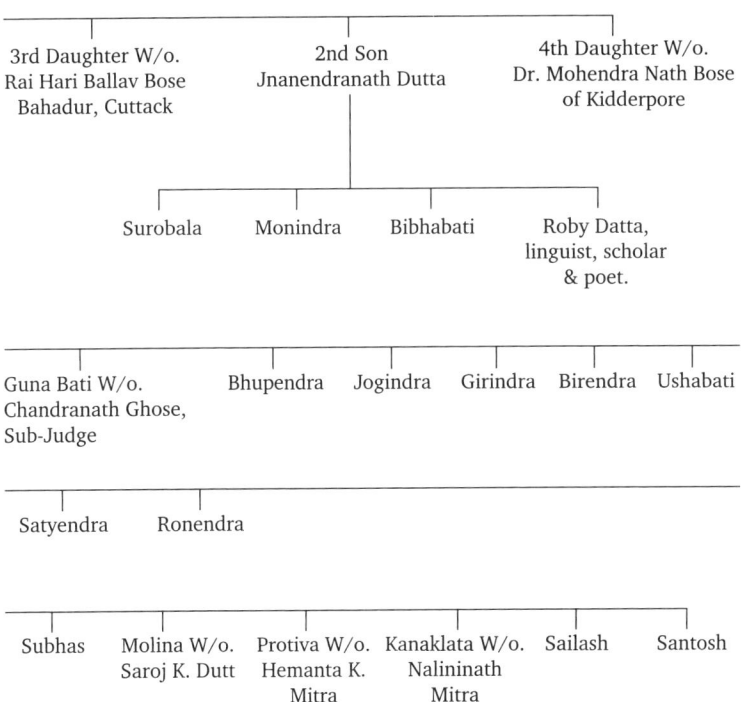

3rd Daughter W/o.
Rai Hari Ballav Bose
Bahadur, Cuttack

2nd Son
Jnanendranath Dutta

4th Daughter W/o.
Dr. Mohendra Nath Bose
of Kidderpore

Surobala   Monindra   Bibhabati   Roby Datta,
linguist, scholar
& poet.

Guna Bati W/o.   Bhupendra   Jogindra   Girindra   Birendra   Ushabati
Chandranath Ghose,
Sub-Judge

Satyendra   Ronendra

Subhas   Molina W/o.   Protiva W/o.   Kanaklata W/o.   Sailash   Santosh
Saroj K. Dutt   Hemanta K.   Nalininath
Mitra   Mitra

APPENDIX 3

JANAKI NATH BOSE

A BRIEF LIFE SKETCH°

by

Subhas Chandra Bose

In a village not far from Calcutta called Kodalia, Janaki Nath Bose was born in 1860. He lost his mother when he was sixteen years old. He passed the Entrance Examination from Albert School of Calcutta. After passing the Entrance Examination he studied for some time in the St. Xavier's College and in the General Assembly College and then left for Cuttack with his elder brother Devendra Nath Bose. Winning scholarships he passed F.A. and B.A. examinations with credit from Ravenshaw College at Cuttack. He was a class-mate of Professor Prafulla Chandra Roy and at the Cuttack College Professor Girish Chandra Bose and Byomkesh Chakravarty were his teachers. After graduation he came to Calcutta to take the Law Examination and at that time he had the good fortune to become familiar with Brahmananda Keshab Chandra Sen, his brother Krishna Vihari Sen and also with Umesh Chandra Dutt, Principal of City College and others. By courtesy of Krishna Vihari Sen he was professor for some time in Albert College and then for about nine months he served as Head Master of the High School in the village of Joynagar in 24 Parganas. He had to face severe financial difficulties during this time.

In 1880 he married Shrimati Prabhabati, grand-daughter of Kashinath Datta and a daughter of Ganga Narayan Dutt of Baranagore near Calcutta. In 1884 he obtained the B.L. degree from the Metropolitan College and returned to Cuttack where he started practising law with the support of Rai Bahadur Hari Ballav Basu, the then Government Pleader of Cuttack. Within a short time he became a very successful and influential lawyer. His father Haranath Bose died in 1895. Some years after the event—in 1901—he was appointed Public Prosecutor of Cuttack. After the death of Rai Bahadur Hari Ballav Basu in 1905, he was appointed the Government Pleader. He was elected the first non-official Chairman of Cuttack Municipality in 1901. In 1912 he was appointed a member of Bengal Legislative Council and the title of Rai Bahadur was conferred on him. In 1916 he was appointed the Government Pleader of the Circuit Court. In 1917, owing to some disagreement with the District Magistrate, he gave up the post of Government Pleader. Thirteen years thereafter, in 1930, as a protest against the repressive measures of the British Raj,

---

° Translated from the original in Bengali.

he renounced the title of Rai Bahadur.

Janakinath spent his professional life in Orissa. He was very closely connected with all philanthropic institutions and activities there. Poor school and college students used to get help from him regularly, month after month and year after year. Indigent neighbours and families in straightened circumstances expected help from him and none was ever disappointed. On every Sunday beggars were fed at his residence. He did not remain satisfied after doing his duty to Orissa and the Oriya people. He was deeply attached to his own village also. Poor relations, nay any every poor villager of Kodalia received his help in times of need and distress. Every year he performed Durga Puja with great pomp and grandeur in the village Kodalia and on that annual occasion he enjoyed the re-union with his fellow villagers. For the progress and the welfare of the villagers he set up two institutions in memory of his parents—the Kamini Charitable Dispensary and the Haranath Library.

Janakinath had all along been very sympathetic to the Indian National Congress. Even during the period when he was a Government Pleader, he used to attend Congress sessions regularly and on account of this he incurred the displeasure of the authorities from time to time. When the non-co-operation movement started, he tried to help the Congress as far as practicable in its constructive programme. He was a patron of *khaddar*, used all kinds of *Swadeshi* goods and was an all-round supporter of *Swadeshi*. He was connected with the first nationalist educational institution of Orissa established by Gopabandhu Das called "Satyavadi Vidyalaya" and he tried his utmost for the upliftment of that institution. Moreover, when his sons devoted themselves to Congress work, he supported them wholeheartedly.

Janakinath, throughout his life, was deeply religious. Over a long period of time he was the President of Cuttack Theosophical Lodge. In 1912, he along with his wife, took spiritual initiation from Pandit Shyama Nath Bhattacharyya of Bagbazar. A few years after the death of the first Guru, he and his wife joined the 'Satsangha' of Thakur Anukul Chandra of Himaitpur and both of them took spiritual initiation there. He became all the more religious as he grew in years. In his life of intense activity and struggle, religious inspiration was the greatest source of sustenance and strength. In his youth he had to fight material want and only through his own efforts and faith in God, could he establish himself in life. Later in life when the untimely death of near and dear ones smote him again and again, only his deep faith in God kept him unperturbed. When his two sons, Suresh Chandra and Subhas Chandra gave up governmental posts, he was not upset in the least—on the contrary, all his life he encouraged his sons in all public welfare activities. Not long before his demise, he had to face two kinds of agony simultaneously, the untimely death of son-in-law, daughter and others and the cruel imprisonment of his two sons Sarat Chandra and Subhas Chandra. But even under such tragic circumstances he remained heroically firm, never losing for a moment his deep faith in God.

Janakinath was a self-reliant man. He prospered in life by virtue of his own hard work and he desired his sons also to be self-reliant. To the best of his ability he arranged for good education for his sons, but he never wanted to curb their freedom. He was a large-hearted man. He felt very deeply for the poor. Before his death he arranged for regular pensions for his old servants and for many unfortunate and indigent persons known to him. In regard to charity while he was generous to a degree, he preferred to keep the matter to himself. He was truthful and a lover of truth. Deep in his heart he hated evil deeds, evil thoughts and evil means. He always remembered and felt indebted to persons who helped him, but never nursed in his mind the thought of misdeeds or harm done to him by others. Nobody ever heard him slandering anybody and jealousy was something completely unknown to him. Moreover, he was extremely polite in his speech. He never had a hard word for anybody—relations, friends, servants, the rich or the poor, elders or youngsters. The ideal he set up as a son, as a husband, as a father, as the patriarch of a big family and as a man is truly rare. The way he did his duty to his family, to his village, to society, to the country and the way he lived his life based on truth and righteousness is truly worthy of emulation by one and all.

APPENDIX 4

PURANDAR KHAN AND MAHINAGAR SAMAJ°

by

Nagendra Nath Bose

Arrangements are being made at Mahinagar to commemorate Purandar. In this connection discussion is taking place regarding the place where Purandar really lived. Some time ago Sarada Charan Mitra, in his booklet 'Purandar Khan' wrote: "The birth-place of Purandar was Sheakhala a village in the police station Chanditola in the district now called Hoogly. Formerly the river Kausiki used to flow by the side of the village Sheakhala. At present only the bed of the dried up river is visible. When the flow of the river stopped the place became extremely unhealthy and so the descendants of Purandar left the place to live somewhere else".

To contradict this observation of Mr. Mitra I contributed an article to the 'Kayastha Patrika' fifteen years ago entitled "A visit to the land of my forefathers". In that article I tried to establish that actually Mahinagar was the birth-place and also the place of social activities of Purandar. It is regrettable that despite my recording of facts after that visit to Mahinagar, Purandar's base of activities, many even now have their doubts about the matter; and to dispel their doubts I am writing the present article.

The founder of the Dakshin Rari Bose dynasty was Dasaratha who had two sons, Krishna and Param. Param migrated to Banga and his descendants came to be classified as Bangaja. Krishna Bose chose Rarh as his place of residence. His son was Bhabanath and Bhabanath's son was Hangsha. Hangsha had three sons, Sukti, Mukti and Alankar. Sukti started living at Baganda, Mukti at Mahinagar and Alankar in Banga. Mukti became the head of the Hindu Society of Mahinagar. This was the period when both Rarh and Gour were under Muslim influence. In the beginning the Kulins used to be chary of, and looked down upon, any socio-political dealings with the Muslims. They were extremely careful about maintaining proper social customs and manners and preserving the biological purity of lineage. Mukti's son was Damodar, his son was Ananta, his son was Gunakar, his son was Lakshman and Lakshman's son was the famous Mahipati Basu, the eleventh one in the genealogical tree stemming from Dasaratha. Coming to know of his endowments, keen intellect and efficiency, he was called by the

---

° Translated from the original in Bengali.
Reprinted from Kayastha Patrika
27th year of publication, 2nd issue, Jaistha, 1335 B.S.

Muslim ruler of Bengal to the capital of Gour. The Muslim King of Bengal was fully satisfied with him and appointed him to a high post, the Minister-in-charge of the Revenue and War.

This post was something akin to the post which in the Hindu period used to be called the post of *Mahasandhi-bigrahik*. Those who could secure such posts during the rule of the Muslims were venerated as kings by the people of their own community. Mahipati was a real leader and when the honorific title of Subuddhi Khan was conferred on him by the Muslim ruler, he came to be regarded as a real ruler by the people of his own community. There is a place now called Subuddhinagar lying about two miles to the south of Mahinagar and about a mile from Baruipur and this ancient site keeps alive even now the memory of Subuddhi Khan. Probably this Subuddhipur was a largesse from the Muslim ruler to Subuddhi Khan. He might have lived here for quite a while.

Mahipati had ten sons among whom the eldest Sureshwar became as famous as his father. His second son Gadadhar lost his status as the son of a Kulin family on account of undesirable activities. The third son Vishnu and the fourth son Ishan, both, were given the status of ordinary chiefs. The fifth one Dasharathi and the Sixth one Sarbeshwar, both, were given the status of Kanistha Kulin and the rest of Mahipati's sons Bisheshwar, Gangadhar, Bhagirath and Parameshwar were given the status of Teojo Kulin.

Ishan Khan, the fourth son of Mahipati topped the list by dint of his scholarship, intellect and wisdom. At the Royal Court of Gour he had the same position and post which his father enjoyed. Ishan Khan had three sons, Govinda, Gopinath and Ballav. The Sultan of Gour conferred on Govinda the honorific title Gandharva Khan, Purandar Khan on Gopinath and Sundarbar Khan on Ballav. During the Muslim period the system was to add some largesse in the form of fief to the conferring of title on some person. The fief which went to Govinda Basu was situated one and half mile to the east of Mahinagar and is known now as Govindapur. The fief which went to Purandar is now called Purandarpur, situated two miles to the North-western corner of Mahinagar.[1] The fief which went to Ballava, was called Bura Mullick, where the famous E. B. Railway Station Mallickpur is situated.

Purandar Khan was the Finance Minister and Naval Commandar of Sultan Hossain Shah. Purandar was closely associated with Sultan Hossain Shah and helped him a great deal during the period of the Sultan's ascendency. As they functioned as ministers for generations from the time of Subuddhi Khan in the court of Muslim rulers, the influence, power, social status and prestige of the family were tremendous. Moreover, as the finance department and the navy were under the control of Purandar, Purandar could enjoy a great deal of autonomy. And because of Purandar's residence in Mahinagar, Mahinagar became a sort of centre of the society of Dakshin Rarhi Kayasthas. At that time Mahinagar lay on the bank of the main course of the Ganges and one could very conveniently go all the way to Gour from Mahinagar by making a journey over the

---

[1] There is another Purandarpur near the house of the Bandopadhyayas of Kalyanpur.

river Ganges. Under the Admiralship of Purandar Khan the navy of the Sultan of Gour commanded this water-way and thus protected the kingdom and property of the Sultan. When Purandar was at the zenith of his power and prestige, he took the initiative in changing the old *Ballali Kulabidhi* to bring about friendly and family relations between the Kulins and Mouliks of the Dakshin Rarhi Kayasthas. He was prepared to unify and bring to a common status the thirteen levels of the Kulins. On the occasion of this work of unification the whole of the Kulina section and the leading Mouliks of the Dakshin Rarhi Kayasthas were invited. In Mahinagar more than a lakh of people gathered during this social function. Before this great gathering, Purandar, with a view to supplying the people invited with pure water, dug a vast tank by appointing a large force of labourers. The place where these large numbers of diggers used to keep the spades after washing them at the end of the day came to be called Kodalia now a suburb of Mahinagar. That big tank of Purandarpur stretching a mile is even now known as the Khanpukur. This tank which was made on the occasion of the unification of thirteen categories of Kayasthas is now mostly boggy and this morass is now choked with wild growth of weeds and hedges. The garden cultivated by Purandar is even now known as Malancha. Some people point to a place where Purandar's stable for the elephants used to stand. As a matter of fact, due to Purandar's residence there Mahinagar became the main centre amongst the six centres of the Dakshin Rarhi Kulin Kayasthas.

Before the rise of Purandar, amongst the Dakshin Rarhi Kayasthas the Ballali custom of maintaning the purity of line through the daughters, that is, to marry all the daughters of a family strictly to Kulins, was prevalent. As a result no daughter of Kulin could be given in marriage to any Moulik. And also as a result of this, any kinship through marriage between the Kulins and Mouliks was almost impossible. Formerly, the leading Kulins had to learn the *Kulashastras* well. Purandar, being himself a leading Kulin, was a scholar on the subject and he knew that before the Sen Kings of Bengal, no bar existed against marital relations between the Kulins and the Mouliks. But after the introduction of the Ballali system of *Kaulinya*, within a few generations the Kulins faced the acute problem of giving in marriage their daughters "properly"—actually a large number of Kulin daughters had to remain spinsters throughout life. Also a gulf was created between the Kulins and the Mouliks. Purandar realized that by imposing such parochialism on society one could only harm society immensely by depriving it of the power which lies in unity. And lack of social unity leads to ultimate destruction. For this reason, conferring with scholars of the system of Kaulinya and with Kulins he brought about unification. In that conference called to deliberate over and take the decision about this unification, Purandar as the leader of the caste introduced a new *Kulapratha*. He knew that the Kayasthas of Bengal had enjoyed kingly positions themselves, had been the favourites of kings and actually were kings. So in a kingly fashion he introduced that new system. As a king might have many sons, but only the eldest son is entitled, by custom and heritage, to the throne and the regal prestige of his father according to the law of inheritance or primogeniture, similarly Purandar made it the custom that only the eldest son of the Kulin family should be given the task of performing the Kulin rites. Other sons, not bound by this, would be allowed to marry girls either from Kulin or from Moulik families. Of course to give daughters in marriage to Kulin bridegrooms and to marry Kulin girls remained a matter of great pride and prestige. For the Mouliks too to give daughters in marriage to Kulin bridegrooms and to have brides from Kulin families became a matter of pride and prestige. As a matter of fact—due to this custom of Mouliks preferring Kulin brides and bridegrooms— the prestige of the Kulins went up.

Previous to this, the prevalence of the custom of keeping Kaulinya by marrying Kulin girls only to Kulin boys, Kulins seeking proper bridegrooms for their daughters had to move within a narrow circle and found the task pretty difficult. And the Mouliks also hesitated to extend due courtesies to the Kulins. Now, in the post-reformation period, as inter-marriage between the Kulins and Mouliks became possible, the Mouliks accepted the Kulapratha introduced by Purandar with a great deal of zest and the Kulins now commanded much more respect of the Mouliks. Previously marriage amongst the Mouliks was endogamous universally; even now the custom is current in Burdwan and Bankura districts. But as soon as Purandar introduced the new system, the Dakshin Rarhi Mouliks inhabiting the coastal regions of the Ganges began practising with zest the custom of marrying their sons and daughters to Kulin families with the idea that thereby they would be able to add lustre to their families. And as a result of this, in six such centres of the Kulins as Mahinagar, Baganda, Akna, Bali, Teka and Barisha and in neighbouring places, the custom of marriage between Mouliks and Mouliks gradually ceased to be in vogue. Owing to the introduction and later prevalence of purandaric reform the Kulin families could get rid almost totally of the problem of failing to give their daughters in marriage properly. Every aristocraric Moulik family became eager to have Kulin brides for their sons and to have Kulin bridegrooms for their daughters and this they came to consider as an essential duty. At that time most of the Dakshin Rarhi feudal chiefs were Mouliks and without a moment's hesitation they all supported the reform introduced by Purandar. After the introduction of inter-marriage between Kulins and Mouliks, a large number of Moulik zamindars gave their daughters in marriage to Kulin boys and then by endowing their Kulin sons-in-law with substantial landed property helped in establishing landed Kulin zamindar families. Quite a large number of documentary evidences are here to prove this point.

Among the Dakshin Rarhi Kayasthas, nine hierarchical groupings have been made—Mukhya, Kanistha, Chha Bhaya, Maddhyangsha, Teoj, Kanistha Dwitiya Putra, Chha Bhaya Dwitiya Putra, Maddhyangsha Dwitiya Putra, Teoj Dwitiya Putra. Among the nine Kulas, the first five ones, i.e., from Mukhya to Teoj, are considered to be the leading ones. The first born son of the Mukhya Kulin attains the status of the Mukhya by the very fact of his birth and he is titled as Janma Mukhya or Mukhya Kulin. In the hierarchy of the Kulas this is the highest one and this too is divided into three categories—Prakrita, Sahaj and Komal. The first one among these categories, i.e., Prakrita, is considered to be higher than the latter two. The Kula of second born son of the Mukhya Kulin is called janmakanistha and the eldest son of this janmakanistha has the Kula status called Chha Bhaya. The third son of the Mukhya Kulin has the Kula status called Maddhyangsha and the fourth has the one called Teoj. From the fifth son downwards the other sons of the Mukhya Kulin have the Kula status called Dwitiya Putra. The persons with such Kula status or names as Kanistha Dwitiya Putra, Chha Bhaya Dwitiya Putra and Teoj Dwitiya Putra are branches of Kulas with the names of Kanistha, Chha Bhaya and Teoj.

The six persons who set up these six centres of the Kulins—Akna and Bali of the Ghoshes, Mahinagar and Baganda of the Boses and Teka and Barisha of the Mitras—are revered as the Prakrita Mukhyas. Later their descendants were accorded the following status: only the eldest son of the Prakrita Mukhya is to be considered Prakrita, the second son is to be considered Sahaja, the third and fourth sons as Komala Mukhya, the fifth one as Kanistha, the sixth one as Chha Bhaya, the seventh one as Teoj, the eighth one as Maddhyangsha and the ninth son as Maddhyangser Dwitiya Po. Up to the time of Mahipati Bose alias Subuddhi Khan, the 11th descendant of Dasaratha Bose the leading Prakrita Mukhya, the above mentioned categorization of the Kula was current. During the period of Purandar Khan this underwent some change and became like this—Mukhya, Kanistha, Chha Bhaya, Maddhyangsha, Teoj, Kanistha Dwitiya Po, Chha Bhaya Dwitiya Po, Maddhyangser Dwitiya Po and Teoj Dwitiya Po— these nine categories were made.

There is no scope here to write in great detail about the history of the Kula-system introduced by Purandar. This much can be asserted here that by the move taken by Purandar the Kulins of Dakshin Rarhi were saved from extinction. Not only Purandar Khan but his eldest son Keshab Khan, the fourteenth in the line from Dasaratha, too brought about greater unification between the Kulins and Mouliks and became famous by this deed. The son of Keshab Khan, Sree Krishna Biswas, the fifteenth in the line from Dasaratha, carried on this job of unification and became famous. This fifteenth one in the line Sree Krishna Basu got the title of Biswas directly from the Sultan of Gour. On the occasion of this title-giving, the Jaigirdari, the lordship of land fief, he got is now called Sreekrishnapur situated to the south of Purandarpur. To the west of this Krishnapur is the village Akna, the centre of the Ghoshes. At present not many relics are left in Akna to demonstrate the ancient fame of the Ghoshes—yet the neighbouring village Ghoshpur stands as a relic to the memory of the Ghoshes.

Ananta Roy was the son of Sree Krishna Biswas. His son was Chand Mullick and the village Chandpur named after him now stands by the side of that canal now silted up and through which once the main current of the river Ganges flowed—to the east of Kodalia.

As the act of unification took place thrice in Mahinagar, it became a place of pilgrimage to those who were socially conscious.

Even two hundred years ago the Ganges used to flow with wide and fast currents by the side of Mahinagar. In the book 'Raimangal' written by Kaviram, an account of that time has been given thus:

Leaving behind Sadhughata the boat moved onwards from Surjapur and then anchored at Baruipur. In appreciation of Her glory the worthy one worshipped the goddess Bishalakshi and then started the journey by boat again. In the course of the journey Malancha was left behind and he moved towards Kalyanpur and in Kalyanpur the traveller bowed down to the god Madhava. Now, there is no point in naming all the villages he passed and just let me mention that the boat reached the Baradaha Ghat. (Raimangal—p. 49)

After the Ganges changed this course, the places on the coast turned unhealthy and an epidemic fever broke out which was the reason why many of the Boses left this place and migrated to healthy and safe places. Though leading Kulin Kayasthas left their ancestral homes, yet the Brahmins who functioned as their preceptors and priests did not think it advisable to move to some other places, leaving behind the rent-free land granted to them. In all these neighbouring places of Mahinagar, Kodalia, Changripota, Rajpur, Harinavi, Langalberia etc. the memory of such eminent and venerable Brahmin pundits as Vidyavachaspati etc. is still alive. In all those places hundreds of famous Brahmin pundits were born and because of the assemblage of so many pundits, Kodalia became as famous as Benaras to the Dakshinatya Vedic society. A verse in Sanskrit is current regarding this— "Kodalia is like Puri and Kashi and Goghata is like Mani Karnika Ghat, because Ramnarayan Tarkapanchanan who was like Vyasa lived there". It should be mentioned that the editor of Somprakash, Dwaraka Nath Vidyabhusan, was a descendant of the family of Ramnarayan Tarkapanchanan who himself was a descendant of Vidyavachaspati. It is not possible to mention in this small article all the names of the famous pundits who lived in that locality.[2]

Among the Kayasthas of that place the name of Rai Bahadur Janakinath Bose of Kodalia (father of the famous Subhas Chandra Bose) and that of Dr. Kartick Chandra Bose are worthy of special mention. Though these two gentlemen do not reside there now, yet as it happens to be their birth-place they often visit it and try to improve it.

About sixteen years ago a number of persons decided to keep alive the memory of Purandar Khan by restoring the big tank dug by Purandar Khan. But as many of them died, the attempt was nipped in the bud. Afterwards, through the efforts of a few Brahmin youths, a library named after Purandar was set up here. On the occasion of the inauguration of that memorial to Purandar Mr. Jatindra Nath Bose and Mr. Amrita Krishna Basu Mallick were present, both of them leading Kulin members of the Mahinagar society. It is undoubtedly true that preserving the memory of Purandar at Mahinagar is a duty which devolves mainly upon the Dakshin Rarhi Kayasthas. But it is a matter of great regret that, though a few meetings were arranged to be held in Calcutta with a view to taking a decision regarding the matter of commemorating Purandar Khan, not to speak of

---

[2] Those who desire to have some knowledge about the revered pundits who lived here, I would refer to the third part of the Vedic chapter of the National History of Bengal.

the general public, even the members of the Committee failed to join the meetings. Only Mr. Jatindra Nath Bose and Rai Bahadur Janakinath Bose took the initiative to carry the plan forward. A plot of land has been purchased thanks to the efforts of Rai Bahadur Janakinath Bose. Bricks have been collected, but the work of building the house has not started yet due to lack of funds. This is the reason why I have been induced to write this essay on the past glorious deeds of Purandar and I am making this appeal to the public that all sympathetic persons having the good of society in their hearts should come forward to preserve the memory of Purandar the defender of our society and the lion-hearted man. Let them help to translate into reality the laudable plan of those who took the initiative by sending money, according to their judgement and capacity at the earliest.

APPENDIX 5

DISCIPLINE IN PRESIDENCY COLLEGE

(a) Government Statement
(b) Report of the Enquiry Committee

(a) GOVERNMENT STATEMENT

A committee, consisting of the Hon'ble Justice Sir Ashutosh Mukherjee, K.T., C.S.I., D.L., the Hon'ble Mr. W. W. Hornwell, M.A., Director of Public Instruction, Bengal, Mr. C. W. Peake, Professor, Presidency College, the Rev. J. Mitchell, M.A., F.R.A.S., Principal, Wesleyan College, Bankura and Mr. Herambachandra Maitra, M.A., Principal, City College, was appointed by this Government in Resolution No. 416, dated the 20th February 1916, and letter No. 442, dated the 21st February 1916 to enquire into the general state of discipline at Presidency College, Calcutta, with special reference to a strike which took place on the 10th January 1916, and to an attack upon Professor Oaten which occurred on the 15th February 1916. The report of the Committee has now been received by Government and is published for general information. The Governor in council desires to tender his thanks to the members of the Committee for their labours, for the care with which they have made the enquiry entrusted to them and for their conclusions and recommendations, which will receive all the consideration which is due to the authority with which they have been made.

2. The Committee have described in detail the two incidents particularly referred to above and the antecedent circumstances which led up to them. With regard to the strike which occurred in January, they are of opinion that it is clearly established that some at any rate of the students' consultative committee entirely failed in their duty, and that so far from assisting the Principal, some members rendered the task of the Principal more difficult by deliberate mis-representations of his attitude. In respect of the assault on Mr. Oaten the Committee are impressed with the gravity of the offence committed by those who organised and carried it out and consider that they should be severely punished. As to the light thrown by these incidents upon the general question of discipline in the College, the view taken is that "it would be unjust to base on these two incidents alone a sweeping condemnation of the entire College, or to conclude that there had been any lack of strenuous and successful efforts on the part of the Principal and the staff to maintain discipline in the institution". The Committee consider that on the other hand, "the true reasons for the present condition of things must be sought for in other directions". They come finally to the conclusion in which the Governor in Council concurs, that no further disciplinary action of a general

nature is required, and that the Governing Body may be left to deal with any individuals who may have been concerned with the assault on Professor Oaten, and also with those members of the Student's Consultative Committee who were implicated in the strike.

3. The Committee have made a careful examination of the general state of discipline at Presidency College. They find that recently there has been some ferment among the students as a body, due, in the main, to political causes, which has resulted in the spread among them of a spirit of insubordination and the existence of what is described as "a spirit of excessive touchiness". The Committee note that there is a tendency among these young men to insist upon what they considered to be their rights without a full realisation of their accompanying responsibilities. These unfortunate conditions are attributed in part to the activities of dangerous revolutionary propagandists, and to the baneful influence of injudicious discussion in the public press of breaches of discipline. They are also in the opinion of the Committee due in part to the irritation caused by the division of the members of the College and between the Indian and the Provincial Educational Services, and to the want of free intercourse between the European Professors and the students, which has led, on four specified occasions in the past four years, to the exhibition of want of tact on the part of the teachers and to an undue sensitiveness on the part of their pupils. The Governor in Council believes that the Committee have accurately summarized the disturbing influences which have been at work, and desires to express his general concurrence in their findings.

4. The Committee then proceeded to make 12 recommendations, each of which has been carefully considered by the Governor in Council. In the first place, he accepts the suggestion that the Governing Body of Presidency College should be reconstituted so as to make it more representative and bring it into closer touch both with Government and with the public. Immediate action will be taken to give effect to this recommendation. The Governor in Council further accepts the views expressed by the Committee as to the departmental system in the College, and also with regard to the desirability of reconstituting the Consultative Committee of students on a basis other than the system of election, which has clearly proved a failure. These views will now be brought to the notice of the Principal and the Governing Body.

5. In their fifth recommendation the Committee deal with the relations between members of the Indian Educational Service and of the Provincial Educational Service and suggest that members of the teaching staff should be appointed not to Services but to posts on an incremental salary. The whole question of the future constitution of the Indian Educational Service and the Provincial Educational Service was discussed very thoroughly before the Public Services Commission, and now awaits the orders to be passed on its report. It will be impossible, therefore, to take any further action in the matter, until the recommendations of the Commission have been dealt with. The Governor in Council is in full sympathy with the views of the Committee that, in order to promote intercourse and foster a better understanding between the European Professors

and the students, the former should possess a competent knowledge of the vernacular and be encouraged to learn a classical Indian language. The Committee's recommendation on this subject will be considered in consultation with the Director of Public Instruction, and after reference to the existing rules governing language examinations. The Committee further advise that the Principal should take an active part in the instruction of the students, and thus come into more direct contact with them. Orders have already been received from the Government of India sanctioning the appointment of two professors of the College as Bursar and Dean respectively, and the Governor in Council hope that in view of the relief which will thus be afforded to the Principal, he may be able to carry out the recommendation made by the Committee. Action will therefore be taken at an early date in furtherance of this proposal of the Committee. The Governor in Council is not prepared to accept without some qualification the suggestion that professors of note should be transferred from the other colleges to the staff of Presidency College. He appreciates, however, the value to the recommendation that graduates of special distinction, with some experience in teaching, should alone be appointed to Presidency College, and suitable action will be taken to give effect to it. The proposals for structural alterations designed to minimise the likelihood of disturbance in the corridors will be referred to the Principal for examination, in direct communication with the Superintending Engineer, with instructions to submit their joint proposals to the Governing Body before they are sent up to Government.

6. The Committee refer in the following terms to the question of discussion in the Press of breaches of discipline in educational institutions:—

"It is essential that a definite pronouncement should be made by Government as to the incalculable mischief likely to result from the injudicious discussion in the Public Press of questions relating to breaches of discipline in educational institutions. At the same time we recognise that the most effective remedy for the situation would be the creation of an 'esprit-de-corps' which would render impossible the ventilation of grievances in the public Press". The Governor in Council emphatically endorses these views, to which he desires to draw the attention of all the editors of newspapers in Bengal. He trusts that they will recognise the grave injury which may be caused to the student community by the public discussion of the grievances of youths who are still "in statu pupillari".

7. The question of the management of the Eden Hindu Hostel, with which the Committee deal in the recommendation will be taken up at once in consultation with the Principal and the Governing Body. The Governor in Council will also take into consideration in communication with the Director of Public Instruction and the Vice-Chancellor and Syndicate of the University, the general recommendations made by the Committee on the subject of hostels.

8. The Committee refer finally to the undesirable character of the present surroundings of Presidency College. Proposals for the removal of the College to a more suitable situation were considered with much care and from all points of view some ten years back, when it was deliberately

decided to retain Presidency College on its present site and elaborate plans were prepared for its future expansion. In accordance with these plans, a considerable area of land has since been acquired and the Baker Laboratories have been built at a large cost. The Governor in Council will, however, examine the papers connected with the previous proposals in the light of the present recommendations of the Committee.

(b) REPORT OF THE COMMITTEE

We, the Committee appointed to enquire into the general conditions of discipline at the Presidency College with special reference to the strike which occurred in January last and the recent attack upon Professor Oaten, have the honour to submit our report and to make recommendations.

The first of the two incidents mentioned took place on the 10th January last. On that date, prizes were distributed to the students of the Hindu and Hare Schools by His Excellency the Governor of Bengal. Some of the Professors of the Presidency College as also some of the students who were ex-students of these schools were invited to the function. The result was that some of the Classes in the College were not held at the appointed hours. There was, besides, one Professor who was late and did not take his class in time. Many of the students of the 3rd Year Class appeared in these circumstances to have been present in one of the corridors contrary to the rule prescribed by the College authorities in this behalf. The particular rule (which appears in a book of instructions supplied to each student) may be set out here in full:—

"To guard against disturbances to classes while lectures are going on, it is a rule of the College that students must not enter the corridors outside the lecture-rooms on the first and second storeys of the College building until the hour for the lectures they have to attend has struck. No student, therefore, should be in the corridors between the sounding of the second gong for lectures and the next hours; nor may students enter unoccupied lecture-rooms, except in accordance with the first part of this rule."

Mr. Oaten was at the time lecturing in one of the rooms adjoining the corridors and felt himself seriously disturbed by the noise outside; he accordingly asked the students several times to go back to their classrooms. They did so, but, later on, in the course of the same hour, the Professor in charge of the class called the rolls and dismissed the students. The boys then left the class-room and came into the corridor again with the professor amongst them. Mr. Oaten was disturbed, came out of his lecture-room and ordered the students back to their class-rooms and pushed some of them. The evidence also shows that he stopped the professor, but the latter established his identity and was allowed to pass through. It is neither necessary for our present purpose nor possible on the evidence to determine with accuracy the exact amount of force used by Mr. Oaten, but the fact remains that the students whose bodies had been "touched" by Mr. Oaten with "an impulsive gesture", as he says, felt aggrieved and lodged a complaint with the Principal. One of the students was Subhas Chandra Bose, the representative of the class on the Students' Consultative

Committee. Here it may be observed in passing that the rule in question does not appear to have been always strictly enforced by every professor of the College, especially when classes were dismissed before the prescribed hour. This is not a matter of surprise when we remember that as many as 80 lectures are delivered in the College in the course of a single day. It should be noted, besides, that on both the occasions which have been brought to our notice the presence of students in the corridor was due to exceptional circumstances. To continue the narrative the Principal asked the students to see Mr. Oaten and advised them to make up the difference with him. This apparently dissatisfied them and the impression rapidly got abroad amongst them that Mr. James lacked sympathy with them and was reluctant to listen to their complaint against Mr. Oaten. This, as we shall presently see, was entirely unfounded and aggrieved students wholly misjudged the real attitude of Mr. James towards them. It now transpires that while on the one hand Mr. James referred the students to Mr. Oaten, on the other hand he privately wrote to Mr. Oaten and hinted that it would be the wise and gentlemanly thing to make it up with the students. Mr. Oaten has not preserved the original letter but this is the impression we gather from his statement as to its contents. The next day Mr. Oaten could not come to the College as he was on guard at Government House. On that day no classes could be held as the students went on strike. It is plain from the evidence that the leading part in this discreditable strike was taken by a few students while of the large majority who kept away from the classes, some did so on account of fear of personal violence and others owing to a lack of moral courage to face the ridicule of their fellow students. Some of the professors, both European and Indian, intervened but not very successfully to bring the students round and induce them to attend their classes. We desire to invite special attention here to the fact that in the organisation of this strike a very prominent part was taken by some at least of the Members of the Students' Consultative Committee; while some fail to assist their Principal to uphold law and order on the occasion of this trouble, others actually spread an unfounded rumour that the Principal had no sympathy for them and thus helped in a large measure to foster discontent and to develop the strike. In the course of the day, a notice was posted by the Principal to the effect that a fine of Rs. 5/- would be imposed upon every student of the college who kept away from his class. This order was issued in accordance with one of the College rules, which may be quoted here 'in extenso':—

"Whenever the students of a class are all found to be absent, unless such absence can be shown to have been accidental and due to misunderstanding every student of the class will incur fine of Rs. 5/-. Should such absence be repeated a second time, the facts will be laid before the Governing Body and such further punishment will be inflicted as the circumstances require".

The next day Mr. Oaten returned to the college. He was interviewed by a select number of students and the matter was amicably settled. The students admitted that there had been on their part a technical breach of rules, while Mr. Oaten expressed regret for what had happened.

Mr. Oaten was enthusiastically cheered by the students when he left the college premises in the afternoon and everything seemed to have ended peacefully. It is now appears that after the strike was over Mr. James called together all the European members of the staff and impressed upon them that they should not on any account touch the person of students, as experience had shown that this invariably led to serious trouble. This demonstrates how utterly unfounded was the impression that Mr. James lacked sympathy towards the students of the College. On the day following the strike, an untoward event, however unexpectedly happened. Mr. Oaten had to lecture to some of his students in history. When he went to his class he found that a dozen students were present, of whom ten had been absent on the day previous. He asked the students who had been absent to leave the class. As Mr. Oaten explained to the Committee, he did so to mark his disapproval of the conduct of his own students who had failed to stand loyally by him. These students thereupon withdrew from the class and complained to the Principal of the treatment they had received at the hands of their professor. The Principal sent the complaint to Mr. Oaten, who replied in writing seeking to justify his action as a disciplinary measure. Mr. James had expressed the opinion before the Committee that the action taken by Mr. Oaten was extremely injudicious, and in that view we all concur. The students of the College in general applied to the Principal on the same day to remit the fine which had been imposed on them. The application was rejected by the Principal with the concurrence of the Governing Body and we have ample evidence that this refusal created considerable discontent among the students. We are informed, however, that the fine was subsequently reduced to a nominal amount in the case of some poor students and partially remitted in the case of others who had attended classes on the second though not on the first day of the strike.

We next come to the second incident, which took place on the 15th February following. On that day there was an accident in the Chemical Laboratory and the Professor of Chemistry was not able to take one of the classes. The lecture was delivered by a substitute, who dismissed the class five minutes before the appointed time. The students passed out of the Laboratory and proceeded along the corridor. The evidence shows that they talked to each other and were possibly somewhat noisy. Mr. Oaten was very near the end of a lecture he was delivering in a room adjoining the corridor. (The room and the corridor, it may be added, are different from those which formed the scene of the first incident.) He came and remonstrated with one of the students. As soon as he turned his back and was about to enter the room, another student in the crowd, Kamalabhusan Bose, called one of his fellow-students, Panchanan by name. There is no reason to suppose that the boy did so with intent to create a disturbance or to annoy Mr. Oaten. Mr. Oaten, however, heard the boy call out in this way, came out of the room, caught hold of him, took him to the steward and had him fined Re. 1/-. The boy asserts that he was caught by the neck and was called a rascal. Mr. Oaten, on the other hand asserts that he took the boy by the arm and denies that he called him a rascal. Whatever might have actually happened, it is certain that the impression quickly got abroad that the boy had been rudely treated. As a matter of fact, the boy forthwith complained to Mr. James that he had been caught by the neck and was called a rascal. Mr. James, thereupon directed the boy to make a written complaint and to see him later in the day. It appears that Mr. James asked Mr. Oaten to see him about the matter and to meet the boy in the Principal's room. The boy appears to have drafted a petition forthwith and to have taken it home with the intention of showing it to his father; this draft has been produced before us; the fair copy was filed before the Principal on the day following. Meanwhile about two hours after this incident and shortly before 3 o'clock Mr. Oaten went to the ground floor of the College premises to post a notice on the Notice Board. He observed a number of students (his own estimate is from 10 to 15) who were assembled near the foot of the staircase. They at once surrounded him, threw him on the floor and brutally assaulted him. Mr. Gilchrist, who was on the first floor, heard a noise and rushed down to help Mr. Oaten, but the assailants disappeared before he could reach the spot. We are not concerned with the question of identification of the actual assailants of Mr. Oaten. In fact that matter is under investigation by the Governing Body of the College; they have, we understand upon evidence taken by them, expelled two of the students of the College on the ground that their complicity in the assault has been proved, and the enquiry has not yet been closed. There can, in our opinion, be no question as to the gravity of the offence committed by the persons who organised and carried out the assault, and whoever is shown to have been implicated in this disgraceful affair deserves severe punishment. We are, however, concerned here with the strike and the assault only in connection with the question of the general conditions of discipline at the Presidency College.

These then are in outline the incidents with special reference to which we are called upon to consider the general conditions of discipline in the Presidency College and to formulate our conclusions. Are we really forced to what, if true, would be a disquieting conclusion, namely, that the general tone of the College is bad because although in ordinary circumstances everything works smoothly, yet, when a dispute occurred between a professor and the students, a considerable proportion of the students behaved as if they were undisciplined? Or is it the right view that there is no ground for anxiety as to the condition of the College because the two incidents mentioned, however discreditable, are due entirely to accidental circumstances and should be regarded only as unfortunate events of an exceptional and isolated character? We are not disposed to take an entirely optimistic view of the situation; at the same time we feel convinced that it would be unjust to base on these two incidents alone a sweeping condemnation of the entire College or to conclude that there had been any lack of strenuous and successful effort on the part of the Principal and the staff to maintain discipline in the institution. The true reasons for the present condition of things must, we think, be sought for in other directions and to these we shall now proceed to refer.

The evidence proves conclusively the presence in the College and the collegiate hostel of a number of turbulent youths whose capacity for mischief is by no means of a restricted character and who are evidently able to make their presence felt whenever there is an occasion calculated to excite the students to an outbreak against authority. The circumstances to which pernicious influence of this class of students may rightly be attributed are not far to seek, and, as will presently appear, they have been in a large measure beyond the control of even the most devoted and efficient Principal. (1) In the first place, we hold it undeniable that during the last ten years there has been a ferment amongst students in general, due mainly to what may be called causes of a political character which need not be described here in detail. This has led in many instances to a manifest spirit of insubordination and a reluctance to render unquestioning obedience to rules and orders promulgated by lawful authority. (2) In the second place, there is baneful influence of obviously injudicious discussions in the public press whenever a case of breach of discipline arises in an educational institution. The harm caused in this way is incalculable. (3) In the third place, we are bound to dwell upon the possibility of a disturbing influence of a very grave character. No evidence is needed in proof of the undoubted fact that revolutionary propagandists have with considerable success carried on their work among students and have from time to time brought into their camp disaffected youths of even considerable ability. To what precise extent the influence of that organisation may have affected the rank and file of Presidency College Students, it is impossible to determine on the evidence before us; but it is significant that the hostel premises have been searched more than once in quite recent years, though on neither occasion was any incriminating article found. We cannot ignore the fact that one student of the college has been prosecuted under the Indian Arms Act and that his conviction was upheld by the High Court. We cannot also overlook the fact that action under the Defence of Indian Act has been taken by Government against more than one student of the institution. Events like these in connection with what is rightly deemed the premier college in this Presidency are undoubtedly calculated to cause serious anxiety amongst all persons truly interested in its welfare and reputation and the gravity of the situation is unquestionably in no way reduced when we bear in mind the character of the assault on Mr. Oaten. It may be conceded that no assault would probably have taken place on the particular day but for what may be called the Kamala incident. Yet it would be idle to disguise the fact that the assault was not committed by a mob of angry students in the heat of the moment but was premeditated and carefully organised. In these circumstances, we are of opinion that special precautions should in future be exercised in the matter of the admission of students to the college, that their conduct there should be carefully watched, and that all suspicious characters should be promptly removed from the rolls by the Governing Body. (4) In the fourth place, the arrangement which divides the staff of the college into two Services—The Indian Educational Service and the Provincial Educational Service—has generated in the mind of many an educated Indian a sense of real grievance which, there is good reason to apprehend, has been reflected upon the minds of students in general. The Indian Educational Service, as is well known, is confined to those who were recruited by the Secretary of State in London and are mainly Europeans; the Provincial Educational Service consists of all those, irrespective of their qualifications, who were appointed by the Local Government. The feeling has thus become prevalent to a considerable extent that young European Professors are unfairly allowed preference over the experienced Indian Professors of equivalent attainments. It is, we think, lamentable that this impression should continue to gain ground, because the inevitable effect is that almost every European professor, when he first enters upon the discharge of his duties starts at an obvious disadvantage and with a certain amount of prejudice against him; he is regarded by the students as a member of an unjustly favoured class, and this feeling is probably shared, though it may be never be expressed, by some of the young professors' Indian colleagues. (5) In the fifth place we cannot refrain from mentioning the harm done by the occasional use of tactless expressions by certain European professors in addressing students. For instance evidence has been given before us to the effect that a professor of the College as chairman of a meeting of students in the Eden Hindu Hostel once said in substance that as the mission of Alexander the Great was to hellenise the barbarian people with whom he came into contact, the mission of the English here was to civilize the Indians. The use of the term "barbarian" in this connection in its literal Greek sense, i.e., "non-hellenic", was misunderstood and engendered considerable bitterness of feeling. It is also plain that, although the true meaning was subsequently explained, the explanation reached only a small portion of those who had heard the original version. We also had evidence to the effect that a young European professor asked certain students in the Presidency College why they were howling like wild beasts; another asked on a different occasion why they were chattering like monkeys; while a third is reported to have enquired of his students why they had behaved like coolies. Only four such instances have been reported to us as having occurred in four years, but reports of these have spread and have not been forgotten. We are convinced that in none of these instances had the professor concerned any ill-will towards the students or a desire to wound their feelings; yet the deplorable fact remains that these unfortunate expressions have been interpreted as an index of ill-will on the part of the professors towards their students or towards Indians in general. We are equally convinced that if a healthier tone had prevailed generally among the students, these expressions would probably not have been interpreted as they have been. But while we wish to emphasize the necessity for caution and tactfulness on the part of professors in their treatment of students, we are inclined to the view that the danger of misunderstanding would be appreciably diminished by natural intercourse between European professors and their students such as is calculated to lead to a better mutual appreciation. We realise, however, that the Presidency College is so located as to render practically impossible, for the present at any rate, such intercourse between the European professors (who are compelled to live far away from the college premises) and their students, the large majority of whom are scattered all over the city. (6) We may finally add that the evidence shows the existence of what may be called a spirit of excessive touchiness amongst students of the rising generation. They have a very keen sense of what they call their rights, but we have unfortunately not gained the impression that they are equally alive to their responsibilities. This characteristic is, in our opinion, a matter for serious concern. If a student has a grievance he can make his submission to his Principal; but he must distinctly realise that the Principal's decision is final and has to be accepted loyally and cheerfully. The position becomes intolerable when a student, who fails to obtain from the authorities of his college what he deems to be just redress, considers that he may take the law into his own hands and even call on his fellow-students to go on strike. Even a tacit acquiescence in so pernicious a doctrine must inevitably lead to defiance of law and order and speedily end in the annihilation not only of all academic but of all civilized communal life. Whilst we recognise that every legitimate grievance should be enquired into, students should be made clearly to understand that a frivolous complaint is in itself a breach of college discipline and will be treated accordingly. With these preliminary observations we proceed to state our recommendations:

(1) The Governing Body of the college should be reconstituted. It should be of a more representative character than at present and should be brought into closer contact with Government on the one hand and the community on the other. The Director of Public Instruction should obviously be a member of the Governing Body and its President 'ex-officio'. The Principal should be an 'ex-officio' member and Secretary. There should be four other members of the staff on the Governing Body, two Europeans and two Indians, all to be nominated by the Director of Public Instruction in consultation with the Principal. Two representatives of the Indian Community and one representative of the non-official European community should also be invited to join the Governing Body; there should be no difficulty in the selection of such representative men as have worked amongst Indian students and are familiar with the conditions of student life in Calcutta, and one of them may very well be appointed Vice-President of the Governing Body.

The College Council which consists entirely of professors and lecturers, should, as hitherto, continue as an Advisory Body which would be consulted by the Principal whenever he desired.

(2) The Consultative Committee of students has, we understand, been disbanded. If the Principal desires to re-constitute the Committee in future, he should himself nominate the members on the recommendation of the professors. The system of election which owed its origin to the natural wish of the Principal to secure a Committee whose views would represent as closely as possible those of the general body of students, has proved a failure, as it has brought on the Committee students of what may be called the demagogue type who are not necessarily the most desirable members from an intellectual and moral standpoint. Mr. Maitra does not share the view indicated in this sentence.

(3) The evidence taken by the Committee clearly shows that some at any rate of the members of the Students' Consultative Committee entirely failed in their duty on the occasion of the strike in January. They had been elected as representative students and occupied a position of some trust and responsibility; yet they neglected to assist the Principal in his

endeavor to deal effectively with the strike. There is also good reason to hold that some of the members deliberately misrepresented the attitude of the Principal at that time and thereby rendered more difficult the settlement of the strike. One of the members has already been expelled by the Governing Body on account of his conduct in connection with the assault on Mr. Oaten; but the action of the members during the strike does not appear to have been yet investigated. The Governing Body should now fully investigate the conduct of each member of the Consultative Committee at the time of the strike, and should take strong action against any members who were found to have been implicated.

(4) The departmental system which has been introduced in the College should be retained; but we strongly advise that a member of a department should not be chosen as its head merely because he is a member of the Indian Educational Service. The professors and lecturers who form the members of a department, it should also be generally understood, stand in the relation of colleagues to each other, and any point of difference that may arise between them should be referred to the Principal for his ultimate decision.

(5) There is a potentiality for grave dissatisfaction in the relations between members of the Indian Educational Service and the Provincial Educational Service. The members of the teaching staff should consequently be appointed, not to Services, but to posts on an incremental salary, and this is also the soundest course to follow from an educational point of view. If effect were given to this recommendation, much of the discontent which now prevails in the Provincial Educational Service would disappear. A healthier tone of comradeship would prevail amongst all the members of the professorial staff, and this could not but produce a beneficial effect upon the students as well.

(6) European professors, more especially the professors of Arts subjects, should possess a competent knowledge of the vernacular and, if their tastes are literary, should receive every encouragement to acquire some knowledge of an Indian classical language. Such knowledge of the vernacular is likely to foster better understanding between teachers and students. As it is difficult for a professor to learn a language in addition to the due performance of his professorial duties, facilities should be given to educational officers appointed in England to obtain a scientific grounding at home, and their duties when they first join should be so arranged as to give them opportunities for acquiring a sound working knowledge of the vernacular.

(7) The Principal should take an active part in the work of instruction of the students and thus come into direct contact with them. A Principal who is constrained to occupy mainly the position of an administrator can hardly be expected to exercise a permanent and effective influence upon the students, as he would unquestionably do if he had the opportunity by direct teaching to impress upon them a full recognition of his high intellectual attainments. In order that the Principal may be able to deliver lectures, he should, we think, be relieved of routine duties as far as possible, which may be delegated to a professor who would hold a position similar to that of the Dean of an English College.

We understand that a scheme has already been drawn up by the Governing Body of the College with a view to give effect to the suggestion we now make, and we trust it will receive early consideration.

(8) We consider that the Indian members of the staff of a college of the standing of Presidency College should be graduates of special distinction and usually with some experience in teaching work, even though this may occasionally involve transfers of professors from other Colleges. Scholars of this stamp alone are likely to be able to command readily the respect of their students and to maintain a position of equality as professors in the company of their European colleagues.

(9) The question of possible structural alterations in the building should be investigated and every effort made (by the erection of additional staircases or other devices of a likely nature) to minimize the likelihood of disturbances in the corridors.

(10) It is essential that a definite pronouncement should be made by Government as to the incalculable mischief likely to result from the injudicious discussion in the public press of questions relating to breaches of discipline in educational institutions. At the same time we recognise that the most effective remedy for the situation would be the creation of an 'esprit de corps' which would render impossible the ventilation of grievances in the public press.

(11) The question of a thorough reorganization of the Eden Hindu Hostel should be immediately taken up for consideration. It is obviously an unsatisfactory arrangement to leave 250 students under one Superintendent, for, however, efficient and devoted he may be, he cannot possibly exercise any real control over his wards. The arrangements contemplated for the provision of residential quarters for the Principal and some European members of the staff in the immediate neighbourhood of the hostel should be made for the accommodation in the hostel of some Indian members of the staff. We regard these recommendations as of such vital importance that we press for the immediate assignment of the necessary funds in spite of the present financial position. This so far as we can judge, is the only means at present feasible, so as to enable the residents of the hostel to have the benefit of social intercourse with the members of the college staff. We observe that the hostel is divided into five wards, each under a professor as a warden. These professors should be encouraged to visit the hostel at intervals, and at such hours of the day, as to make it possible for them to have friendly intercourse with the students under their charge. We desire, finally, to sound an emphatic note of warning in reference to the building of hostels in the future. The evidence has convinced us that a large hostel with inadequate supervision is a source of grave danger to a college, and we strongly advocate that no hostel should accommodate more than 40 or 50 students in charge of a resident Superintendent, preferably a member of the college staff.

(12) While we have made the above recommendations for the construction of certain additional residential quarters in the neighbourhood of the present hostel, and while we consider that this provision is essential so long as the college continues in its present position, yet we desire

to place it on record as to our emphatic opinion that the situation of the college is most distinctly unsuitable on account of its surroundings, both from the point of view of the congested character of the neighbourhood and the impossibility of adequate expansion in the future even at an enormous cost. The problem of the creation of a University town and the removal of the college to a more healthy and commodious site in the immediate neighbourhood of Calcutta and with easy reach of the Indian community whose boys receive instruction in the institution is by no means impossible of solution. The question is one of grave importance and we feel convinced that unless it is approached and solved in a generous and statesmanlike spirit, there is no real hope for radical improvement; it is imperative that the large majority of the students—in fact all who do not reside with their parents or natural guardians—should be removed from unhealthy influences and every possible facility be given for a free social intercourse between the students and the members of the staff, both European and Indian.

We understand that with a view to indicate their unqualified disapproval of the lamentable events which have happened in the college during the last two months, the Government of Bengal have directed that the College should be deemed closed for the remainder of the current academical session, subject to the reservation that the annual examination of the 1st and 3rd year students will be held in due course on such dates as may be specified by the Principal and that the students in the M.A. and M.Sc. classes will be sent up for their respective examinations on the dates prescribed by the University authorities. In view of the action so taken by the Government, which will have operated as a punishment upon all the students of the College we are of opinion that no further disciplinary action need be taken in respect of the college as a whole, though individual delinquents implicated in the strike and the assault on Mr. Oaten should be suitably dealt with by the Governing Body.

The 3rd April
1916.

Ashutosh Mookherjee
W. W. Hornell
C. W. Peake
J. Mitchell
Herambachandra Maitra.

APPENDIX 6

[Netaji evidently intended to write out a complete account of the two incidents involving Professor Oaten in the Presidency College, Calcutta, in 1916. An incomplete account is available relating to the first incident and is published below.—*Editor*]

THE PRESIDENCY COLLEGE TROUBLE—A True Version

by

Subhas Chandra Bose

On Monday some 8 or 10 ex-students of the Hindu and Hare Schools, now belonging to the 3rd year B.A. class, were invited to the School Prize Distribution Ceremony. The meeting broke up at about 12-15 p.m. and the students were returning. They had been informed previously that Prof. R. N. Ghosh would not take his English class (from 12 to 1 o'clock). But while returning they met the Steward who informed them that as Mr. Ghosh had come, he would probably take his class. As they were passing along the corridor of the room in which Mr. Oaten was teaching, Mr. Oaten came out, obstructed them, catching one or two by the hand, and insultingly ordered them to go away. The students most becomingly went down with the intention of applying to the Principal. In the meantime the students already assembled in the 3rd year class room. Seeing that it was twentyfive minutes past twelve, they thought of going down to inform the Professor. When they were coming out they were met by Mr. Oaten who threatened them with a fine of 5 Rupees if they left the room before one o'clock and sent them back in the same insulting manner though they informed him of their intention and assured him that they would not make any noise. A little before 12-25 p.m. Prof. Ghosh came and formally dismissed the class. The students asked him if they could go down, in spite of Mr. Oaten's threat, with Prof. Ghosh's permission, to which he replied in the affirmative. The students while coming away were met by Mr. Oaten and told him that their class was dismissed and they would undertake to make no noise. In spite of this, Mr. Oaten ordered them to go back and wait till one o'clock and adding injury to verbal insult actually gave them rough pushes. The students went back. At one o'clock Mr. Oaten went to them and added some more threats, saying that a Professor had the power to fine students. He regretted that that power was not utilized so long and said that thenceforth it would be made use of. The students made an application to the Principal and the same day the Principal had a long talk with some of the aggrieved students and told them to withdraw the application and patch up the matter with Mr. Oaten. Personally three only agreed to see Mr. Oaten regarding their personal grievance, but the class as a whole did not. The next day the three students waited on Mr. Oaten but he could not unavoidably come. The class as a whole remained so dissatisfied on getting no promise of redress and the dissatisfaction spread so widely that the whole body of students refused to attend classes till their grievance was attended to. The strike lasted for two days and on the third day Mr. Oaten spoke to the students and brought the unpleasant incident to an end.

APPENDIX 7

SUBHAS CHANDRA BOSE

Obiit 1945

Did I once suffer, Subhash, at your hand?
Your patriot heart is still'd! I would forget!
Let me recall but this, that while as yet
The Raj that you once challenged in your land
Was mighty; Icarus-like your courage planned
To mount the skies, and storm in battle set
The ramparts of High Heaven, to claim the debt
Of freedom owed, on plain and rude demand.
High Heaven yielded, but in dignity
Like Icarus, you sped towards the sea.
Your wings were melted from you by the sun,
The genial patriot fire that brightly glowed
In India's mighty heart, and flamed and flowed
Forth from her Army's thousand victories won.

E. FARLEY OATEN

This poem was written about 1947. It was printed and published by the author in a collection of his poems entitled "Song of Aton and other Verses" in 1967. A holograph copy of the poem was presented to the Netaji Research Bureau by the author in June 1969.

APPENDIX 8

SCOTTISH CHURCH COLLEGE

PHILOSOPHICAL SOCIETY

[Minutes of meetings as recorded by Subhas Chandra Bose, fourth year honours student in philosophy and Secretary of the Society, in 1918]°

The fifth meeting of the Society came off on the 7th of March with Prof. K. D. Chatterjee in the chair. Mr. M. L. Himatsingka read an interesting paper on the "Origin of Evil". The essayist tried to look at the problem from the theistic standpoint, leaving other points to shift as best as they could for themselves. He said that we are not made machines, so we want freedom of will. There must be various possibilities to choose and herein the possibility of sin lies.

Many critics rose to address the meeting. Almost all of them contended that as inscrutable are the ways of God we cannot fully know why God created sin and evil. "Wait and see" should be our motto.

The President then, in the course of a very beautiful speech, said that we must not hold with Pascal that every change of climate means change of morality, but there is an absolute ideal. Now if we deeply consider the fact that the most High was capable of creating us good then the question which puzzles all is why God in that case created evil at all? We must, to arrive at a satisfactory conclusion, fully endorse the views of Schopenhauer and Hartmann that evil is not really evil but 'partial evil is universal good'. Evil is a means to something good. As Leibnitz puts it, "Evil is a metaphysical necessity; the world is the best possible world with the presence of evil and we can by no means know what form a better world would take". With a vote of thanks the meeting broke up.

We offer a cordial welcome to the students who have recently joined the Third Year Class and have taken up philosophy. It would sit very well upon them to make a point of attending the meetings of the above Society, and as philosophy will stand with all its charms before them, we are looking forward confidently for their co-operation to make this Society a brilliant success.

SUBHAS CHANDRA BOSE
Secretary

° Published in the Scottish Church College Magazine, July 1918.

September 1918

PHILOSOPHICAL SOCIETY

Since our last report we have been able to hold four meetings. There has always been a large attendance and what delights us most is the enthusiasm of our third year friends.

"Faith and Reason" was the subject of the first meeting and Mr. Kiran Kumar Bhattacharya was the essayist. The essayist held that reason could at least give us scientific knowledge but scientific knowledge was all based on hypothesis and could not give us the whole truth regarding the nature of the world. Faith alone could give us a solution of the ultimate problems of life, and without faith morality and religion were not possible. There was a very interesting discussion and the President wound up the proceedings with an excellent address. Religion, he held, comes through faith but should be justified by Reason. Faith and Reason are not contradictory but they are simply different ways of approaching the same truth.

In the next meeting, Mr. Jadunath Das read his paper on "Who is the Father of Modern Philosophy?"—and Dr. Urquhart was in the chair. The essayist first enumerated the main characteristics of Modern Philosophy and proceeded to examine how far Bacon or Descartes possessed them. Because philosophy, he said, was void of content and his method also was faulty. His contribution was negative. Descartes's philosophy had a positive content and he treated almost all the problems of modern philosophy.

Consequently Descartes ought to be regarded as the founder of Modern Philosophy. After a lively fight between Baconians and Cartesians, the President's speech came as a reconciliation. According to the President, Bacon and Descartes must be taken together to be the Fathers of Modern Philosophy.

The subject of the next debate was "The Philosophical Basis of Indian and European Civilization". Mr. Binoy Rakhit was the essayist and Prof. Ewan was in the chair. The essayist tried to maintain that the Indian civilization was essentially spiritualistic whereas European civilization was materialistic. The abuse of science was in great measure responsible for this in Europe. He hoped that the civilization of the future would be a harmonious blending of Indian and European culture. It was urged by the critics that it was not fair to hold that India had neglected the material aspect and Europe the spiritual aspect of civilization. The synthesis of spiritual and material interests had been attempted both here and in Europe. The President said that European civilization was based not on Materialism but on Christianity. The performance of so-called secular duties was in fact the service of God.

The fourth meeting, since the opening of this session, came off on 6th September, Dr. Urquhart presiding. Mr. Subhas Chandra Bose read his paper on 'A Defence of Idealism'. The essayist supports Idealistic Monism of the Hegelian type but differed from Hegel and Schopenhauer in conceiving of the Absolute not as pure Reason or pure Will but as Spirit in all its fulness, striving through all the processes of the world to rise into the bliss of self-consciousness in the life of man. He held that such a view could reconcile both Science and Religion and supplement the popular and scientific conception of things with the metaphysical.

Mr. M. L. Himatsingka read his criticism of the paper and an interesting discussion followed. The President in his closing speech referred to two difficulties in a Hegelian type of philosophy (1) The relation between eternity and time, (2) the freedom of the human will.

With a vote of thanks to the chair the meeting broke up.

SUBHAS CHANDRA BOSE
Secretary

REFERENCES AND GLOSSARY

Abanindranath—Abanindranath Tagore, well-known Bengali painter

Adwaitacharya—the great Vaishnava who anticipated the appearance of Shri Chaitanya

Ahalya Bai—Holkar Queen (1765–1795) known for her piety and administrative ability

Ami—Sarat Chandra Bose's second son Amiya

Arabinda—Arabinda Mukherji, a student worker of the Jugantar party in its early days

Ashu Babu—Ashutosh Mukherji (Sir), the then Vice-Chancellor of Calcutta University

Babu—Bengali Hindu gentleman

Baidyanath (dham)—a place of pilgrimage in Bihar

Balananda—Swami Balananda, a well-known Sadhu who had his monastery in Deoghar, Bihar

Ballali Kulabidhi—rules prescribed by Ballal Sen of Bengal for the different castes of Hindu Society

Bardidi—eldest sister Pramila

Bardada—eldest brother Satish Chandra Bose

Bartaman Bharat—Swami Vivekananda's work entitled *India Today*

Basumati—a Bengali daily and monthly publication

Belur—a town near Calcutta where monasteries of the Ramakrishna Mission are situated

Belghurria—a town near Calcutta

Beni Babu—Beni Madhav Das, Head-Master, Ravenshaw Collegiate School, Cuttack, when Netaji joined it

Bharatvarsha—a Bengali periodical

Bidhu—Bidhu Bhusan Roy (Dr.), later Khaira Professor of Physics, Calcutta University

Bijaya—the immersion day of Goddess Durga

Bimal—eldest son of eldest sister Pramila

Bolpur—the village in West Bengal where Tagore established his 'Santi-Niketan'

Bowdidi—sister-in-law (elder brother's wife)

Brahmin, Brahman—one belonging to the priest caste

Brahmachari—one practising self-control

Brahmacharya—the practice of self-control

Brahmananda—Swami Brahmananda, a direct disciple of Ramakrishna Paramhansa

Capt. Gray—Commanding Officer, University Unit of India Defence Force (1917)

Chaitanya (Shri)—the greatest Vaishnava saint (1485–1533)

Chandi—a form of Goddess Durga; here, refers to Chandimangal, a book of psalms glorifying the goddess

Charu—Charu Chandra Ganguly, fellow-student and friend of Netaji
Choto Mamima—youngest maternal aunt
Chotdada—brother Dr. Sunil Chandra Bose
C. Cozajee (Professor)—Head of the department of Economics, Presidency College
Cuttack—the former capital city of Orissa where Netaji was born

Dada—elder brother
Dakshineshwar—a place near Calcutta by the Hooghly river well-known for the Kali Temple where Ramakrishna worshipped
Darshan—divine audience
Deoghar—a place of pilgrimage in Bihar (the same as Baidyanathdham)
Dharma—religion
Dharmapala—a great king of Bengal who ruled towards the end of first century A.D.
Dhiren—Dhirendra Nath Dhar, a contemporary of Netaji in Cambridge
Didi—eldest sister Pramila
Durga—Hindu goddess
Durga Bati—Rajput Queen (sixteenth century) known for her beauty and valour

Girish, Girishda—Girish Banerjee
Gita—the Bhagavat Gita, which contains the essence of Hindu philosophy and may be regarded as the Bible of the Hindus
Goari—home town of Hemanta Kumar Sarkar in Nadia, West Bengal
Godavari—a river in South India
Gopali—younger brother Sailesh Chandra Bose
Gurudev—religious preceptor

Hemendu—Hemendu Sen, a friend of Netaji's younger days
Hardwar—a place of pilgrimage in Uttar Pradesh
Haripada—Haripada Vishnu
Hazaribagh—a town in then Bihar, present-day Jharkhand
Hem Babu—Hem Sarkar, Professor of English, Ravenshaw College, Cuttack
Hemkut Parbat—a Himalayan peak tinged with bright red (gold)

Jagadish Babu—Jagadish Chandra Bose, the eminent scientist
Jamai Babu—brother-in-law, elder sister's husband
Jugalda—Jugal Kishore Adhya (Dr.)

Kali—Hindu goddess
Kanchi Mama—maternal uncle Satyendra Nath Dutt (Dr.)
Kashi—the holy city of Benaras
Khandagiri—historic caves near Bhubaneshwar, Orissa
Khatriya—the warrior caste
Krishnanagar—a town in West Bengal
Kulapratha—the custom of a family
Kulasastra—family rules

Kulin—a person of a special social status conferred by Ballal Sen of Bengal
Kunti Devi—the mother of the Pandavas (Mahabharata)
Kurseong—a hill station near Darjeeling
Kusha—one of the twin sons of Rama and Sita (Ramayana)

Laba—one of the twin sons of Rama and Sita
Lama—Buddhist monk
Lakshmana—half-brother of Rama (Ramayana)
Lily—fourth sister
Lord Hari—another name of Lord Krishna

Madhusudan—Michael Madhusudan Dutt, well-known Bengali poet
Maha-Pandit—a very learned person
Mama—maternal uncle
Mamima—maternal aunt
Mantra—holy word
Maya—the theory that the world as perceived through the senses is an illusion
Meera Bai—well-known preacher of the Radha-Krishna cult (fifteenth century)
Mejabowdidi—sister-in-law Bivabati, wife of Sarat Chandra Bose
Mejdada—second brother Sarat Chandra Bose
Mejdidi—second sister Sarala Bala Dey
Mejajamaibabu—second elder sister's husband

Nada, Nadada—fourth brother Sudhir Chandra Bose
Nagen Thakur—family priest
Narayana—another name of Lord Krishna
Natun Mamababu—fifth maternal uncle
Nilmoni—Nilmoni Senapati (I.C.S.), a contemporary of Netaji in Cambridge
Nilratan Babu—Nilratan Sircar (Sir), an eminent Calcutta physician

Panda—a priest attached to a temple
Panchabati—the forest in Deccan where Rama, Sita and Lakshmana spent a part of their exile (Ramayana)
Pandit—a learned person
Parija (Prankrishna)—Netaji's contemporary who later became a well-known scientist
Pishamahasaya—paternal uncle
Prafulla—Netaji's contemporary who later became a doctor
Prafulla Chandra—Prafulla Chandra Ray (Sir), well-known Bengali chemist and philanthropist
Priya Ranjan—Priya Ranjan Sen, Netaji's contemporary who later became Professor of English, Calcutta University
Pramatha—Pramatha Nath Sarkar, a contemporary of Netaji
Pronams—obeisance
Puja—worship
P.R.S.—Premchand Roychand Scholarship (Calcutta University)

Rabindranath—Rabindranath Tagore
Raghua—family gardener at Cuttack
Rakshasa—a monster
Raja of Aal—the head of a native State in Orissa
Rama—the principal character in the Ramayana
Ramayana—Hindu epic
Ramakrishna—Ramakrishna Paramhansa, the great Hindu saint
Ramkrishna Mission—Religious Order founded by Swami Vivekananda
Rangamamababu—maternal uncle, Birendra Nath Dutt
Ranen Mama—maternal uncle, Ranendra Nath Dutt
Rishi—a sage

Sadhana—spiritual exercise
Sama Veda—the third of the four Vedas
Sankaracharya—the great Hindu Philosopher (eighth century)
Sannyasi—a monk
Santipur—a town in West Bengal
Sarada—the oldest family maid who looked after Netaji in childhood
Saroj Babu—Sarojendra Kumar Dutt, fourth brother-in-law of Netaji
Sati—Youngest brother Santosh Chandra Bose
Satyen Dhar—elder brother of Dhiren Dhar
Satyen Mama—maternal uncle Satyendra Nath Dutt (Dr.)
Sealdah—One of the railway stations of Calcutta
Sejajamaibabu—third elder sister's husband Radha Binode Roy (Dr.)
Sejdada—third elder brother Suresh Chandra Bose
Sejdidi—third elder sister
Senchal—a beauty spot near Darjeeling
Sita—the consort of Rama (Ramayana)
Shiva—Hindu god, consort of Parvati
Sloka—psalm
Sudra—one of the four castes in old Hindu society
Sureshda—Suresh Chandra Banerjee (Dr.) well-known political leader of
    later days
Surhit—Surhit Chandra Mitra (Dr.)
Sushil Dey—Dr. Sushil Dey, Senior Professor of English and later Head of
    the Department of Sanskrit, Dacca University

Taraporewalla (Dr.)—Professor of Comparative Philology, Calcutta
    University

Udaigiri—historic caves near Bhubaneshwar, Orissa

Valmiki—the Hindu sage who wrote the Ramayana
Vaishya—one of the four castes of old Hindu society
Vaishnava—the Hindu sect which worships God as Love in the form of
    father and protector

Vedas—the ancient Hindu scriptures
Yoga—union with Godhead; the word is used to indicate the goal as well
    as the means
Yogi—one who practices Yoga

INDEX